THE GOVERNING LAW OF COMPANIES IN EU LAW

The manner in which the governing law of companies is determined has attracted much attention from academics and practitioners alike ever since the European Court of Justice began receiving references for preliminary rulings regarding the compatibility of protective conflict of corporate law norms with the EC Treaty provisions concerning freedom of establishment. Although recent developments have been less controversial than the ground-breaking judgment in *Centros*, they have not only consolidated the general thrust of liberalisation occasioned by the Court of Justice, but have added new dimensions to the regulatory landscape. These developments include amendments to the European constitutional order enshrined in the Lisbon Treaty, European legislation on cross-border mergers, the proposed statute for a European Private Company, the judgment of the Court of Justice in *Cartesio* and a Commission communication that contemplates the introduction of legislation on the governing law of companies.

This book examines these recent developments and appraises the current law, as well as the foreseeable trajectory of the law, within a theoretical setting that addresses the socio-economic and legal-theoretical concerns associated with choices of the governing law of companies. In addition to considering the present and probable future state of EU law, the book also develops new theoretical perspectives and proposes novel solutions to long-standing dilemmas. In particular, it suggests that the use of information technology may render possible previously impossible compromises between party autonomy and the proper locus of prescriptive sovereignty.

Volume 9 in the series Studies in Private International Law

Studies in Private International Law

Volume 1: Electronic Consumer Contracts in the Conflict of Laws
Sophia Tang

Volume 2: Foreign Currency Claims in the Conflict of Laws
Vaughan Black

Volume 3: Jurisdiction and Judgments in Relation to EU Competition Law Claims
Mihail Danov

Volume 4: Cases and Materials on EU Private International Law
Stefania Bariatti

Volume 5: International Commercial Disputes: Commercial Conflict of Laws in English Courts
Jonathan Hill and Adeline Chong

Volume 6: International Child Abduction: The Inadequacies of the Law
Thalia Kruger

Volume 7: Mediating International Child Abduction Cases
Sarah Vigers

Volume 8: International Antitrust Litigation: Conflict of Laws and Coordination
Edited by Jürgen Basedow, Stéphanie Francq and Laurence Idot

Volume 9: The Governing Law of Companies in EU Law
Justin Borg-Barthet

The Governing Law of Companies in EU Law

Justin Borg-Barthet

·HART·
PUBLISHING

OXFORD AND PORTLAND, OREGON
2012

Published in the United Kingdom by Hart Publishing Ltd
16C Worcester Place, Oxford, OX1 2JW
Telephone: +44 (0)1865 517530
Fax: +44 (0)1865 510710
E-mail: mail@hartpub.co.uk
Website: http://www.hartpub.co.uk

Published in North America (US and Canada) by
Hart Publishing
c/o International Specialized Book Services
920 NE 58th Avenue, Suite 300
Portland, OR 97213-3786
USA
Tel: +1 503 287 3093 or toll-free: (1) 800 944 6190
Fax: +1 503 280 8832
E-mail: orders@isbs.com
Website: http://www.isbs.com

British Library Cataloguing in Publication Data
Data Available

ISBN: 978-1-84946-296-9

Typeset by Hope Services, Abingdon
Printed and bound in Great Britain by
Lightning Source UK Ltd

To Catriona

SERIES EDITORS' PREFACE

Private international law of companies is an important topic that is in danger of being neglected by private international lawyers – witness its omission from the latest edition of *Cheshire, North and Fawcett, Private International Law* 14th edn (Oxford, Oxford University Press, 2008) by James Fawcett and Janeen Carruthers. Justin Borg-Barthet's book helps to avoid this neglect. It does so not by writing a doctrinal work but rather by writing a more theoretical, yet practical, book. The author immersed himself in theories of corporate governance in order to be able to analyse how far it is appropriate to extend the principle of party autonomy in the field of private international law of corporations. Not surprisingly he rejects a simplistic unlimited party autonomy model in favour of a more nuanced and limited application of that principle.

The practical outworking of the author's theoretical analysis of what private international law of companies should be is set in the particular context of the European Union. The author does not make the mistake of confusing the 'is' and the 'ought'. Instead he devotes the second part of the book to a careful explanation of the current law on private international law of companies at the European Union level. The author skilfully guides the reader through the relevant secondary legislation affecting companies in the EU, including optional supranational business vehicles. He then provides a pathway through the Court of Justice of the European Union's case law on the freedom of establishment of companies and how this limits the room for manoeuvre of national private international law of companies in the EU. The Court's case law is divided into three parts: (1) the conservatism of the Daily Mail case (ie little or no interference with national private international law); (2) the radical case law from Centros to Sevic Systems that seemed to be moving towards the Court of Justice occupying the field of private international law of companies by its deregulatory case law on the Treaty right to freedom of establishment; and (3) the acknowledgment in the Cartesio case that there are limits to what the Court of Justice is willing to regulate through its case law on freedom of establishment in relation to private international law of companies.

In the last part of the book Justin invites the various branches of the EU legislature to consider a series of ideas rooted in the theoretical analysis from the first part of the book as to appropriate EU legislation on private international law of companies. Given that the Stockholm programme acknowledges the 'need to explore whether common rules determining the law applicable to matters of company law . . . could be devised' it is a good time to be offering constructive and detailed ideas for new EU legislation on the private international law of companies.

This book should be of interest to a wide range of people. Apart from specialists in private international law it should be read by company lawyers, those with an interest in corporate governance, and European Union lawyers and policy makers with an interest in freedom of establishment, civil justice, the internal market and company law.

Paul Beaumont
Jonathan Harris

PREFACE

The laws that regulate companies, both nationally and transnationally, require technical analysis. This book engages with this need and sets out to diagnose the current state of EU law concerning the governing law of companies. However, there is a lot more to corporate law and the governing law of companies. The way that societies organise companies says much about how they wish to organise power and wealth. This is especially challenging in a transnational context. European company law also concerns questions about the balance to be struck between the rights of states and the polities within those states on the one hand, and the economic freedoms upon which the internal market is built on the other.

The writing of this book began prior to the financial crisis. It is tempting to suggest that the crisis vindicates the book's challenge to contractarian approaches to transnational company law; but that temptation must be resisted. The history of corporate law suggests that current economic conditions are often used as a pretext to justify given approaches to the corporate form. Still, the financial crisis invites us to reconsider the basis upon which we organise our social and economic life through the law. This book suggests alternatives to unbridled economic liberalism.

The book is based on a PhD thesis that was completed at the University of Aberdeen in 2011. I am thankful to Aude Fiorini (University of Dundee) who supervised me in the earlier stages, when guidance was paramount and confidence was realistically low. Aude continues to read much of my work and to offer intellectual rigour, and I am thankful for her selfless guidance and support. Professor Paul Beaumont took over as lead supervisor when Aude moved to the University of Dundee, and Professor John Paterson provided continuity as second supervisor. Their insight and varied expertise helped me to develop ideas and to communicate them better.

Professor Beaumont's confidence in the thesis enabled me to think of the work as a publishable monograph. I am thankful to him and his co-editor, Professor Jonathan Harris (King's College London), for the opportunity to present this work to a wider audience, as well as for the helpful conversations about aspects of the thesis. Mel Hamill, Tom Adams, Richard Hart (Hart Publishing) and two anonymous reviewers have also been tremendously helpful and patient.

The examiners of my PhD, Professor Janet Dine (Queen Mary, University of London) and Dr Sophia Tang (University of Aberdeen) made helpful suggestions regarding changes that could be made between PhD and monograph. They also made the day of my viva voce examination memorable for all the right reasons. Professor Janet McLean (University of Auckland), Dr Daniel Carr (University of

Edinburgh) and Professor Peter McEleavy (University of Dundee) also read parts of this work. Their encouraging comments and advice about style and substance were invaluable.

My fiancée Catriona Mallia proofread several chapters of the thesis. Her attention to detail was particularly helpful, as was her boundless patience, care and encouragement during the completion of my PhD and this book. The book is dedicated to her, with thanks and love.

Dr Adrian Mallia's authoritative instruction on the classification of property in corporate restructuring provided unexpected, extensive ideas – *kollox ghallimtni.*

Finally, I am also thankful to my parents, Carmen and Tony Borg Barthet, and family. 'Last but not least' is a clichéd phrase, but certainly a pertinent addition to the previous sentence. They endured and encouraged throughout the long gestation of an unlikely academic career.

Justin Borg-Barthet

CONTENTS

Series Editors' Preface vii
Preface ix
Table of Cases xv
Table of Legislation xvii

1 Introduction 1
1.1 Aims 1
1.2 Scope 3
1.3 A History in Brief 4
1.3.1 International and Regional Unification 6
1.4 Are Conflicts of Corporate Laws Still Relevant? 8
1.5 Provisional Conclusions 12

2 The Principle of Party Autonomy 13
2.1 Introduction 13
2.2 A Global Movement Towards Party Autonomy? 16
2.3 Analogies with Contract Law 19
2.3.1 *Lex Societatis or Lex Contractus?* 20
2.3.2 Displacing Contractual Covenants – Protection of the Weaker Party 21
2.3.3 A Standard Form Contract? 25
2.3.4 Reincorporation as Novation 27
2.3.5 Provisional Conclusions 29
2.4 Economic Analyses of the Conflict of Corporate Laws 30
2.4.1 The Authority of Entrepreneurs: Direction, and Monitoring of Team Production 30
2.4.2 The Firm as a Nexus of Contracts, or a Nexus of Specific Investments 33
2.4.3 Property Rights and the Nature of Shareholding 36
2.4.4 Efficiency: Choice of the Best Law 39
2.4.5 Efficiency: Legal Certainty 41
2.5 Conclusions 48

3 The Plural Aims of Conflict of Corporate Laws 49
3.1 Introduction 49
3.1.1 The Real Seat Theory 50

3.1.2 The Incorporation Theory 51
3.2 Targeted Protective Mechanisms 52
3.2.1 Shareholders' Rights 52
3.2.2 The Limits of Shareholders' Liability 57
3.2.3 Creditor Protection 62
3.2.4 Employees 65
3.2.5 Accountability of Directors 68
3.3 Enduring Divergence in Corporate Law, and Potential Exceptions in Private International Law 69
3.4 Conclusions 71

4 *Party Autonomy in European Law* 73
4.1 Introduction 73
4.2 The Constitutional Treatment of Party Autonomy 74
4.3 The Origins and Purpose of Article 50 78
4.3.1 Article 50(2)(g) after *Centros* 81
4.4 The Substantive Effects of Harmonisation on Party Autonomy 85
4.4.1 The Cross-Border Merger Directive 87
4.4.2 The Works Council Directive 90
4.4.3 The Directives that Never Were, and a New Basis for Harmonisation 92
4.5 Supranational Business Vehicles 95
4.5.1 Introduction 95
4.5.2 The Societas Europaea (SE) 95
4.5.3 The Societas Privata Europaea (SPE) 99
4.6 Conclusions 103

5 *The Freedom of Establishment Judgments* 104
5.1 Introduction 104
5.2 *Centros* et al in Context: the Treaty Provisions, the 1968 Convention and *Daily Mail* 105
5.2.1 The 1968 Convention 106
5.2.2 The TFEU 109
5.2.3 *Daily Mail* 111
5.3 The ECJ's Liberalising Judgments 113
5.3.1 *Centros* 113
5.3.2 *Überseering* 117
5.3.3 *Inspire Art* 120
5.3.4 *de Lasteyrie du Saillant*, *Marks and Spencer*, and *Cadbury Schweppes* 123
5.3.5 *Sevic Systems* 125
5.4 *Cartesio* 127

5.4.1 AG Maduro's Opinion 127
5.4.2 The Court's Judgment 131
5.5 The Present State of EU Law 135
5.6 Conclusions 138

6 Options for Future Development 142
6.1 Introduction 142
6.2 Option 1: the Status Quo 143
6.3 Option 2: the Status Quo Ante 146
6.4 Option 3: Unification or Supranationalisation of Corporate Law 147
6.5 Option 4: a New Regulatory Framework 149
6.5.1 Legal Basis 150
6.5.2 Aims and Principles 151
6.5.3 An Electronic Solution 158
6.5.4 Substantive Matters to be Included in Future Legislation 159
6.5.5 Legal Certainty 165
6.5.6 An Obligation to Incorporate 'Foreign' Companies 166
6.5.7 Determining the State of the Real Seat, and Applying its Laws 167
6.5.8 Enforcement Mechanisms: the Challenge of the Privity of Contract 169
6.6 Conclusions 169

7 Concluding Remarks 171
Bibliography 175
Index 185

TABLE OF CASES

Court of Justice of the European Union

Case 8-74 *Procureur du Roi v Benoît and Gustave Dassonville* [1974] ECR 837 124

Case 120/78 *Rewe-Zentral AG v Bundesmonopolverwaltung für Branntwein* [1979] ECR 649 .... 113, 138

Case 270/83 *Commission v France* [1986] ECR 273 105

Case 79/85 *DHM Segers v Bestuur van de Bedrijfsvereniging voor Bank- en Verzekeringswezen, Groothandel en Vrije Beroepen* [1986] ECR 2375 105

Case 218/86 *SAR Schotte GmbH v Parfums Rothschild Sarl* [1987] ECR 4905 60

Case 81/87 *The Queen v HM Treasury and Commissioners of Inland Revenue, ex parte Daily Mail and General Trust plc* [1988] ECR 5483 .... 8, 76, 105, 153

Case C-214/89 *Powell Duffryn plc v Petereit* [1992] ECR I-01745 .... 19, 78, 164

Case C-55/94 *Reinhard Gebhard v Consiglio dell'Ordine degli Avvocati e Procuratori di Milano* [1995] ECR I-4565 .... 76, 116

Case C-212/97 *Centros Ltd v Erhvervs-og Selskabsstyrelsen* [1999] ECR I-01459 .... 1, 8, 49, 56, 64, 74, 76–77, 104, 110, 113–16, 121–22, 132, 136–37, 151–53, 155, 163

Case C-86/00 *HSB-Wohnbau Ltd* [2001] ECR I-5353 117

Case C-447/00 *(Reference for a preliminary ruling from the Landesgericht Salzburg): Holto Ltd* [2002] ECR I-735 117

Case C-208/00 *Überseering BV v Nordic Construction Company Baumanagement GmbH* (NCC) [2002] ECR I-9919 .... 8, 15, 74, 76–77, 104, 114–15, 118–19, 132, 136–37, 152–54

Case C-167/01 *Kamer van Koophandel en Fabrieken voor Amsterdam v Inspire Art Ltd* [2003] ECR I-10155 .... 8, 56, 74, 104, 155

Case C-9/02 *Hughes de Lasteyrie du Saillant v Ministère de l'Économie, des Finances et de l'Industrie* [2004] ECR I-2409 .... 123, 153

Case C-442/02 *CaixaBank France v Ministére de l'Économie* [2004] ECR I8961 135

Case C-446/03 *Marks & Spencer plc v David Halsey (Her Majesty's Inspector of Taxes)* [2005] ECR I-10837 .... 123–25, 153

Case C-196/04 *Cadbury Schweppes plc, Cadbury Schweppes Overseas Ltd v Commissioners of Inland Revenue* [2006] I-7995 .... 123, 125, 153

Case C-411/03 *Sevic Systems AG* [2005] ECR I-10805 .... 8, 74, 76–77, 87, 104, 125–27, 134, 136–37, 143, 153

Case C-341/05 *Laval un Partneri Ltd v Svenska Byggnadsarbetareforbundet* [2007] ECR I-11767 76
Case C-438/05 *International Transport Workers' Federation v Viking Line ABP* [2007] ECR I-10779....76, 135
Case C-210/06 *Cartesio Oktató és Szolgáltató bt* [2008] ECR I-9641 ....1, 8, 27, 29, 50, 73–78, 82, 88, 93–94, 98, 104–06, 110, 123–25, 127–37, 140, 143, 145, 153–54
Case C-258/08 *Ladbrokes Betting & Gaming Ltd, Ladbrokes International Ltd v Stichting de Nationale Sporttotalisator* [2010] ECR I-0000....140
AG Tesauro in Case C-214/89 *Powell Duffryn plc v Petereit* [1992] ECR I-01745....19–21, 23, 78, 164
AG La Pergola in Case C-212/97 *Centros Ltd v Erhvervs-og Selskabsstyrelsen* [1999] ECR I-01459.... 15, 76, 115, 151, 153–54
AG Colomer in Case C-208/00 *Überseering BV v Nordic Construction Company Baumanagement GmbH (NCC)* [2002] ECR I-9919....114–15, 119, 132
AG Mischo in Case C-9/02 *Hughes de Lasteyrie du Saillant v Ministère de l'Économie, des Finances et de l'Industrie* [2004] ECR I-2409....123
AG Tizzano in Case C-411/03 *Sevic Systems AG* [2005] ECR I-10805....126
AG Maduro in Case C-210/06 *Cartesio Oktató és Szolgáltató bt* [2008] ECR I-9641....94, 98, 124–25, 128, 131, 134

United Kingdom

Borland's Trustee v Steel Brothers & Co Limited [1901] 1 Ch 279....37
Macaura v Northern Assurance Company [1925] AC 619....37
Lazard Bros. & Co v Midland Bank Ltd. [1933] AC 289....5
Kuenigl v Donnersmarck [1955] 1 QB 515....5
Gasque v Inland Revenue Commissioners [1940] 2 KB 80....5
DHN Food Distributors v Tower Hamlets LBC [1976] 1 WLR 852....60
Arab Monetary Fund Appellants v Hashim and Others Respondents (No 3) [1991] 2 AC 114....5
Westland Helicopters Ltd v Arab Organisation for Industrialisation [1995] QB 282....5
Macmillan Inc v Bishopgate Investment Trust plc and others (No 3) [1996] 1 WLR 387....38
Lubbe et al v Cape Industries plc [1997] 4 All ER 335....60, 70

Other Jurisdictions

Paramount Communications, Inc v Time, Inc, Delaware Supreme Court 571 A.2d 1140....11
Liechtenstein AG BGH 21 March 1986, BGHZ 97....45, 167
Chilon Valeurs Inc c Financial Construction Company Inc ATF 117 II 497....68

TABLE OF LEGISLATION

Treaties and Conventions

Treaty of Lisbon amending the Treaty on European Union and the Treaty establishing the European Community, signed at Lisbon, 13 December 2007 [2007] OJ C306/1 .... 1, 150
Treaty on the Functioning of the European Union (TFEU) 3, 7, 73, 74, 78, 80, 82, 84, 87, 95, 104, 106, 109–15, 120–22, 125, 128, 132–33, 136–8, 140, 151, 153, 155, 172
EC Treaty 3, 104, 114, 117, 119, 122, 150
Hague Convention of 1 June 1956 concerning the recognition of the legal personality of foreign companies, associations and institutions 6
Hague Convention on Choice of Court Agreements 2005 .... 17, 27
EC Convention on the Mutual Recognition of Companies and Bodies Corporate of 29 February 1968, Bulletin of the European Communities, Supplement 2/69, 7–18 .... 7, 106–08, 141
Hague Convention of 23 November 2007 on the International Recovery of Child Support and Other Forms of Family Maintenance 158
Hague Protocol of 23 November 2007 on the Law Applicable to Maintenance Obligations 17
Protocol Concerning the Interpretation by the Court of Justice of the Convention of 29 February 1968 on the Mutual Recognition of Companies and Legal Persons (signed at Luxembourg on 3 June 1971), Bulletin of the European Communities, Supplement 4/71, 6–16 108

Secondary Legislation of the European Union

Council Directive (EEC) 1968/151 of 9 March 1968 on co-ordination of safeguards which, for the protection of the interests of members and others, are required by Member States of companies within the meaning of the second paragraph of Article 58 of the Treaty, with a view to making such safeguards equivalent throughout the Community [1968] OJ L 065/8 .... 80, 85
Council Directive (EEC) 1977/91 of 13 December 1976 on coordination of safeguards which, for the protection of the interests of members and others, are required by Member States of companies within the meaning of the second paragraph of Article 58 of the Treaty, in respect of the formation of public limited liability companies and the maintenance and alteration

of their capital, with a view to making such safeguards equivalent [1977] OJ L26/1 ....63, 80, 85
Council Directive (EEC) 1978/855 of 9 October 1978 based on Article 54 (3) (g) of the Treaty concerning mergers of public limited liability companies [1978] OJ L-295/36....................127
Council Directive (EEC) 1978/660 based on Article 54 (3) (g) of the Treaty on the annual accounts of certain types of companies [1978] OJ L222/11 163
Council Directive (EEC) 1983/349 based on the Article 54 (3) (g) of the Treaty on consolidated accounts [1983] OJ L193/1 ....60, 163
Council Directive (EEC) 1984/253 based on Article 54 (3) (g) of the Treaty on the approval of persons responsible for carrying out the statutory audits of accounting documents [1984] OJ L126/20 163
Council Directive (EEC) 1989/666 concerning disclosure requirements in respect of branches opened in a Member State by certain types of company governed by the law of another State [1989] OJ L395/36....................163
Council Directive (EEC) 1993/13 on unfair terms in consumer contracts [1993] OJ L095/29 ....22, 27
Council Directive (EC) 1994/45 on the establishment of a European Works Council or a procedure in Community-scale undertakings and Community-scale groups of undertakings for the purposes of informing and consulting employees [1994] OJ L254 .... 3, 10, 85, 90, 144
Council Regulation (EC) 44/2001 on jurisdiction and the recognition and enforcement of judgments in civil and commercial matters [2001] OJ L12/1 ....17, 158
Council Directive (EC) 2001/86 supplementing the Statute for a European company with regard to the involvement of employees [2001] OJ L 284/22 ...95
Council Regulation (EC) 2157/2001 on the statute for a European company (SE) [2001] OJ L294/1 .... 3, 10, 95, 130, 145
Council Regulation (EC) 2201/2003 concerning jurisdiction and the recognition and enforcement of judgments in matrimonial matters and the matters of parental responsibility, repealing Regulation (EC) No 1347/2000 [2003] OJ L 338/1 17
Directive (EC) 2005/56 of the European Parliament and of the Council of 26 October 2005 on cross-border mergers of limited liability companies [2005] OJ L310/1 ....1, 3, 10, 56, 65, 68, 85, 87, 125, 141, 144, 145, 151, 164
Directive (EC) 2007/36 of the European Parliament and of the Council of 11 July 2007 on the exercise of certain rights of shareholders in listed companies [2007] OJ L184/17....................3, 10, 57, 85
Directive of the European Parliament and of the Council (EC) 101/2009 on coordination of safeguards which, for the protection of the interests of members and third parties, are required by Member States of companies within the meaning of the second paragraph of Article 48 of the Treaty, with a view to making such safeguards equivalent [2009] OJ L258/11 163

Regulation of the European Parliament and the Council (EC) 864/2007 on the law applicable to non-contractual obligations (Rome II) [2007] OJ L 199/40 17
Regulation (EC) 593/2008 of the European Parliament and of the Council on the Law Applicable to Contractual Obligations (Rome I) [2008] OJ L177/6).... 16
Council Regulation (EC) 4/2009 on jurisdiction, applicable law, recognition and enforcement of decisions and cooperation in matters relating to maintenance obligations [2009] OJ L 7/1........17
Directive (EC) 2009/38 of the European Parliament and of the Council of 6 May 2009 on the establishment of a European Works Council or a procedure in Community-scale undertakings and Community-scale groups of undertakings for the purposes of informing and consulting employees (recast) [2009] OJ L122/28........85, 90

State Legislation

L. 31 maggio 1995, n218 (Italy)........6, 50
Testo Unico della Finanza (Italy) 154
Codice Civile (Italy)........164
Gesetzes zur Modernisierung des GmbH-Rechts und zur Bekämpfung von Missbräuchen (MoMiG) (Germany)........10, 63, 82
Loi n°2003-721 du 1 août 2003 pour l'initiative économique (France).... 10, 63, 82
Loi fédérale du 18 décembre 1987 (Switzerland) 65
Companies Act 2006 (UK) 11, 66, 161, 164
Ley Orgánica 3/2007, de 22 de marzo, para la igualdad efectiva de mujeres y hombres (Spain) 11
California Corporations Code........47, 54, 58, 68
New York Business Corporation Law........55

Reports and Legislative Proposals

Draft Fifth Directive on the structure of public limited companies and the powers and obligations of their Organs [1972] OJ C 131 92
Draft Ninth Directive on links between undertakings and in particular on groups. Not published 92
Commission (EC) Proposal for a Council Regulation on the statute for a European private company COM (2008) 396/3..... 1, 10, 15, 20, 99, 100–02, 145
Commission (EC), '"Think Small First": A "Small Business Act" for Europe' (Communication) COM (2008) 394, 19 June 2008........99, 102
Commission (EC), 'An area of freedom, security and justice serving the citizen' (Communication) COM (09) 262 final, 10 June 2009 ...... 1, 8, 94, 107, 124, 142
Commission (EC), 'Green Paper: The interconnection of business registers' (Communication) COM (09) 614 final, 04 November 2009 158

Council of the European Union, 'The Stockholm Programme – An open and secure Europe serving and protecting the citizens' Document 17024/09 142
Commission (EC) Proposal for a Regulation of the European Parliament and of the Council on jurisdiction, applicable law, recognition and enforcement of decisions and authentic instruments in matters of succession and the creation of a European Certificate of Succession COM (2009) 154 final 17
Commission (EU) Proposal for a Council Regulation implementing enhanced cooperation in the area of the law applicable to divorce and legal separation COM (2010) 104 final 17
Council of the European Union, 'Proposal for a Council Regulation on a European private company – Political agreement' 1061/11 DRS 84 SOC 432 ....99, 145, 154
M Giuliano and P Lagarde, 'Report on the Convention on the law applicable to contractual obligations' [1980] OJ C282/01 21
Permanent Bureau of the Hague Conference on Private International Law, 'Preliminary Document No 5 – Draft Business Plan for the Development of iSupport' (2009) <http://www.hcch.net/upload/wop/maint_pd05e2009.pdf> accessed 30 August 2011 ....158–59, 166
Restatement (Second) of Conflict of Laws 122
Conseil allemand pour le droit international privé, 'Proposition du Deustcher Rat für Internationales Privatrecht en vue de l'adoption d'une réglementation du droit international des sociétés au niveau européen/national' (2006) *Révue Critique* 712 149
Proposition de loi (No 2140) relative à la représentation équilibrée des femmes et des hommes au sein des conseils d'administration et de surveillance et à l'égalité professionnelle 11
Projet de Loi Pour l'Initiative Économique <http://www.assemblee-nationale.fr/12/pdf/projets/pl0507.pdf> accessed 30 August 2011 64
Entwurf eines Gesetzes zur Modernisierung des GmbH-Rechts und zur Bekämpfung von Missbräuchen (MoMiG), 23 May 2007 ....10, 63, 82
Treasury Committee, 'Women in the City' HC (2009-10) 482 11
Message concernant une loi fédérale sur le droit international privé, du 10 novembre 1982 (no 294.2) per B Dutoit, *Commentaire de la loi fédérale du 18 décembre 1987* (Helbing und Lichtenhahn Frankfurt-sur-le-Main 1996) ...16

1

Introduction

1.1 Aims

The manner in which the governing law of companies is determined has attracted much attention from academics and practitioners alike since the European Court of Justice began to receive references for preliminary rulings concerning the compatibility of protective conflict of corporate law norms with the EC Treaty provisions concerning freedom of establishment.[1] Although recent jurisprudential and legislative developments have been less controversial than the groundbreaking judgment in *Centros*,[2] they have not only consolidated the general thrust of liberalisation occasioned by the Court of Justice, but have added new dimensions to the regulatory landscape. The most recent of these developments include amendments to the European constitutional order enshrined in the Lisbon Treaty,[3] European legislation on cross-border mergers,[4] the proposed statute for a European Private Company,[5] the judgment of the ECJ in *Cartesio*,[6] and a Commission communication that considers the introduction of legislation on the governing law of companies.[7]

[1] See eg A Looijestijn-Clearie, 'Centros Ltd – A Complete U-Turn in the Right of Establishment for Companies?' (2000) *International and Comparative Law Quarterly* 621, 621–42; E Micheler, 'Recognition of Companies Incorporated in other EU Member States' (2003) *International and Comparative Law Quarterly* 521, 521–34; WF Ebke, 'The European Conflict-of-Corporate-Laws Revolution: Uberseering, Inspire Art and Beyond' (2004) *International Lawyer* 813, 813–53; WG Ringe, 'No Freedom of Emigration for Companies?' (2005) *European Business Law Review* 621, 621–42; B Angelette, 'The Revolution that Never Came and the Revolution Coming – *De Lasteyrie du Salliant, Marks & Spencer, Sevic Systems* and the Changing Corporate Law in Europe' (2006) *Virginia Law Review* 1189, 1189–1223; V Korom and P Metzinger, 'Freedom of Establishment for Companies: the European Court of Justice confirms and refines its *Daily Mail* Decision in the *Cartesio* Case C-210/06' (2009) *European Company and Financial Law Review* 147, 147–60; J Borg-Barthet, 'A New Approach to the Governing Law of Companies in the EU: A Legislative Proposal' (2010) *Journal of Private International Law* 589, 589–621; J Armour and WG Ringe, 'European Company Law 1999–2010: Renaissance and Crisis' (2011) *Common Market Law Review* 125, 125–74.

[2] Case C-212/97 *Centros Ltd v Erhvervs-og Selskabsstyrelsen* [1999] ECR I-01459.

[3] Treaty of Lisbon amending the Treaty on European Union and the Treaty establishing the European Community, signed at Lisbon, 13 December 2007 [2007] OJ C306/1.

[4] Directive 2005/56/EC of the European Parliament and of the Council of 26 October 2005 on cross-border mergers of limited liability companies [2005] OJ L310/1.

[5] Commission (EC), 'Proposal for a Council Regulation on the statute for a European private company' COM (2008) 396/3.

[6] Case C-210/06 *Cartesio Oktató és Szolgáltató bt* [2008] ECR I-9641.

[7] Commission (EC), 'An area of freedom, security and justice serving the citizen' (Communication) COM (09) 262 final, 14.

This book accounts for these recent developments and appraises the current law, as well as the foreseeable trajectory of the law, within a theoretical setting that addresses the socio-economic and legal-theoretical concerns associated with choices of the governing law of companies. In addition to consideration of the present and foreseeable state of EU law, the book develops new theoretical analyses and proposes novel solutions to some long-standing dilemmas. In particular, it is suggested that the use of information technology may render possible the previously impossible compromises between party autonomy and the proper locus of prescriptive sovereignty.

The central thesis is that the argument for private ordering serves to be qualified because both the existing legal basis and the theory underpinning party autonomy are imperfect. It is therefore proposed that European legislation should be introduced to provide a sound and certain legal basis for corporate mobility. Under current conditions, this should account for the competing claims of private ordering and the political peculiarities of each Member State. To this end, chapter 6 articulates a legislative proposal which strikes a balance between the integrationist agenda of the European Union and the ability of Member States to safeguard the interests of various stakeholders in corporate law.

The legislative proposal is based on a number of logical steps which are established in the book's earlier chapters. This chapter introduces relevant issues through an appraisal of the historical development of the law, as well as an overview of relevant corporate law and conflicts theory. Chapter 2 evaluates the cogency of the principle of party autonomy in the conflict of corporate laws through analogies with contractual choice of law and reference to corporate legal theory; Chapter 3 highlights interests which the private international laws of some states protect in preference to party autonomy. Having identified that private autonomy in choice of corporate law is a matter of legislative choice rather than dogma, Chapter 4 addresses the place of autonomy in the European Union's legal order. Chapter 5 appraises the jurisprudential evolution of conflict norms in the EU and illustrates that a failure to legislate coherently and comprehensively has vested the task of harmonisation in the wrong hands, namely those of the judicial branch of the Union. It is argued in that chapter that negative harmonisation has occurred against the express wishes of Member States that intended a more controlled and refined process of liberalisation. In addition, the present state of the law is internally incoherent and requires rationalisation. Chapter 6 then analyses options that are open to European legislators. An alternative to the current thrust of liberalisation is proposed in a manner that accounts for the genuine concerns of both protectionist and liberal policies. It is suggested that the use of information technology could facilitate a workable solution to replace the zero-sum conflict between the predominant choice of corporate law doctrines. Finally, Chapter 7 includes brief concluding remarks.

1.2 Scope

This book analyses the law and theory concerning the governing law of companies in Europe. It does not set out to define companies with precision, but addresses companies with a profit-making purpose, since it is only these companies that enjoy the right to freedom of establishment as defined in article 54 TFEU (article 48 EC). Excluded from this work is the law of insolvency, which is a discipline that merits analysis in its own right. Similarly, the tax implications of corporate freedom of establishment are only addressed where they are directly relevant to a study which is concerned with the implications of corporate mobility for the mechanics of corporate law itself. The problems are addressed principally from the perspective of European Union law, in particular with regard to its limiting effects on the laws of the Member States. Occasional references are also made to other jurisdictions where the law is illustrative of a broadly applicable principle, or a potential legislative concern.

The norms of EU law pertaining to the governing law of companies do not emanate from a private international law instrument that stands alone, but from the Treaty itself,[8] as well as the regulations and the directives of the Union that harmonise the private international law of companies in specific circumstances.[9] The Treaty basis for harmonisation therefore adds a constitutional dimension to the present study. In particular, it is pertinent to address the constitutional value of party autonomy. In addition, the harmonisation of substantive company law reduces the scope for conflicts of laws since the said conflicts are, in some respects, as between laws that have been transposed with a common purpose. Because the harmonisation of laws has a direct impact on the extent to which the determination of the governing law is of practical consequence, harmonisation may reduce the policy motivations for protective conflict of laws mechanisms. Accordingly, an analysis of the conflict of corporate laws must necessarily refer to constitutional foundations of EU company law and the laws of the Union that harmonise the company laws of the Member States. Thus, while the principal focus of this book remains the private international law of the Union, it is also necessary to address European law norms which have no direct bearing on the manner in which the governing law of companies is determined.

[8] Arts 49, 50 and 54 TFEU (arts 43, 44 and 48 EC). Art 293 of the EC Treaty, which has now been repealed, is addressed in view of its influence on the judgments of the ECJ which have shaped EU law in its present state.

[9] Council Directive (EC) 1994/45 on the establishment of a European Works Council or a procedure in Community-scale undertakings and Community-scale groups of undertakings for the purposes of informing and consulting employees [1994] OJ L254; Council Regulation (EC) 2157/2001 on the statute for a European company (SE) [2001] OJ L294/1; Directive (EC) 2005/56 of the European Parliament and of the Council of 26 October 2005 on cross-border mergers of limited liability companies [2005] OJ L310/1; Directive (EC) 2007/36 of the European Parliament and of the Council of 11 July 2007 on the exercise of certain rights of shareholders in listed companies [2007] OJ L184/17.

In order to further inform discussion concerning the dichotomy between liberal and protective conflict of corporate laws, this work analyses the underlying corporate law values that inform private international law theory and practice. Conflicts of corporate laws, arguably more than any other commercial area of private international law, must account for the fact that the corporate form is intended to serve both private and public goods.[10] The balance that is struck as between those goods, or indeed the manner in which the aggregate of those goods is best served, is subject to a value judgment by the legislators of each state. Indeed, corporate law is a highly regulated area of private law in any jurisdiction, and the selection of the governing law of companies therefore affects the full spectrum of matters that are regulated by corporate law. An understanding of corporate legal theory is therefore required if one is to properly devise a broadly acceptable system for the determination of the governing law of companies. Accordingly, this book also addresses discussions that are more commonly associated with corporate legal theory in order to better inform the discussion of concerns associated with the extent of states' prescriptive jurisdiction over corporations.

1.3 A History in Brief

Prior to the judgments of the Court of Justice, the vast majority of Member States adopted the real seat theory, which prescribes that a company is to be established under the law of the state in which its operational headquarters is situated. A minority of Member States adopted the incorporation theory, which dictates that a company is governed by the law of the state in which it is formally incorporated, regardless of whether it is connected thereto in any manner other than by virtue of the act of incorporation.[11]

The crux of the theoretical controversy between the real seat and incorporation theories stems from a disagreement regarding the extent to which a company is an expression of individual autonomy, or whether it is a result of the concession of the legal fiction of separate juridical personality by a state.[12] This is redolent of the debate between contractarians and concession theorists in the corporate law camp.[13] While

[10] J Dine, *The Governance of Corporate Groups* (Cambridge, Cambridge University Press, 2000) 3–29.

[11] For an overview of the two theories, see S Rammeloo, *Corporations in Private International Law: A European Perspective* (Oxford, Oxford University Press,2001) 11–20; E Rabel, *The Conflict of Laws: A Comparative Study*, vol II, 2nd edn (University of Michigan, 1960) 31–46; FJ Garcimartín Alférez, 'Cross-Border Listed Companies' (2007) 328 *Recueil des Cours de l'Académie de Droit International* 13, 48–55.

[12] Ebke (n 1) 817–18; E Stein, 'Conflict-of-Laws Rules by Treaty: Recognition of Companies in a Regional Market' (1970) *Michigan Law Review* 1327, 1333; F Guillaume, 'The Law Governing Companies in Swiss Private International Law' (2004) *Yearbook of Private International Law* 251, 257; A Johnston and P Syrpis, 'Regulatory Competition in European Company Law after *Cartesio*' (2009) *European Law Review* 378, 389–90.

[13] Dine (n 10) 67.

the truth is quite clearly that companies are the result of both private agreement and the assent of the state, philosophical differences in emphasis have resulted in different approaches to the extent to which incorporators should be free to select a company's governing law.[14] Consequently, both the real seat and incorporation theories have merit, and neither theory is flawless. Rather, the theories are grounded in divergent understandings of some elements of the nature and purpose of companies, and the extent of failure to bridge the gap between the theories lies in a dialogue that is often conducted at cross-purposes.[15]

It appears that the incorporation theory predates the real seat theory. As early as the eighteenth century, the United Kingdom recognised the incorporation theory as an instrument to grant free choice of corporate law to promoters of companies.[16] It is uncontroversial in UK company law that the domicile of a limited company is the place of registration or the country in which it was incorporated, and that 'in so far as nationality can by analogy be applied to a juristic person, its nationality is determined in an inalienable manner by the laws of the country from which it derives its personality.'[17] Similarly, in the nineteenth century, French promoters of companies are known to have set up companies under foreign laws in order to escape the stricter provisions of French law.[18] The emergence of the real seat theory can probably be traced back to the nineteenth century.[19] The admission of the possibility of the existence of a company outside the jurisdiction that gave it its legal personality led to the problem of recognition of companies and their governing laws in much the same form as the problem persists presently. Whereas companies were previously only allowed to be set up for a specific purpose and limited duration, the emergence of open registers was closely followed by corporate mobility.[20] The policy motivations for the emergence of the theory appear to be quite clear: in order to protect against the encroachment of corporate forms that were deemed to be lax, French law adopted the *théorie du siège réel* whereby companies are to be incorporated under the laws of the state in which their real seat, as opposed to their nominal seat, is situated. The theoretical foundations are somewhat more complicated. At a time when nationality was the principal connecting factor in private international law, and states set out to control their nationals, it became the norm that one could only be the subject of one

[14] ibid; Y Hadari, 'The Choice of National Law Applicable to the Multinational Enterprise and the Nationality of Such Enterprises' (1974) *Yale Law Journal* 1, 19–21.

[15] See RR Drury, 'The Regulation and Recognition of Foreign Corporations: Responses to the Delaware Syndrome' (1998) *Cambridge Law Journal* 165, 182–83.

[16] J Dammann, 'A New Approach to Corporate Choice of Law' (2005) *Vanderbilt Journal of Transnational Law* 51, 59; Drury (n 15) 178–88; Hadari (n 14) 19–21.

[17] *Kuenigl v Donnersmarck* [1955] 1 QB 515. See also *Gasque v Inland Revenue Commissioners* [1940] 2 KB 80; *Lazard Bros & Co v Midland Bank Ltd* [1933] AC 289; *Arab Monetary Fund Appellants v Hashim and Others Respondents (No 3)* [1991] 2 AC 114; *Westland Helicopters Ltd v Arab Organisation for Industrialisation* [1995] QB 282.

[18] Dammann (n 16) 59; Drury (n 15) 187–88.

[19] Angelette (n 1) 1193–94.

[20] ibid.

sovereign, namely the state of which one was a national.[21] Since companies were considered to be nationals of the state in which they had their operational headquarters, it followed that companies may only be the subject of that state, and incorporation under any other law was therefore precluded.[22]

1.3.1 International and Regional Unification

The need to harmonise rules on recognition of companies and to thereby provide a sound legal basis for businesses to operate transnationally was acknowledged at an early stage in the process of European integration. Efforts have been made to unify this area of private international law both globally through the Hague Conference, as well as at the regional level in the European Community. However, none can be said to have successfully bridged the ideological divide between the protective real seat theory and the autonomy-oriented incorporation theory. Two conventions were adopted by varying formations among the founding Member States, but neither mustered sufficient ratifications to enter into force.

The 1956 Hague Convention[23] was only ratified by three states, namely Belgium, France and the Netherlands. Luxembourg and Spain were also signatories, but never ratified the agreement. Spain was the only signatory from outside the EC. The Convention provided a somewhat unworkable solution, which did little more than to acknowledge the status quo. Contracting states would have been bound to recognise companies incorporated in other contracting states,[24] unless the state in which recognition was sought adopted the real seat theory.[25] In the latter case, states could depart from the incorporation theory, and refuse recognition if a company had its seat in a state which adopted the real seat theory.[26] Curiously, the Convention did not require states which applied the real seat theory to make a declaration to this effect, or that application of the real seat theory was to be allowed only by way of reservation. Thus little guidance was to be provided to stakeholders. Accordingly, the only bridging which the Convention would have occasioned was that real seat states would have been bound to acknowledge the existence of companies established in states which adopt the incorporation theory, and having their operational headquarters in such states. This was already the case in most real seat states which either legislated indifference to companies having their headquarters in other jurisdictions, or acknowledged the rights of other states to adopt their own rules on recognition of companies.[27]

[21] Rammeloo (n 11) 11.
[22] ibid.
[23] Hague Convention of 1 June 1956 concerning the recognition of the legal personality of foreign companies, associations and institutions (hereinafter 'Hague Convention').
[24] Hague Convention art 1.
[25] Hague Convention art 2.
[26] ibid.
[27] By way of example, Italian law adopts the incorporation theory in respect of companies that do not have their seat in Italy: L 31 maggio 1995, n 218 art 25; German law uses renvoi to refer the matter of recognition to the state in which the company's seat is situated: Rammeloo (n 11) 12 and 179.

The members of the European Community signed a Convention on the Mutual Recognition of Companies and Bodies Corporate in 1968.[28] The Convention was intended to remedy a situation in which it was deduced that freedom of establishment and enjoyment of other market freedoms were precluded by diverse rules on the recognition of companies, and where, despite the apparent liberalism of articles 49 and 54 TFEU (articles 43 and 48 EC), it was not expected that the Treaty itself would directly provide the basis for mutual recognition.[29]

The Convention required that the legal personality of companies established in a Member State must be recognised throughout the Community.[30] However, this was subject to the proviso that Member States could refuse to recognise companies established in the Community but not having a genuine link with the economy of any Member State.[31] This would guard against the automatic recognition of companies which were formally products of the laws of a Member State, but which were in fact operated from outside the Community. In addition, Member States could apply their own laws to companies having their real seat within their territory but established elsewhere in the Community.[32] Accordingly, two laws could be incumbent on the same company, namely the law of the state in which the company was incorporated, and the state in which the company's real seat was situated. The Convention did not prescribe clear limitations concerning which aspects of corporate law could be included in the scope of the mandatory rules that a Member State would apply. Effectively, this would have enabled the state in which a company's real seat was situated to prescribe the conditions under which a pseudo-foreign corporation would operate, a situation not dissimilar to the application of the real seat theory, save to the extent that the law would be formally bifurcated. The Convention did not provide a mechanism for the resolution of any conflicts between the two applicable laws, and it appears that the drafters did not foresee the possibility that the incumbency of two laws might expose the company and its officers to irreducible conflicts of obligations and a concomitant choice between suffering the penalties imposed by one state or another.[33]

The Convention was ratified by five of the founding Member States. However, the Netherlands refused to ratify the Convention, motivated by that country's adoption of the incorporation theory in 1959,[34] shortly before negotiations towards

[28] EC Convention on the Mutual Recognition of Companies and Bodies Corporate of 29 February 1968, Bulletin of the European Communities, Supplement 2/69 7–18 (hereinafter 'EC Convention 1968').

[29] M Goldman, 'La nationalité des sociétés dans la Communauté économique européenne' (1969) *Travaux du Comité français de droit internationale privé* 215, 219–26; Stein (n 12) 1329–31.

[30] EC Convention 1968 art 1.

[31] EC Convention 1968 art 3.

[32] EC Convention 1968 art 4.

[33] See Rammeloo (n 11) 36. For a discussion of conflicts of obligations in corporate law, see DA DeMott, 'Perspectives on Choice of Law for Corporate Internal Affairs' (1985) *Law and Contemporary Problems* 161, 172–79; AE Anton and PR Beaumont, *Private International Law: A treatise from the standpoint of Scots law*, 2nd edn (Edinburgh, W Green, 1990) 703.

[34] Drury (n 15) 181–82. T Ballarino, 'Sulla mobilità delle società nella Comunità Europea. Da *Daily Mail à Überseering*: norme imperative, norme di conflitto e libertà comunitarie' (2003) *Rivista delle società* 669, 670. In addition to the Netherlands' objections to the content of the Convention, there is

the adoption of the Convention began. The Dutch refusal to ratify the Convention rendered the instrument a dead letter. The absence of harmonisation was perceived as authority for Member States to retain their own conflict rules.[35] This view was endorsed by the European Court of Justice in its judgment in *Daily Mail*.[36]

As noted above, legislation has since been introduced in respect of some areas of the private international law of companies.[37] Plans are now afoot to introduce legislation of general application in the European Union.[38] However, they remain at an embryonic consultative phase. The most significant developments in the discipline which have led to a degree of unification of private international law have been occasioned by the European Court of Justice.[39] The judgments of the Luxembourg Court have gradually articulated limitations to the prescriptive jurisdiction of the Member States whereby companies incorporated under the laws of one Member State must be fully recognised by every other Member State. In addition, the ECJ has suggested that Member States may not impede changes in a company's governing law by requiring dissolution and reincorporation.[40]

1.4 Are Conflicts of Corporate Laws Still Relevant?

Companies have played an essential role in the social and economic organisation of territories ever since early British corporations were established to colonise the empire and to establish fiefdoms by and for the Crown.[41] Enlightened thinking accelerated the privatisation of economic governance.[42] The consequence of privatisation is that companies play a role that was previously considered to be public. This role grows as the generation and distribution of wealth are entrusted to private actors.[43] Nevertheless, private governance is highly regulated, and the

some evidence to suggest that the Netherlands was in no mood to be accommodating, following General De Gaulle's veto of the accession of the United Kingdom to the Community. See Stein (n 12) 1337.

[35] A Santa Maria, *European Economic Law* (Netherlands, Kluwer, 2009) 11; Rammeloo (n 11) 36–37; Stein (n 12) 1330.

[36] Case 81/87 *The Queen v HM Treasury and Commissioners of Inland Revenue, ex p Daily Mail and General Trust plc* [1988] ECR 5483.

[37] See n 9.

[38] Commission (EC), 'An area of freedom, security and justice serving the citizen' (Communication) COM (09) 262 final, 14.

[39] Centros (n 2); Case C-208/00 *Überseering BV v Nordic Construction Company Baumanagement GmbH* (NCC) [2002] ECR I-9919; Case C-167/01 *Kamer van Koophandel en Fabrieken voor Amsterdam v Inspire Art Ltd* [2003] ECR I-10155; Case C-411/03 *Sevic Systems AG* [2005] ECR I-10805; *Cartesio* (n 6).

[40] *Cartesio* (n 6) paras 110–12.

[41] J McLean, 'The Transnational Corporation in History: Lessons for Today?' (2004) *Indiana Law Journal* 363, 363–72.

[42] For an account of the introduction of limited liability in its historical context, see D Loftus, 'Capital and Community: Limited Liability and Attempts to Democratize the Market in Mid-Nineteenth-Century England' (2002) 45 *Victorian Studies* 93, 93–120.

[43] See Dine (n 10) 114–16.

approach to regulation is not uniform. The emergence of divergences in corporate law illustrates the fact that legislators are aware that the regulation of enterprise helps to define the social and economic construct of their territories.

However, there exist pressures on the relevance of conflicts of corporate laws, which should be addressed prior to delving deeper into a study of the discipline. First, the above-noted developments in EU law restrict the application of protective norms. Notwithstanding historical differences, there appears to be a significant degree of convergence on a singular, liberal model, insofar as conflicts within the EU are concerned. In this respect, suffice it to note at this juncture that there remain significant theoretical and legal questions to merit attention. However, substantive corporate law itself presents a further challenge. The policy motivations for a protective approach to the governing law of a company are, arguably, being gradually diminished in a related convergence on a singular model of corporate governance.

Of late, eminent corporate law scholars have proclaimed the end of history of corporate law.[44] They claim that there is a growing international consensus in favour of the shareholder primacy model which suggests that corporations are established for the benefit of shareholders, and that all other interests in the corporate form are ancillary to those of shareholders: 'just as there was rapid crystallization of the core features of the corporate form in the late nineteenth century, at the beginning of the twenty-first century we are witnessing a rapid convergence on the standard shareholder-oriented model as a normative view of corporate structure and governance'.[45] The impact of the predicted end of history of corporate law could be particularly significant for the discipline of the conflict of corporate laws. Although differences will remain in terms of specific substantive issues and private international law questions will therefore remain relevant, as indeed is the case in the United States, where conflicts of corporate laws have not been eliminated, notwithstanding significant convergence on the nature and purpose of the corporation,[46] the global acceptance of one broad model of corporate governance would have the net effect of reducing the policy justifications for protective conflicts norms. Accordingly, if the thesis that further corporate law reform will bring forth further substantive convergence is correct,[47] competition for incorporations would likely be the chief remaining policy motivation of any great consequence in choice of corporate law.

Proponents of the end of history thesis cite the failure of alternative models of corporate governance, legal competition, the emergence of an influential and organised shareholding class, and the influence of academia as reasons for the dominance of the shareholder model.[48] They take the view that it is unlikely that

[44] H Hansmann and R Kraakman, 'The End of History for Corporate Law' (2001) *Georgetown Law Journal* 439.

[45] ibid 443.

[46] See generally DeMott (n 33) 161–98.

[47] See generally Hansmann and Kraakman (n 44).

[48] ibid 443–53.

the development will be reversed.[49] Recent amendments to corporate laws in a plurality of European states lend credence to the view that there is an increased international consensus on the nature and purpose of the corporate form. Notable developments include the reform of the German GmbH, the French *société à responsabilité limitée* (SARL) and the Dutch BV.[50] Those civilian systems are fast approaching a model that is more akin to the United Kingdom's private company, that is a model that defers matters of corporate governance to the will of the shareholders. In addition to the national developments, the nascent European Private Company also closely follows the shareholder-primacy model and makes express reference to the contractual covenants of the shareholders.[51]

Despite a significant degree of convergence on the shareholder primacy model, and despite liberalisation in the conflict of laws camp, much like Fukuyama's political end of history, Hansmann and Kraakman's proclamation of the 'end of history for corporate law' was premature at best. It is conceded that the prevalent debate regarding corporate governance has been steered in the direction of the maximisation of shareholder value. However, there is also compelling evidence that the end of history is not nigh. In Europe there remain several states that include workers in the governance of firms to varying degrees.[52] At a supranational level there are harmonising and unifying measures that account for the place of workers in the firm, as well as the protection of other non-shareholder constituencies.[53] Indeed, Hansmann and Kraakman acknowledge the fact that European harmonisation of corporate law has been driven by a desire to stave off the shareholder primacy model.[54] Moreover, the continuing deference to non-shareholder constituencies is not merely an old-world phenomenon. Twenty-nine states in the USA have adopted constituency statutes which allow or oblige managers to consider the interests of non-shareholder constituencies in their decisions.[55] Even in

[49] ibid 443.

[50] Gesetzes zur Modernisierung des GmbH-Rechts und zur Bekämpfung von Missbräuchen (MoMiG); Loi n°2003-721 du 1 août 2003 pour l'initiative économique art 1; Dutch Ministry of Justice http://english.justitie.nl/currenttopics/pressreleases/archives2006/-Simplified-Formation-of-BVs-for-Smaller-companies-and-Start-up-Businesses.aspx. For academic commentary see: J Armour, 'Legal Capital: An Outdated Concept?' (2006) *European Business Organization Law Review* 5, 26; M Miola, 'Legal Capital and Limited Liability Companies: The European Perspective' (2005) *European Company and Financial Law Review* 413, 445; M Becht, C Mayer and F Wagner, 'Where do firms incorporate? Deregulation and the cost of entry' (2008) *Journal of Corporate Finance* 241, 252.

[51] Commission (EC), 'Proposal for a Council Regulation on the statute for a European private company' COM (2008) 396/3 recital 4.

[52] M Andenas and F Wooldridge, *European Comparative Company Law* (Cambridge, Cambridge University Press, 2009) 417–47.

[53] Council Directive (EC) 1994/45 on the establishment of a European Works Council or a procedure in Community-scale undertakings and Community-scale groups of undertakings for the purposes of informing and consulting employees [1994] OJ L254; Council Regulation (EC) 2157/2001 on the statute for a European company (SE) [2001] OJ L294/1; Directive (EC) 2005/56 of the European Parliament and of the Council of 26 October 2005 on cross-border mergers of limited liability companies [2005] OJ L310/1; Directive (EC) 2007/36 of the European Parliament and of the Council of 11 July 2007 on the exercise of certain rights of shareholders in listed companies [2007] OJ L184/17.

[54] Hansmann and Kraakman (n 44) 454.

[55] A Winkler, 'Corporate Law or the Law of Business? Stakeholders and Corporate Governance at the End of History' (2004) 67 *Law and Contemporary Problems* 109, 123.

Delaware, the standard-bearer of accommodating corporate law, there are situations where directors are entitled to take account of considerations other than shareholder value. The judgment in *Paramount Communications v Time*[56] is a case in point. The court held that Time's directors were within their rights to refuse to put a tender offer to a shareholder vote, notwithstanding that the acceptance of the tender would increase shareholder value in the short term. The directors opted instead for a merger with Warner Brothers, which had the net effect of rendering Time's shareholders a minority in a company that was heavily burdened by debt. The court reasoned that the directors were entitled to take protective action to safeguard the philosophy and practices of the corporation, notwithstanding that this would have negative short-term repercussions on shareholders. In the United Kingdom, another bastion of shareholder value, recent amendments to the Companies Act provide that the discretion of directors is not to be exercised exclusively for the benefit of shareholders. Whereas the principal duty is 'the success of company for the benefit of members as a whole', directors must also, as far as possible, have regard to other considerations, including: (a) the long-term effects of decisions, (b) the interests of employees, (c) relationships with suppliers and customers, (d) the impact of the company on the community and the environment, (e) the company's goodwill and (f) fairness between members of the company.[57]

In addition to long-standing divergences in corporate law, new divisions are emerging in Europe in respect of gender issues in corporate law. In much the same manner as socialism and conservative values led to divergences in the past, contemporary developments reflect new political sensibilities which provide compelling evidence that new lines will continue to be drawn between corporate legal cultures. France,[58] Spain[59] and Norway[60] have taken the view that the law should prescribe gender balance in the boards of certain companies, and similar developments are in the offing in other European states.[61] In contrast, a Treasury Report in the United Kingdom acknowledges the problem of under-representation of women, but suggests that equality should not be enforced through corporate laws.[62] This illustrates a continuing division regarding which matters are to be dealt with at the core of corporate law, and which should be left to other laws or to the market. Accordingly, convergence on a particular corporate model will continue to be counterbalanced by the permanence of some old divisions and the emergence of new divisions which reflect diverse approaches to the purpose of companies and the manner in which they are to be regulated.

[56] *Paramount Communications, Inc v Time, Inc*, Delaware Supreme Court 571 A 2d 1140.

[57] Companies Act 2006 s 172.

[58] Proposition de loi (No 2140) relative à la représentation équilibrée des femmes et des hommes au sein des conseils d'administration et de surveillance et à l'égalité professionnelle.

[59] Ley Orgánica 3/2007, de 22 de marzo, para la igualdad efectiva de mujeres y hombres art 75.

[60] See A Belcher, 'Board Diversity: Can Sex Discrimination Law Help?' (2005) *Northern Ireland Legal Quarterly* 356, 359–61.

[61] S Terjesen and V Singh, 'Female Presence on Corporate Boards: A Multi-Country Study of Environmental Context' (2008) *Journal of Business Ethics* 55, 62; C Villiers, 'Achieving Gender Balance in the Board Room: Is it Time for Legislative Action in the UK?' (2010) *Legal Studies* 533, 534.

[62] Treasury Committee, *Women in the City* (HC 2009–10) 482.

1.5 Provisional Conclusions

In view of the foregoing, it is submitted that the conflict of corporate laws remains a discipline that merits academic and legislative attention. In an environment where broad doctrinal controversies have been replaced by a case-by-case judicial development of European conflicts theory, it is all the more necessary to take stock of the state of development of the law and to determine whether the direction of legislative development is in harmony with the corporate law goals of the Union and its Member States. It is also necessary to evaluate whether the law is normatively and substantively coherent. This exercise will enable the elaboration of legislative solutions which are theoretically sound, widely acceptable and practically effective.

2

The Principle of Party Autonomy

2.1 Introduction

The judgments of the European Court of Justice have required Member States to adopt the incorporation theory in respect of the recognition of companies established under the laws of other Member States. The incorporation theory is sometimes characterised simply as that recognition theory which determines a company's governing law with reference to the jurisdiction in which the company is formally constituted.[1] Although this explanation is accurate, it does not represent the theory's principal distinguishing claim. Indeed, the real seat theory also, quite logically, requires concurrence of the governing law and formal constitution.[2] Rather the most significant distinction between the two theories is the extent to which they permit party autonomy in the election of a company's governing law and the situation of the company's seat.[3]

Under the incorporation theory, promoters of companies are at liberty to select any state in which to incorporate a company. They are not restricted in their choice by other connecting factors such as the situation of the company's seat. The formal argument is that companies are born of the law of their domicile, which in English law is considered to be the law of the state of their formal constitution.[4] Yet

[1] Y Hadari, 'The Choice of National Law Applicable to the Multinational Enterprise and the Nationality of Such Enterprises' (1974) *Yale Law Journal* 1, 7–8; S Rammeloo, *Corporations in Private International Law. A European Perspective* (Oxford, Oxford University Press, 2001) 16; B Dutoit, *Commentaire de la loi fédérale du 18 décembre 1987* (Frankfurt-sur-le-Main, Helbing und Lichtenhahn, 1996) 418–19; D Coester-Waltjen, 'German Conflict Rules and the Multinational Enterprise' (1976) *Georgia Journal of International and Comparative Law* 197, 203; V Korom and P Metzinger, 'Freedom of Establishment for Companies: the European Court of Justice confirms and refines its *Daily Mail* Decision in the *Cartesio* Case C-210/06' (2009) *European Company and Financial Law Review* 125, 140.

[2] RM Buxbaum, 'The Origins of the American "Internal Affairs" Doctrine Rule in the Corporate Conflict of Laws', in HJ Musielak and K Schurig (eds), *Festschrift für Gerhard Kegel* (Berlin, Kohlhammer, 1987) 86.

[3] WF Ebke, 'The European Conflict-of-Corporate-Laws Revolution: Überseering, *Inspire Art* and Beyond' (2004) *The International Lawyer* 813, 817–18; E Stein, 'Conflict-of-Laws Rules by Treaty: Recognition of Companies in a Regional Market' (1970) *Michigan Law Review* 1327, 1333; F Guillaume, 'The Law Governing Companies in Swiss Private International Law' (2004) *Yearbook of Private International Law* 251, 257; A Johnston and P Syrpis, 'Regulatory Competition in European Company Law after *Cartesio*' (2009) *European Law Review* 378, 389–90.

[4] P Reymond, 'Les personnes morales et les sociétés dans le nouveau droit international privé suisse', in F Dessemontet (ed), *Le nouveau droit international privé suisse. Travaux des journées d'études organisées par le Centre de droit de l'entreprise les 9 et 10 octobre 1987, à l'Université de Lausanne* (Lausanne, Cedidic, 1988) 143, 149; Ebke (n 3) 817–18.

underlying this is a premise founded in corporate legal theory which suggests that it is the shareholders who establish corporations, and that they do so for their own ultimate benefit.[5] Company statutes are therefore viewed principally as contractual instruments which govern the rights and obligations arising from the relationship thereby established.[6] The intercession of the state is viewed as a secondary factor of far lesser importance.[7] Notwithstanding doctrinal controversy in the corporate law camp, proponents of the incorporation doctrine are eager to advance the view that the private aspects of corporate law should extend freedom of choice in free and competitive international markets – 'to do so would be consistent with the highly contractualized view of corporation law that dominates the contemporary view of the subject'.[8] As a consequence of an essentially private conception of companies, the determination of the proper law of a company must rely on the contractual interests of the incorporators, as opposed to the interests of any state in governing the company's affairs, or the interests of those who contract with the company.[9]

In contrast, the real seat theory proposes that autonomy in the choice of the *lex societatis* should be limited to the law of the state in which promoters intend to set up their company's headquarters.[10] Thus the principal distinction is between the liberal contractual approach of the incorporation theory and the territorial approach of the real seat theory. The real seat model errs on the side of the state's prerogative to regulate corporate affairs within its territory, and to guard against avoidance of the laws of the state whose 'economic, political, social, and cultural life' the corporation is most intimately connected with.[11] The real seat theory does not deny freedom of choice entirely, provided that markets in products and services are unencumbered by barriers to international trade. It is, however, severely limited to the extent that incorporators are free to select a territory in which to establish the company's central office and to determine the governing law accordingly.[12] In reality, this brings several externalities to bear on individual freedom, not least the unquantifiable factor of an individual's attachment to a personal and cultural context.

[5] DA DeMott, 'Perspectives on Choice of Law for Corporate Internal Affairs' (1985) 48 *Law and Contemporary Problems* 161, 195–96; DM Majchrzak, 'Corporate Chaos: Who Should Govern Internal Affairs?' (2001) *Thomas Jefferson Law Review* 83, 87–88; S Lombardo, 'Conflict of Law Rules in Company Law after *Überseering*: An Economic and Comparative Analysis of the Allocation of Policy Competence in the European Union' (2003) *European Business Organization Law Review* 301, 320–22; MJ Whincop, 'Conflicts in the Cathedral: Towards a Theory of Property Rights in Private International Law' (2000) *University of Toronto Law Journal* 41, 52–54; EM Iacobucci, 'Toward a Signaling Explanation of the Private Choice of Corporate Law' (2004) *American Law and Economics Review* 319, 319–20; Hadari (n 1) 19–20.

[6] J Dine, *The Governance of Corporate Groups* (Cambridge, Cambridge University Press, 2000) 3–29, 67; B Audit, *Droit International Privé*, 3rd edn (Paris, Economica, 2000) 910.

[7] ibid.

[8] DeMott (n 5) 196.

[9] ibid.

[10] WF Ebke, '*Centros* – Some Realities and Some Mysteries' (2000) *The American Journal of International Law* 623, 635; WF Ebke, 'The "Real Seat" Doctrine in the Conflict of Laws' (2002) *The International Lawyer* 1015, 1028.

[11] ibid.

[12] ibid.

Yet the term 'party autonomy' appears only sporadically in the discourse of European private international law of companies. It is seldom referred to in the judgments of the Court of Justice, and then only obliquely.[13] Nor does any reference to party autonomy yet appear in any European measures for the approximation of corporate law, whether substantive or conflicts-related; there exists but one overt mention of 'contractual freedom' in the preamble to a proposed regulation.[14] The scarcity of legislative or judicial references to party autonomy belies the factual state of affairs. The notion that promoters of companies should be free to select the governing law of a company is indeed firmly embedded following *Centros*[15] – it is now commonplace for companies to be set up under a law other than that of the state in which they operate principally.[16]

The gulf between the language of the law and reality may arguably be explained with reference to the surreptitious nature of the harmonisation of European private international law of companies. Harmonisation is occurring under cover of the fundamental freedoms, rather than through direct engagement with conflicts questions. The result is that much of the discussion of recent developments in EU law fails to engage deeply with the question of whether party autonomy merits its emerging status as a core principle of European conflicts of corporate laws. The chapter therefore sets out to unpack the principle and evaluate the extent to which party autonomy may in fact form an appropriate basis for the unification of European private international law of companies, and as such as a possible instrument of substantive approximation of laws through legal competition.

The discussion is set out as follows: section 2.2 contextualises the discussion with reference to a global movement towards the furtherance of private ordering across the full spectrum of private international law and sketches a taxonomy of relationships in which private international law tends to favour autonomous election of the applicable law and/or choice of forum. In section 2.3 the contractual paradigm of corporate choice of law is discussed with reference to limits to party autonomy in contractual choice of law. Certain limits to autonomy in contractual choice of law are found to be applicable to corporate choice of law. Section 2.4 then explores the extent to which theories of the firm support the case for increasing autonomy. In the final analysis, it is argued that, although there is a compelling case for party autonomy, it is not entirely convincing, particularly upon consideration of internationally diverging views on the nature and purpose of the firm. The discussion that

[13] See Case C-208/00 Überseering *BV v Nordic Construction Company Baumanagement GmbH* (NCC) [2002] ECR I-9919 para 62. Overt reference to party autonomy was made in the Opinion of AG La Pergola in Case C-212/97 *Centros Ltd v Erhvervs-og Selskabsstyrelsen* [1999] ECR I-01459 para 20; this was not reflected in the judgment of the Court: See Johnston and Syrpis (n 3) 395–96; M Gestri, 'Mutuo Riconoscimento delle Società Comunitarie, Norme di Conflitto Nazionali e Frode alla Legge: il caso *Centros*' (2000) *Rivista di Diritto Internazionale* 71, 90.

[14] Draft Council Regulation on the statute for a European private company COM (2008) 396/3 recital 3.

[15] Case C-212/97 *Centros Ltd v Erhvervs-og Selskabsstyrelsen* [1999] ECR I-01459.

[16] See M Becht, C Mayer and HF Wagner, 'Where do Firms Incorporate?: Deregulation and the cost of entry' (2008) *Journal of Corporate Finance* 241, 242.

follows in chapter 3 sets out a non-exhaustive exposé of substantive limitations to party autonomy in the laws of a number of states.

2.2 A Global Movement Towards Party Autonomy?

Discussion of the emergent principle of party autonomy in European choice of corporate law may be situated in the context of a wider preponderance of freedom of choice in private international law. There is an increased global acceptance that party autonomy may supplant predefined rules as a means to connect transactions and disputes to a jurisdiction. Rules that are steeped in the territorial principle of jurisdiction, such as the real seat theory,[17] are increasingly becoming optional rather than prescriptive, and one can certainly discern a growing movement that situates party autonomy at the heart of private international law.[18] The discussion in this section is intended to facilitate a better understanding of: (i) whether the growing influence of party autonomy is inexorable in the broader discipline of private international law, and (ii) whether there is a discernible taxonomy of relationships where party autonomy is given a free rein. After identifying limits to the scope of party autonomy in private international law generally, the discussion in the following sections of this chapter considers how such limits may apply to private international law of companies.

Until recently, widespread acceptance of party autonomy in private international law was limited to contract law, where the universal basic tenet of private ordering in the municipal sphere[19] is readily accepted in the transnational sphere.[20] Yet there is now ample evidence that party autonomy is becoming a pervasive principle of private international law that extends far beyond contract. Relatively uncontroversial instruments that consecrate the principle include the Hague

[17] See Message concernant une loi fédérale sur le droit international privé, du 10 novembre 1982 (no 294.2) per B Dutoit (n 1) 17; H Muir Watt and LG Radicati di Brozolo, 'Party Autonomy and Mandatory Rules in a Global World' (2004) *International Law Forum* 90, 91–96.

[18] M Lehmann, 'Liberating the Individual from Battles between States: Justifying Party Autonomy in Conflict of Laws' (2008) *Vanderbilt Journal of Transnational Law* 381, 386–90; PJ Borchers, 'Contract and Tort Law: Categorical Exceptions to Party Autonomy in Private International Law' (2008) *Tulane Law Review* 1645, 1648–51; G Rühl, 'Party Autonomy in the Private International Law of Contracts: Transatlantic Convergence and Economic Efficiency' in E Gottschalk et al (eds), *Conflict of Laws in Globalized World* (Cambridge, Cambridge University Press, 2007) 155–58; E Friedler, 'Party Autonomy Revisited: A Statutory Solution to a Choice-of-Law Problem' (1989) *Kansas Law Review* 471, 474–79.

[19] T Weir (tr), K Zweigert and H Kötz, *An Introduction to Comparative Law,* 3rd edn (Oxford, Oxford University Press,1998) 324–26.

[20] The point of departure in discovering the governing law of a contract is a determination of whether the parties have designated a law applicable to their agreement. See eg Regulation (EC) 593/2008 of the European Parliament and of the Council on the Law Applicable to Contractual Obligations (Rome I) [2008] OJ L177/6 (hereinafter 'Rome I Regulation') art 3. For academic commentary, see M Reiman, 'Savigny's Triumph? Choice of Law in Contracts Cases at the Close of the Twentieth Century' (2008) *Virginia Journal of International Law* 571, 575–78; Rühl (n 18) 155–58; P Nygh, *Autonomy in International Contracts* (Oxford, Oxford University Press,1999) 13.

Convention on Choice of Court Agreements, which gives effect to exclusive choice of court agreements in civil and commercial matters,[21] as well as European legal instruments such as the Brussels I Regulation, which recognises prorogation clauses.[22] The growing tide in favour of autonomous election of the governing law of a dispute or relationship is evidenced in the deference to party autonomy in family law matters, and matters related to succession: the recent Hague Protocol on the Law Applicable to Maintenance Obligations contains a clause that limitedly empowers parties to designate the law applicable to their dispute;[23] the EC Maintenance Regulation adopts the rules on applicable law in the Hague Protocol,[24] and allows parties to choose a court from a defined list of connected jurisdictions;[25] similarly, the proposed EC Succession Regulation allows limited choices of law;[26] the Brussels II *bis* Regulation also allows limited prorogation of jurisdiction in matters relating to the parental responsibility and child abduction;[27] perhaps most controversially, in a socially and religiously diverse Europe, the Rome III Regulation allows parties limited choice of law in respect of matters relating to divorce and legal separation.[28] Indeed, party autonomy has been admitted in areas of law that were previously considered to be incompatible with that principle, including tort,[29] personal status, and procedural law.[30]

Justification for a movement towards party autonomy is to be found in an emphasis on the *private* nature of private international law. When one considers the parties that have an interest in private international law questions on a case-by-case basis, it is usually individuals rather than states and their legal systems that are directly affected by a dispute. Where states are party to a private international law dispute, it is not in their regulatory capacity but in their capacity *iure gestionis* where they are to be treated as any private actor:

> The justification of party autonomy has to start by recalibrating the problem of conflicts. The issue is not, as most theories suggest, a struggle between states for the application of their respective laws. It is important to move beyond that idea and instead think about

[21] Hague Convention on Choice of Court Agreements 2005.

[22] Council Regulation (EC) 44/2001 on jurisdiction and the recognition and enforcement of judgments in civil and commercial matters [2001] OJ L12/1 (hereinafter 'Brussels I Regulation') art 23.

[23] Hague Protocol of 23 November 2007 on the Law Applicable to Maintenance Obligations art 8.

[24] Council Regulation (EC) 4/2009 on jurisdiction, applicable law, recognition and enforcement of decisions and cooperation in matters relating to maintenance obligations [2009] OJ L 7/1 art 15.

[25] ibid art 3.

[26] Commission (EC), 'Proposal for a Regulation of the European Parliament and of the Council on jurisdiction, applicable law, recognition and enforcement of decisions and authentic instruments in matters of succession and the creation of a European Certificate of Succession' COM (2009) 154 final arts 5, 16 and 17.

[27] Council Regulation (EC) 2201/2003 concerning jurisdiction and the recognition and enforcement of judgments in matrimonial matters and the matters of parental responsibility, repealing Regulation (EC) No 1347/2000 [2003] OJ L 338/1 art 12.

[28] Council Regulation (EU) 1259/2010 implementing enhanced cooperation in the area of the law applicable to divorce and legal separation [2010] OJ L343/10 art 5.

[29] Regulation of the European Parliament and the Council (EC) 864/2007 on the law applicable to non-contractual obligations (Rome II) [2007] OJ L199/40 art 14.

[30] Lehmann (n 18) 386–88.

when and why conflict problems start in the first place: conflicts of laws begin with a dispute between individuals.[31]

The case for characterising the conflicts process as essentially private is certainly compelling. Conflicts of laws do begin with a dispute between individuals, and it is those individuals who are most directly interested in the solution to their dispute.

Contemporary justifications for party autonomy are seated in the liberal philosophies of the enlightenment.[32] Autonomy was premised on the notion that the public good was best served by individual freedom to serve one's own ends and to thereby generate wealth: 'It is not from the benevolence of the butcher, the brewer, or the baker that we expect our dinner, but from their regard to their own interest.'[33] It follows that markets should be free, and that individuals should prescribe their rights and obligations on the basis of their own evaluation of risks and opportunities.[34] This is particularly poignant in the context of European economic integration which was, in part, inspired by Adam Smith's view that individuals should be politically and economically liberated from the state.[35] Given this broad acceptance of contractual liberty following Western Europe's embrace of liberal philosophy, it appears that the point of departure must be that autonomy is to be respected.

Yet, the extent of a movement towards the furtherance of party autonomy in private international law must be qualified. Party autonomy is not an absolute good and is not enforced without exception. It must be balanced with the rights of third parties and the interests of states in the governance of their territories. The above-mentioned instruments limit party autonomy to a defined material scope of a private nature. By definition, excluded from the scope of these instruments are all matters that are *iure imperii*. Several private law matters are also excluded, or the extent of autonomy limited by the application of mandatory rules. These invariably either reflect a strong State interest, such as the integrity of public records,[36] or the desire of some states to protect particular societal interests or norms such as matrimonial relationships[37] and consumer welfare.[38] In the latter cases individual liberty is curtailed or negated in order that other goods may be safeguarded. The furtherance of party autonomy is therefore limited to such areas of law as are deemed to be of a purely private nature. Where a legal relationship relates to the social construct of a territory, affects parties other than the contractors, or where there is a perceived imbalance between contractors, the law must balance individual liberty with such other goods as are relevant to the matter.

[31] Lehmann (n 18) 413; see also DeMott (n 5) 195–96.

[32] PS Atiyah, *The Rise and Fall of Freedom of Contract* (Oxford, Clarendon, 1979) 292–321; Nygh (n 20) 7–8.

[33] A Smith, *The Wealth of Nations: Books I and II* (London, Penguin, 1999) 119.

[34] Nygh (n 20) 7–8.

[35] I Ward, *A Critical Introduction to European Law*, 3rd edn (Cambridge, Cambridge University Press, 2009) 113–20.

[36] Brussels I Regulation art 22(3).

[37] Brussels I Regulation art 2(a).

[38] Rome I Regulation art 6.

As a matter of principle, if one is to conform to the growing consensus in private international law, the pertinent test for party autonomy in corporate law is therefore the extent to which corporate law qualifies to be treated as a matter in which the autonomous will of individuals should be given a free rein, or if there are policy reasons for the limitation of autonomy, whether for the protection of third parties or overriding State interests.

2.3 Analogies with Contract Law

This section employs analogies with contract law to evaluate the cogency of the contractual paradigm of choice of corporate law and to determine whether the said paradigm should be refined. In *Powell Duffryn* the European Court of Justice found that intra-company relationships were akin to a contract. It reasoned as follows:

> The setting up of a company is the expression of the existence of a community of interests between the shareholders in the pursuit of a common objective. In order to achieve that objective each shareholder is assigned, as regards other shareholders and the organs of the company, rights and obligations set out in the company's statutes . . . for the purposes of the application of the Brussels Convention, the company's statutes must be regarded as a contract covering both the relations between the shareholders and also the relations between them and the company they set up.[39]

The Advocate General, whose Opinion the Court endorsed generally, conceded that 'a resolution of a majority at a meeting of the company . . . in principle resists inclusion in any contractual classification'.[40] However, he then dismissed the contractual-institutional dichotomy as merely theoretical and found that a company resolution was in fact a contract for the purposes of the Brussels Convention.[41] The judgment in *Powell Duffryn* concerned prorogation of jurisdiction rather than choice of law, but it is noteworthy for present purposes because it is the Court's most potent statement to date in support of the contractual paradigm of transnational corporate law.[42] As noted above, several proponents of free choice in the election of the governing law of companies employ contractual analogies to support their thesis.[43] For the sake of the argument, this section accepts the premise that a corporate statute is a contractual instrument. From that point of departure it goes on to illustrate that a corporate statute is similar to those classes of contract in which the legislator intervenes to limit party autonomy, whether in European private international law or through the harmonisation of substantive law.

[39] Case C-214/89 *Powell Duffryn plc v Petereit* [1992] ECR I-01745 para 10.

[40] *Powell Duffryn* (n 39) para 4 (AG Tesauro).

[41] ibid.

[42] However, the Court itself conceded that the judgment was motivated by the utilitarian purpose of furthering certainty and avoiding multiple grounds of jurisdiction in the context of the Brussels Convention: *Powell Duffryn* (n 39) para 20.

[43] DeMott (n 5) 195–96; Majchrzak (n 5) 87–88; Lombardo (n 5) 320–22; Whincop (n 5) 52–54.

2.3.1 *Lex Societatis* or *Lex Contractus*?

Prior to delving deeper into contractual analogy, it is pertinent to distinguish the private international law of corporations from that of contracts. The thesis that conflicts of corporate laws should be resolved with reference to contractual principle begs the question as to why the private international law of contract is not applied to determine a company's governing law. If one takes the suggestion that choices of corporate law should be adhered to as contracts at face value, there is a principled argument that the 'contract' between incorporators should be capable of being governed by the same principles as any other contract. In default, there is an implicit admission that corporate law is a distinct discipline that is at least capable of being regulated in its own right as a matter of conflicts theory. Why then is it that the private international law of contract is not applied to corporations?

The laws of several states[44] and a judgment of the European Court of Justice emphasise contractual aspects of the corporate statute.[45] The proposed Statute for a European Private Company also refers to the maximisation of 'the contractual freedom of shareholders' in selecting both the situation of the company's operational headquarters and the company's governing law.[46] Indeed, it has been posited in the work of eminent scholars that the governing law of a company is to be called the *lex contractus.*[47] Accordingly, it is not theoretically inconceivable that the governing law of a company should be determined with reference to the *lex contractus.* If the applicability of contractual principle were not plausible, there would have been no need to explicitly exclude corporate law from the scope of application of the Rome I Regulation[48] and the Convention that it replaces,[49] as is in fact the case. The drafters of the Rome Convention found that it was necessary to exclude from the operation of that instrument 'questions governed by the law of companies . . . such as the creation, by registration or otherwise, legal capacity, internal organization or winding up of companies . . . and the personal liability of officers and members as such for the obligations of the company'.[50] By implication, one could safely conclude that the drafters felt that if corporate law were not excluded explicitly, the internal affairs of corporations might have been deemed to be included in the scope of the convention. In fact, the Giuliano-Lagarde report

[44] See AG Tesauro in *Powell Duffryn* (n 39) para 4.

[45] *Powell Duffryn* (n 39).

[46] Commission (EC), 'Proposal for a Council Regulation on the statute for a European private company' COM (2008) 396/3 recital 3.

[47] Cansacchi suggests that the *lex contractus* of a company is to be determined either by reference to the place in which the constitutive act of the company was perfected or by reference to the law of the common nationality of all of the subscribers to the company's statute: G Cansacchi, 'Le choix et l'adaptation de la règle étrangère dans le conflit des lois' (1953) II *Recueil des Cours de l'Académie de Droit International* 81; see also A Santa Maria, 'Problemi attinenti al diritto internazionale privato e processuale delle società' (1987) *Rivista delle Società* 1473, 1476.

[48] Rome I Regulation art 1(2)(f).

[49] Rome Convention art 2(e).

[50] ibid.

does not state that corporate law should not be governed by a contracts convention because corporate law is implicitly not contractual. Rather, the drafting group 'thought it inadvisable, even in the original preliminary draft, to include companies, firms and legal persons within the scope of the Convention, especially in view of the work being done on this subject within the European Communities.'[51] The report therefore indicates that contractual choice of law norms could be applicable to the conflict of corporate laws, but that this was inadvisable because corporate law was being addressed in the context of the Community's harmonisation programme. The concern that the Rome Convention might be applied to companies is also reflected in German law, where the only occasion where the legislator has felt the need to enact a written law regarding the governing law of companies is in the transposition of article 2(e) of the Rome Convention.[52]

Yet in reality there is no doubt that the private international law of corporations is distinct from the private international law of contract; the intervention of the State is a *sine qua non* for the formation of a company.[53] This is not so for most contractual transactions, which may be completed without public involvement. In fact, the system for the maximisation of party autonomy in transnational corporate law is to connect a company to its governing law by looking to the place of incorporation, the *lex incorporationis*. The governing law is therefore determined by looking to the place where the administrative act of incorporation has perfected the agreement among promoters of companies, without which mere agreement is inconsequential. One does not explore contractual parallels applicable in the absence of choice, such as the place of the characteristic performance of the contract. The distinction between conflicts of corporate laws and contract law is therefore patent. The *lex contractus* is not applicable to companies, despite the fact that contractual liberty is cited as one of the merits of and justifications for the incorporation theory. Accordingly, the analysis below addresses contractual analogies with choice of corporate law in the knowledge that the two disciplines are distinct, but also aware that there is ample doctrinal common ground and that the inspiration for party autonomy in corporate choice of law is indeed to be found in contractual principle.

2.3.2 Displacing Contractual Covenants – Protection of the Weaker Party

As the ECJ observed in *Powell Duffryn*,[54] when one acquires a share in a company one freely assumes all of the rights and obligations attaching to that share.[55] The

[51] M Giuliano and P Lagarde, 'Report on the Convention on the Law Applicable to Contractual Obligations' [1980] OJ C282/01.

[52] See Ebke 2002 (n 10) 1017–18.

[53] Santa Maria (n 47) 1476–77.

[54] *Powell Duffryn* (n 39).

[55] ibid paras 27–28.

applicability of contractual principle to the governing law of companies therefore appears to be incontrovertible insofar as shareholders are concerned. However, the contractual paradigm fails to account for the fact that European contract law limits the applicability of contractual clauses that are deemed to be oppressive to parties in a weaker negotiating position, such as consumers.[56] The libertarian foundations of contract law are thus displaced in exceptional circumstances where the legislator identifies a market failure that calls for the intervention of the State on behalf of a vulnerable party to a contract whose consent may be partially vitiated by said vulnerability.[57] The Rome I Regulation adds a further layer of protection in addition to harmonised national laws. As regards consumer contracts, it provides that, in default of choice, contracts shall be governed by the law of the consumer's habitual residence. Choices of law that derogate from the default rule 'may not, however, have the result of depriving the consumer of the protection afforded to him by provisions that cannot be derogated from by agreement by virtue of the law which, in the absence of choice, would have been applicable by virtue of the law' of his habitual residence.[58] It is submitted that if shareholders could be assimilated with the weaker party in contracts, the central premise of the contractual paradigm of corporate law must be qualified. This sub-section shows that it is in fact unrealistic to deem all shareholders to be informed contractors, and that there are sufficient similarities between a consumer and certain classes of shareholder to call for the refinement of the contractual paradigm, by accounting for the potential limitations to party autonomy in contract law itself.

The Unfair Contract Terms Directive defines a 'consumer' as 'any natural person who . . . is [transacting] for purposes outside his trade, business or profession.'[59] The notion that a shareholder, who is by definition an entrepreneur, could be considered to be analogous with a consumer is not immediately obvious. As investors in companies, shareholders are 'part of the apparatus of producers rather than consumers'.[60] As such, prima facie, shareholders resist categorisation as consumers. However, closer examination indicates that 'consumer-shareholders', that is shareholders whose ordinary business is not the buying and selling of shares or the administration of relevant businesses, suffer an informational imbalance that is similar to that of an inexpert consumer.[61] Indeed, shareholders who invest via intermediaries 'are also consumers – of financial services, namely the services of

[56] Council Directive (EEC) 1993/13 on unfair terms in consumer contracts [1993] OJ L095/29 (Unfair Contract Terms Directive) art 3.

[57] TC Hartley, *International Commercial Litigation: Texts, Cases and Materials on Private International Law* (Cambridge, Cambridge University Press, 2009) 566; CGJ Morse, 'Consumer Contracts, Employment Contracts and the Rome Convention' (2000) *International and Comparative Law Quarterly* 1, 1.

[58] Rome I Regulation art 6.

[59] Unfair Contract Terms Directive art 2(b); substantively identical definitions are employed in art 15 of the Brussels I Regulation and art 6 of the Rome I Regulation.

[60] See BW Harvey and DK Perry, *The Law of Consumer Protection and Fair Trading*, 6th edn (London, Butterworths, 2000) 64.

[61] ibid; Justice, *The Protection of the Small Investor* (Cambridge, Justice Educational and Research Trust, 1992) 9–10; P Cartwright, 'Consumer Protection in Financial Services: Putting the Law in Context' in P Cartwright (ed), *Consumer Protection in Financial Services* (London, Kluwer, 1999) 6.

advisers, brokers, dealers, managers etc',[62] while shareholders generally are viewed in a similar light through the prism of company law.[63] Surely if one is to accept the contractual paradigm of the conflict of corporate laws, one must also accept that restrictions to party autonomy in contract law itself may apply to certain subscribers to the corporate contract.

The informational imbalance suffered by some shareholders is perpetuated and exacerbated by the fluidity and longevity of the corporate statute. The pliability of the rights and obligations of shareholders constitutes a major departure from contractual principle. Indeed, the more strictly contractual corporate laws of most nineteenth-century states did not allow any changes to the founding covenants in a company statute.[64] This was in keeping with general principles of contract law whereby contractual covenants may only be altered with the express consent of all parties thereto.[65] In that legal environment, rights and obligations were as clear and foreseeable as the quality of their drafting permitted. Nowadays, shareholders' relations with one another and with the company may change at the behest of the majority controlling the company from time to time. This calls to mind the above-quoted passage from AG Tesauro's Opinion in *Powell Duffryn*: 'a resolution of a majority at a meeting of the company . . . in principle resists inclusion in any contractual classification'.[66] Since some shareholders are in fact akin to consumers, the fact that rights and obligations may change to the point of becoming unrecognisable, without the consent of all shareholders, must be viewed in a similar light to unilateral alteration of consumer contracts – that is, that clauses which enable the seller or service provider unilaterally to alter the terms of a contract may be regarded as unfair and as such may be set aside by mandatory state law.[67]

The longevity of the corporate contract is also of consequence to the treatment of intra-company relationships. The law of contract generally governs relationships that are transient, the lacunae in which can often be resolved with reference to the express intention of the parties. Where relationships are indefinite, such as in the case of employment contracts, the law intervenes to compensate for inevitable lacunae by superimposing norms that reflect the political consensus in the states concerned.[68] The extent of intervention of the law is such as to render these particular contractual relationships legal disciplines in their own right. More pertinently for present purposes, it also creates differences in national laws, based on the political consensus in each state, such as to justify limitations to party autonomy in transnational law.[69] In much the same manner, subscription to

[62] AC Page and RB Ferguson, *Investor Protection* (London, Weidenfeld and Nicolson, 1992) 14.
[63] ibid 13.
[64] A Conard, 'Fundamental Changes in Marketable Share Companies' in *International Encyclopedia of Comparative Law*, vol XIII: Business and Private Organizations, ch 6 (1972) 6.
[65] ibid.
[66] *Powell Duffryn* (n 39) para 4 (AG Tesauro).
[67] The Unfair Contract Terms Directive, Annex para (j).
[68] See N Selwyn, *Selwyn's Law of Employment*, 15th edn (Oxford, Oxford University Press 2008) 76; H Kötz and T Weir (tr), *European Contract Law*, vol I (Clarendon, Oxford 1997) 127.
[69] See Rome I Regulation art 8.

shares does not constitute subscription to a fixed set of rights and obligations, but subscription to rights and obligations that can be altered under particular conditions. Further, the parties to the corporate contract are likely to change during that time. The substitutability of the parties creates an element of blind trust that is unparalleled in other contractual instruments and that therefore calls for further refinement of the contractual paradigm. This is mitigated, to some extent, by the fact that entity shielding and the limitation of liability reduce monitoring costs between shareholders.[70] However, in practice, the value of shareholders' investments and shareholders' ability to participate effectively in the company remains vulnerable to those who control the company from time to time.[71]

The shareholders' vulnerability to loss of autonomy and authority over their investment has additional consequences.[72] If one accepts the incorporators' right to select a governing law and to regulate the corporation accordingly, their decision to empower directors to control an enterprise, and indeed to choose an alternative jurisdiction in which to reincorporate a company,[73] should be enforced in the same manner as any other lawful agreement freely entered into. Yet jurisdictions that are otherwise liberal in their approach to party autonomy adopt outreach statutes designed to protect the rights of shareholders by extraterritorially enforcing rights or by superimposing obligations on directors of pseudo-foreign companies.[74] This evidences legislators' preference for the limitation of the effects of the choice of law as a contractual covenant in cases where the said covenant is not beneficial to shareholders as a broad class.

As against the argument for characterising a minority shareholder as a weaker contracting party, it could be argued that shareholders in public companies have the peculiar ability to terminate their contract unilaterally without thereby incurring any penalty. The ability to sell shares without the approval of other contractors qualifies the extent to which shareholders are in fact the weaker contractual party. However, the dependency arising from minority status means that the value of shares depends on the decisions of those controlling the corporation.[75] Indeed, agency costs such as the misallocation of funds or the alteration of minority rights may reduce the real value of shares and thereby create an insurmountable disincentive to the termination of the relationship between dissatisfied shareholders and the company. The continued autonomy of shareholders may therefore be severely impeded by their vulnerability to factors over which they have no effective control.

[70] H Hansmann, R Kraakman and R Squire, 'Law and the Rise of the Firm' (2006) *Harvard Law Review* 1335, 1350.

[71] D Kershaw, *Company Law in Context: Text and Materials* (Oxford, Oxford University Press, 2009) 582–85.

[72] Shareholders tend to choose corporate governance models that favour director supremacy: see LA Stout, 'Bad and Not-So-Bad Arguments for Shareholder Primacy' (2002) 75 *Southern California Law Review* 1189, 1202.

[73] See DeMott (n 5) 181.

[74] See section 3.2.1.

[75] Kershaw (n 71) 582–85.

In view of the potential vulnerability of shareholders, it is submitted that the corporate statute can indeed be compared to a contract in which some shareholders may be deemed to be a weaker party that should be protected by mandatory rules. This approach is not free of theoretical shortcomings in view of the fact that shareholders constitute a broad class of persons that have varying degrees of vulnerability and, arguably, suffering varying degrees of rational apathy – from institutional investors to uninformed savers, and from controlling majority shareholders to the holders of non-voting shares.[76] However, it is not the purpose of this section to address the minutiae of corporate law. Rather, it is intended to illustrate that the broad statement of the contractual paradigm is capable of qualification on the basis of contemporary contractual principle. Moreover, the theoretical difficulty posed by diversity among shareholders is not unique – one could say the same of consumer contracts in which some consumers are better informed and better placed to protect their interests than others. It is therefore submitted that it is plausible to refine the contractual paradigm by also accounting for the vulnerability of minority shareholders. Effectively, this could result in a denial of party autonomy in corporate choice of law on the basis of contractual principle itself, as understood in contemporary European law.

2.3.3 A Standard Form Contract?

In addition to the possible application of principles of the law of consumer protection to shareholders, contract law may allow for the protection of other stakeholders by way of exception to party autonomy. Some difficulty is posed by the fact that all persons who willingly interact with a company do so with the benefit of the knowledge, or at least the possibility of having the knowledge, of its constitutional foundations, including the content of the law by which the company is governed. In theory, one may therefore employ contractual mechanisms to charge the company for any risks inherent in the chosen corporate form.[77] However, it is also arguable that the statutes drawn up by the promoters of a company and their choice of governing law act as a standard form contract that all future stakeholders in corporate life will be bound by.[78] By way of example, minority shareholders who subscribe to shares after a company has been incorporated have only such rights to dividend payments as are enshrined in the corporate statute and the law of the land, or rather the chosen land. Creditors are protected by capital maintenance

[76] For a discussion of the problem of rational apathy, and its pervasiveness, see SM Bainbridge, 'Director Primacy and Shareholder Disempowerment' (2006) *Harvard Law Review* 1735, 1745; LA Bebchuk, 'The Case for Increasing Shareholder Power' (2005) *Harvard Law Review* 833, 891; R Romano, 'Answering the Wrong Question: The Tenuous Case for Mandatory Corporate Laws' (1989) *Columbia Law Review* 1599, 1611.

[77] See SE Woodward, 'Limited Liability in the Theory of the Firm' in DA Wittman (ed), *Economic Analysis of the Law: Selected Readings* (Oxford, Blackwell, 2003) 153.

[78] See O Hart, 'An Economist's Perspective on the Theory of the Firm' (1989) *Columbia Law Review* 1757, 1764.

rules, but they must take or leave them as they appear in the law or the company statute. Employees similarly must accept any such provision for participation in the governance of a firm as the employing company's governing law provides.

If one accepts that persons other than shareholders may indeed be stakeholders in the company's development, it follows that the corporate contract creates conditions that the said stakeholders must accept or reject as a whole.[79] Conversely, if one is of the view that such persons are external to the company, an analogy with a natural person is better suited than one with a contractual template. When one transacts with a natural person one must accept that person's circumstances as a non-negotiable fact, and it is equally arguable that those circumstances are the canvas to which every other contractual condition is applied. The economic nature of companies is discussed in further detail in section 2.4 of this chapter. At this juncture, it is merely submitted that it is not helpful to assimilate a natural person and a company without taking the special legal features of corporations into account. Even if one accepts equivalence between legal personality endowed by law and legal personality acquired at birth, the privilege of the limited liability of a company's shareholders must rationally call for some refinement of the analogy between natural and legal persons. In effect the limitation of the incorporators' liability constitutes a transfer of risk from the entrepreneur to his or her creditors.[80] In view of the risk incurred by creditors, the laws of every state have, to varying degrees, concurred with those economic theorists who argue that creditors are an integral part of the company and that the agreement between shareholders must provide for the inclusion of their interests in the considerations of corporate decision-makers.[81] Corporate statutes and the laws upon which they are founded also create non-negotiable conditions that delimit the rights of third parties. Crucially, these conditions vary from one state to another, and creditors are therefore directly affected by choices of corporate law. The contractual paradigm thus rests on the assumption that third parties such as creditors have agreed to be bound by the conditions of the contract between the shareholders and the law of the said contract, an assumption that gives rise to some 'theoretical difficulty' in view of the principle of the privity of contract.[82] If one accepts this analogy, the effect of choices of corporate law on third parties in a weaker negotiating position provides an arguable case for the limitation of the effects of the incorporators' autonomy.

Insofar as shareholders other than the original subscribers are concerned, it is patently the case that the corporate statute can be equated with a standard form contract that they may take or leave. If one also accepts that shareholders can be equated with consumers, as is argued in the immediately foregoing subsection, it

[79] See L Enriques and M Gelter, 'Regulatory Competition in European Company Law and Creditor Protection' (2006) *European Business Organization Law Review* 417, 429.

[80] Woodward (n 77) 153.

[81] J Armour, G Hertig and H Kanda, 'Transactions with Creditors' in R Kraakman and others (eds), *The Anatomy of Corporate Law. A Comparative and Functional Approach*, 2nd edn (Oxford, Oxford University Press, 2009) 115.

[82] ER Latty, 'Pseudo-Foreign Corporations' (1955) *Yale Law Journal* 137, 138.

follows that the argument for the refinement of the contractual paradigm of corporate law is strengthened further. The contractual paradigm of choice of corporate law may therefore also be refined to account for contractual limitations to the effects of standard form contracts – limitations that stem from the understanding that standard form contracts do not necessarily constitute an expression of the will of both parties, since one party would not have had the opportunity to contribute to the covenants contained therein but could only accept or refuse the agreement as a whole.

However, it is not clear that third parties other than consumers, who are protected by consumer protection legislation regardless of corporate law,[83] can be equated with parties to a standard form contract who are deemed worthy of protection in the general law of contract. European private international law does not generally preclude choices of law and prorogation of jurisdiction through standard form contracts.[84] Nor does the Hague Choice of Court Convention contain any restriction concerning standard form contracts in business-to-business transactions.[85] It is only if one accepts the view of the firm as a broad nexus of contracts, and if one also accepts that parties such as suppliers and employees are weaker parties in that nexus,[86] that the analogy in this sub-section can be extended to non-shareholder constituencies.

2.3.4 Reincorporation as Novation

The tenuous nature of the contractual paradigm of corporate choice of law is most striking when one considers the implications of a change in the governing law of existing companies. Freedom of incorporation in its fullest form includes freedom of reincorporation in a state other than the original state of incorporation. The ECJ has suggested that Member States may not prevent a company from changing the situation of its seat if this is accompanied by a change in governing law.[87] Thus a company established under the laws of one Member State may change its governing law without the need of winding up and being established anew.

If the contractual paradigm is accepted, there is no overt difference between changing the governing law of a company and changing the governing law in the general law of contract. Parties may agree to amend or insert a new governing law clause in a contract and otherwise leave the contract unaffected and in continued operation, and the facility to do so is recognised unqualifiedly in the Rome I Regulation.[88]

However, it is submitted that the difference is considerable, and such as to render reincorporation more akin to novation than to a mere change in the governing

[83] Council Directive (EEC) 1993/13 on unfair terms in consumer contracts [1993] OJ L095/29.
[84] See Brussels I Regulation; Rome I Regulation.
[85] Hague Convention on Choice of Court Agreements 2005 art 3.
[86] See section 2.4.2.
[87] Case C-210/06 *Cartesio Oktató és Szolgáltató bt* [2008] ECR I-9641 paras 111–13.
[88] Rome I Regulation art 3(2).

law of a continuing legal relationship. Contracts are not generally terminated and replaced by new contracts when the governing law is changed. In contrast, the original corporate contract is terminated and replaced by a new corporate contract when a company is reincorporated. The relationships between shareholders and between shareholders and the company are replaced by a new set of rights and obligations. It is therefore more accurate to say that the fiction of the legal personality of the company and the external relations of the company are all that remain unaffected. The company's contractual relationships with third parties proceed unchanged, while the contractual relationships within the company are replaced by new covenants. Moreover, the replacement of the rights and obligations within the company may go so far as to render parties such as employees third parties where they were previously considered to be bearers of rights under the corporate contract.

Further distinctions are notable in respect of the requirement of consent and perfection. In the general law of contract a change in the governing law requires only a meeting of the minds of the parties to the contract. It does not require an act of the organs of the states whose laws governed the contract prior to and after the change in the governing law. In contrast, reincorporation requires states to formalise the act of the parties. It does not, however, necessarily require the consent of all of the parties to the corporate contract. Some shareholders might not express consent to changing the governing law, and indeed there might be express opposition to it. Subscription to shares in the company as originally constituted is therefore not only a contract with flexible rights and obligations, but also an undertaking to accept that the limits of rights and obligations may be altered to such an extent that the law governing those limits may be changed, notwithstanding one's opposition to such a change. This puts a severe strain on the notion that a company is a creature of contract and that as such, party autonomy should be safeguarded.

Moreover, the general law of contract is not as diverse from one state to another as are company laws. While there are discernible divisions between contract law in the civil law and common law traditions, those divisions do not reveal contrasting aims to a degree that is comparable to the differences between corporate law regimes. Nor is the law of contract as highly regulated as company law. The vulnerability of minority shareholders to less favourable choices of law is therefore patent when compared to a choice of law in contract. As such, if one accepts that a company statute constitutes a contract between shareholders, one must also accept that transnational contractual principles that limit party autonomy to protect the weaker party may be applied *mutadis mutandis* to corporate choice of law. A minority shareholder acquires few rights and accepts majority control of the company. That shareholder also accepts that the control of the majority of shares may change hands from time to time without his or her consent. Accordingly, the minority shareholder is not effectively contracting with a particular natural person but with such natural persons as may from time to time own shares in the company. In the absence of uniform rules on minority shareholder protection, it would be abusive to impose upon that minority such a lack of certainty that the rights attaching to the shares held could be varied at will by the majority through a change in the governing law.

The vast disparity between the effects of a change in the governing law of contracts and that of companies renders contractual analogy somewhat difficult. Nevertheless, here too one can rely on contract law to refine contractual analogy. Whereas the ECJ's obiter statement in *Cartesio* vests the choice of accepting reincorporation in the destination state,[89] European transnational law of contract requires that the extinction of obligations be governed by the law of the contract.[90] Accordingly, if one accepts that reincorporation may terminate and replace obligations, European contractual principles would require that the conditions governing the termination be prescribed by the existing law of the company, as opposed to that which it proposes to be governed by prospectively. Hence another example of the disconnect between the broad-brush approach of the contractual paradigm of transnational corporate law and the finer details of transnational contract law.

2.3.5 Provisional Conclusions

In the final analysis there is no clear argument based on contractual liberty that can of itself resolve the myriad issues at stake when determining the governing law of companies. If it is conceded that corporate law is principally contractual, there remains the hurdle of the applicability of limitations to contractual freedom. As illustrated above, the protection of weaker parties to the contract, as well as the protection of third parties, could justify limitations to party autonomy in corporate choice of law on the same bases as in the private international law of contract. Accordingly, the contractual nature of a corporation, if accepted, should not necessarily lead one to the conclusion that incorporators should be free to choose a governing law without restriction. That argument over-simplifies contractual choice of law, and disregards the reality that party autonomy is not an absolute good and is not applied absolutely. Indeed, party autonomy is never absolute in municipal corporate law, because the corporate 'contract' is always supplemented, or indeed supplanted, by the company laws that give birth to corporations as amended from time to time. Moreover, to say that the law should not limit party autonomy at all would be to ignore the fact that the law must have a role to play, as evidenced by the requirement of public faith for the statutory contract and legal privileges of the corporate form to become effective. While there is no question of the existence of a contractual element in the corporation's constitutive instrument, there is also the equally important act of the state granting recognition to that instrument and granting the benefit of fictitious legal personality to the corporation and limited liability to the shareholders. Still more importantly, if one

89 *Cartesio* (n 87) paras 111–13.

90 Rome I Regulation art 12(1).

were to set aside the strains on the contractual paradigm itself, there would remain ample contractual doctrine to support the limitation of autonomy.

2.4 Economic Analyses of the Conflict of Corporate Laws

The previous section explored analogies with transnational contract law and showed that the contractual paradigm of the conflict of corporate laws may be refined. However, this alone does not suffice to qualify the role of party autonomy – in addition to contractual claims, freedom of choice is also predicated on economic principle. This section addresses the economic claims that support unrestricted choice of corporate law in order to establish whether there exists an economic imperative for the furtherance of party autonomy.

Three major economic claims are made in favour of party autonomy. The more commonly stated claim is that regulatory competition, which is a corollary of party autonomy, increases efficiency in corporate law and related legal and administrative services.[91] The second claim, which is stated less often but which is central to the first, is that the economic nature of the company is such that party autonomy in transnational corporate law should be given a free rein.[92] Finally, the most compelling and irresistible claim is that party autonomy serves to maximise legal certainty and thus eliminates unnecessary costs.[93]

2.4.1 The Authority of Entrepreneurs: Direction, and Monitoring of Team Production

It is pertinent to premise this discussion with an understanding of the economic assumptions made by jurists who advocate party autonomy in the conflict of corporate laws. These authors cite Coase's seminal work on the economic nature of the firm,[94] the focus of which is the question of what motivates the entrepreneur

[91] See eg Lombardo (n 5) 331–33; JC Dammann, 'Freedom of Choice in European Corporate Law' (2004) *Yale Journal of International Law* 477, 536–41; J Dammann and H Hansmann, 'Extraterritorial Courts for Corporate Law: ECGI Law Working Paper No 43/2005' (2005) http://papers.ssrn.com/sol3/papers.cfm?abstract_id=724165, 1, 6; S Deakin, 'Legal Diversity and Regulatory Competition: Which Model for Europe?' (2006) *European Law Journal* 440, 441–42; R Romano, 'Law as a Product: Some Pieces of the Incorporation Puzzle' (1985) *Journal of Law, Economics and Organization* 225, 227–32.

[92] See eg Whincop (n 5) 52–54; Lombardo (n 5) 314–22; Iacobucci (n 5) 319–20.

[93] Majchrzak (n 5) 86–89; J Israël, *European Cross-Border Insolvency Regulation: A Study of Regulation 1346/2000 on Insolvency Proceedings in the Light of a Paradigm of Co-operation and a* Comitas Europaea (Oxford, Intersentia, 2005) 125.

[94] Whincop (n 5) 52–54; Lombardo (n 5) 314–22; Iacobucci (n 5) 319–20. Some theorists who address the nature of the firm in their analysis of private international law take a broader view and construct their analysis accordingly. By way of example, Garcimartín Alférez defines a firm as 'a nexus of relationships among different actors': FJ Garcimartín Alférez, 'Cross-Border Listed Companies' (2007) 328 *Recueil des Cours de l'Académie de Droit International* 13, 47.

to forgo the price mechanism and opt instead for internalising factors of production within a firm.[95] The question is addressed from the perspective of economic efficiency and does not overtly address the attainment of other goals.[96] This approach is useful because entrepreneurship is self-evidently a vital factor in an analysis of the emergence of any business vehicle. Yet the entrepreneur's motivation cannot suffice to resolve issues of corporate governance, whether in municipal or transnational law. Posing the question of why firms emerge will not elicit an answer to the question of how a company should function and be governed, any more than asking why states emerge elicits incontrovertible answers regarding political systems of government: 'Even economists . . . will admit that [economic] theories are – naturally – reductionist in their view of the firm, and some would suggest that what they leave out renders their ready acceptance in practice problematical.'[97] Reliance on economic theory must therefore be qualified at the outset. Nevertheless, there is an irresistible value in understanding the economic nature of companies and how this could inform regulatory behaviour.

When investigating the economic explanation for the existence of firms, Coase observes that there is a cost in using the price mechanism, namely that of discovering prices for each transaction and negotiating contracts individually.[98] Where the commercial relationship between the entrepreneur and the relevant factor of production is not transitory, the entrepreneur will choose to replace a series of contracts entered into under market conditions with a single long-term contract.[99] This also enables contracting parties within the firm to hedge costs, thus averting the risk of adverse fluctuations in price.[100] However, the price mechanism continues to exist outside the firm, and the entrepreneur retains the option to revert to the open market in the event that the firm becomes costlier than the market.[101] The entrepreneur assumes a hierarchical role within a firm, as other factors of production subjugate themselves to his or her direction in exchange for fixed remuneration.[102] Voluntary subjugation can be explained either because other factors of production also eliminate costs through their association with the firm, or because their attitude to risk is such that they prefer a fixed income to the open market.[103]

[95] RH Coase, 'The Nature of the Firm' (1937) *Economica* 386, 386–405.

[96] Although Coase's methods do not indicate any overt desire to attain socially driven ends, this is not to say that it is completely divorced from the pursuit of social goods. Proponents of conservative corporate policy suggest that the maximisation of efficiency through the pursuit of a single unequivocal goal – profit and shareholder wealth – has a ripple effect that benefits all of the interests in the firm. See H Hansmann and R Kraakman, 'The End of History for Corporate Law' (2001) *Georgetown Law Journal* 439, 450–51.

[97] J Paterson, 'The Company Law Review in the UK and the Question of Scope: Theoretical Concerns, Practical Constraints and Possible Directions' in R Cobbaut and J Lenoble (eds), *Corporate Governance. An Institutional Approach* (Netherlands, Kluwer Law International, 2003) 150.

[98] Coase (n 95) 390–91.

[99] ibid.

[100] ibid.

[101] ibid 392.

[102] ibid 390–91.

[103] ibid; Coase also points out that there are fiscal incentives that encourage the growth of firms, such as the exemption of intra-firm activity from sales taxes (ibid 393). However, his economic analysis does

The assumption of a hierarchical construct of the firm which is reliant on the direction of the entrepreneur is particularly significant when considering whether the governance of firms should be designed to benefit non-shareholder stakeholders. It has been argued that, although 'Coase's basic analysis says nothing explicit about corporate governance . . . the very focus on authority as the "essence" of the relationship between employer and employee seems to close the door to any form of corporate governance that involves co-determination.'[104] This is certainly a tenable interpretation. Entrepreneur-investors, the incorporators for the purposes hereof, are the focal point of Coase's economic theory – the purpose of the corporation is the maximisation of the entrepreneurs' wealth.

Entrepreneurs' authority, if absolute, should be such as to allow them to seek efficiencies in the firm with the maximisation of their own wealth in mind. This is consistent with theorists who refined Coase's approach by shifting the emphasis from direction to team production, which is made up of several inputs that contribute to the firm's productivity.[105] Alchian and Demsetz observe that Coase's theory of the firm requires refinement, because it is so broad as to include factors of production such as sub-contractors within a firm.[106] What is more, Coase did not consider the cost of shirking within a firm.[107] They therefore suggest that the firm arises to deal with team production, which requires monitoring in order to deter shirking.[108] Monitoring is a burdensome, unappealing exercise, and the monitor must be incentivised to carry out this task, without shirking duties herself. Hence, the following features, among others: (i) the existence of one party who is common to all other inputs; (ii) the right of that party to be a residual claimant, and 'to sell his central contractual residual status'; and (iii) the right 'to renegotiate any input's contract independently of contracts with other input owners'.[109] Thus, in common with Coase, the point to which the firm will extend beyond that centre occupied by the residual claimant will depend on the residual claimant's economic judgment – where there are efficiencies to be made by bypassing the price mechanism, the relevant factor of production will be internalised; where this is not the case, the price mechanism will prevail.[110] For the purposes of the present discussion the crucial economic lesson is that conservative economic theory dictates that the extent to which the firm will include factors of production

not address the social phenomena of power and capital and the consolidation thereof through fiscal incentives that maximise rewards.

104 Paterson (n 97) 145.

105 A Alchian and H Demsetz, 'Production, Information Costs and Economic Organization' (1972) *American Economic Review* 777, 779–81.

106 ibid 784.

107 ibid.

108 ibid 781–83. In larger firms, such as corporations with dispersed share ownership, the task of management is delegated because it would be too bureaucratic for every shareholder to participate in every decision. What is more, the return on the investment and the risk associated with bad decisions is too small for shareholders to have an incentive to invest their time in the management of companies (ibid 787–89). This problem of 'rational apathy' is explored further in section 3.2.1.

109 ibid 783.

110 Coase (n 95) 393–98.

in its internal structure depends on the judgment of the residual claimant to the firm's assets, as opposed to the judgment of third parties or regulators. Entrepreneurs are tasked with evaluating efficiencies, and the measure of efficiency is the extent to which a given choice will be of benefit to the entrepreneur rather than any other stakeholder.[111] If this approach to the economic reality of the company is justified then there is a strong case for incorporators to be allowed to select the law that will govern their enterprise and to use that choice of law as a means to maximise efficiencies for their own benefit, and to allow them to exercise the most effective organisation of team production.

However, even if it is conceded that authority is central to the firm, it remains arguable, although somewhat tenuously, that one could conform to the notion of authority without adopting governance structures that operate on the basis of absolute authority. In Germany, where employee co-determination exists in the fullest form in which it is practised today, the balance of power within certain companies remains marginally tilted in favour of shareholders. Thus, despite the inclusion of employees in decision-making processes, authority in the governance of firms is retained by entrepreneurs.[112] The notion of hierarchy is not denied entirely but it is significantly diminished in one dimension of its expression. Authority remains in the employment dimension of the firm. Accordingly, that alteration does not necessarily displace Coase and Alchian and Demsetz's theories because authority is broadly retained. In sum, the most conservative of economic theories of the firm are capable of multifarious, if somewhat strained, interpretations when applied to the practice of corporate law and corporate choice of law. This poses some difficulty, albeit surmountable, for the thesis that economic theory supports conflicts rules that are based entirely on the will of entrepreneurs.

2.4.2 The Firm as a Nexus of Contracts, or a Nexus of Specific Investments

If it can be argued that theories of the firm which focus on authority are capable of being interpreted in a manner that does not vindicate a particular conflict of laws theory, literature that characterises the firm as a nexus of contracts confirms that the company is not a unitary concept for the purposes of municipal and transnational law.

[111] ibid.

[112] Co-determination does not create parity, but only quasi-parity between representation of employees and shareholders. Where the number of employee-representatives equals the shareholder-representatives on the supervisory board, the chairman, who is generally elected by the shareholders, has a casting vote in the event of a tie. That noted, there are matters where employees have an effective power of veto – the appointment and reappointment of management board requires the approval of two-thirds of the supervisory board – and it is significant that these include the appointment of the management board, as this does impact upon the hierarchical design: L Enriques, H Hansmann and R Kraakman, 'The Basic Governance Structure: The Interests of Shareholders as a Class', in Kraakman and others (n 81) 85.

Jensen and Meckling observe that 'most organizations are simply legal fictions which serve as a nexus for a set of contracting relationships among individuals.'[113] It follows that the firm is a locus for balancing the contractual interests of all contracting parties.[114] This balancing occurs in a manner that is comparable to the market, and the firm is a result of a 'complex equilibrium process.'[115] To these authors, asking what is the function of a firm, or whether it has any social responsibility, is as nonsensical as asking whether the wheat market has a social responsibility. They also reject questions about what is internal and external to the firm.[116] However, they betray their understanding of the question when they observe that there is 'only a multitude of complex relationships (i.e. contracts) between the legal fiction (the firm) and the owners of labor, material and capital inputs and the consumers of output.'[117] Clearly, the firm itself is a contract between investors.

Rajan and Zingales develop the thinking about the firm further by defining the firm as a nexus of specific investments. This accounts for the fact that in order for an enterprise to be productive, it requires not only the investment of capital, but also the investment of specialised skills. However, the acknowledgement of the role of the skills of employees was not, initially, taken into account for the purposes of the governance of corporations. This was instead left to employment law.[118] An employee's power lay in the ability to specialise, to thereby become indispensible, and to bargain on the basis of the possibility of withdrawing specialised skills from the firm.[119] Rather, the focus of theoretical analysis was the definition of the agency problems within the firm – how to theorise the relationship between management and ownership. This constitutes a departure from the theories proposed by earlier scholars. However, the implications for the basic structure of companies are not significantly different.

Notwithstanding their conservative approach to a firm's governance, Rajan and Zingales' insights may be drawn upon by progressive theorists who view the role of stakeholders as one which merits a set of enforceable rights. Freeman suggests that those who stand to gain or lose from corporate decisions are to be considered stakeholders in the firm, and that 'corporations shall be managed in the interests of its stakeholders'.[120] Stakeholders include management, the local community, customers, employees, suppliers and owners. Freeman does not suggest that all stakeholders should have a role in the management of companies. Instead, directors should owe a duty of care to all stakeholders, who in turn should have legal

[113] MC Jensen and WH Meckling, 'Theory of the Firm: Managerial Behavior, Agency Costs and Ownership Structure' (1976) *Journal of Financial Economics* 305, 310.

[114] ibid 311.

[115] ibid.

[116] ibid.

[117] ibid.

[118] M Blair, 'Firm-Specific Human Capital and Theories of the Firm' in M Blair and MJ Roe (eds), *Employees and Corporate Governance* (Washington DC, Brookings Institute, 1999) 70.

[119] RG Rajan and L Zingales, 'Power in a Theory of the Firm' (1998) *Quarterly Journal of Economics* 387, 388.

[120] RE Freeman, 'A Stakeholder Theory of the Modern Corporation' in TL Beauchamp and NE Bowie (eds), *Ethical Theory and Business*, 5th edn (New Jersey, Prentice Hall, 1997) 67.

means to enforce rights. This is in sharp contrast to those theorists who suggest that contracts are the only appropriate instrument for non-shareholders to bargain their rights and obligations.

The merits of Freeman's approach are debated extensively in the literature. Criticisms include the suggestion that the model should be developed more fully in order to identify a hierarchy among stakeholders in order to guide management in its decision-making. Who should be the principal beneficiaries of this strategy is also a matter of controversy.[121] Others develop the stakeholder model further and suggest that stakeholders should have a role in the governance of companies, rather than being mere beneficiaries of the decisions of stakeholder-regarding management.[122] This ensures procedural justice in corporate decision-making, in addition to the substantive justice which Freeman's model seeks to ensure.[123] It is noteworthy that early advocates of stakeholder models of corporate governance are at least equally inclined to reliance on unscientific methods as are proponents of a shareholder model. [124] This suggests that much of corporate legal theory is based on the elaboration of political instinct. This lends credence to the suggestion that economic theory provides insights into the nature and purpose of firms, but that arguments about choice of law which are based on economic theory tend to rely on incomplete assumptions. A stakeholder model of the private international law of companies would equally be questionable if it were premised on dogmatic suggestions about what a firm is, or what it should be.

Transaction cost economics might add credence to the stakeholder model, but this too is open to interpretation. Williamson suggests that corporate governance should be reserved to those who contribute specific assets to the firm.[125] This would appear to include employees, whose investment of specialisation cannot be resold to other firms who do not need the specialised skill set.[126] However, to Williamson, the key question is how best to enable stakeholders to secure their stake in the firm, rather than situating their claim within the governance structures of companies.[127] In Williamson's view, employees are best served by tuning and fine-tuning contractual mechanisms, whereas the governance of the firm is better reserved for the 'natural residual claimants', namely shareholders.[128]

In contrast, Blair's views on firm-specific human capital offer arguably the most compelling case against employing economic theory as a justification for party autonomy in corporate choice of law. Blair observes that an employee's stake in the firm is 'very difficult to protect by means of explicit contracts . . . Other institutional arrangements are needed, and these arrangements often have the effect of

[121] See Paterson (n 97) 151–52, and the references therein.

[122] AF Alkhafaji, *A Stakeholder Approach to Corporate Governance* (New York, Quorum Books, 1989) 111 per Paterson (n 97) 153.

[123] NE Bowie, *Business Ethics: A Kantian Perspective* (Oxford, Blackwell, 1999) 112–13.

[124] See Paterson (n 97) 154.

[125] OE Williamson, *The Economic Institutions of Capitalism* (New York, Free Press, 1985) 313–14.

[126] ibid.

[127] ibid.

[128] ibid.

tying the fortunes of the employee together with those of the firm.'[129] The firm is then defined as a relationship of trust. In order for trust to be maintained, participants in the firm must be involved in the development of the firm.[130] In Blair's view, the opportunity cost incurred in specialisation merits participation in the governance of companies.

This alternative understanding of the nexus of contracts that makes up the firm puts a severe strain on the notion that the corporate contract is, or should be, merely a private agreement between shareholders, and consequently upon the notion that shareholders may freely choose a company's governing law. If one accepts that non-shareholder constituencies make an investment in the company, the argument that a company is a private instrument for the benefit of shareholders becomes controversial. This alternative view therefore limits the extent to which it is tenable to argue that hierarchy and party autonomy should define the manner in which the governing law is selected. The corporate contract is no longer a mere private agreement between shareholders at the apex of the corporate hierarchy, but a social contract between the various stakeholders, the parties to which are many and varied. However, the nexus of specific investments that makes up the firm has not led to the elaboration of a single model of governance. Rather, progressive theorists add further controversy because they propose a variety of methods to protect stakeholders. Divergent views on the limitations to party autonomy are borne out both by virtue of the application of the real seat theory which protects particular stakeholder models, as well as by virtue of mandatory rules that incorporation states employ to limit the perceived negative outcomes associated with the application of the incorporation doctrine within their territories.[131]

2.4.3 Property Rights and the Nature of Shareholding

Another aspect of the economic justification for party autonomy is the assumption that shareholders are the residual claimants to a company's assets and as such that they are the owners of the company.[132] If the rights of shareholders may be characterised as ownership rights in companies, the point of departure for a choice of law regime should, presumably, be that they are entitled to use and abuse their property as they please. Arguments opposing shareholders' rights to use, abuse and enjoy the fruits of the company would bear the logical burden of proof. It would follow that, as co-owners, the shareholders may agree how they wish to govern their common property. They would be entitled to regulate the internal affairs of the company and there would be a principled argument that they are entitled to contractually agree amongst themselves as to which law should govern the corporation.

[129] Blair (n 118) 63.

[130] ibid 86. For further discussion of the role of trust in the firm, see J Kay and A Silberston, 'Corporate Governance' (1995) *National Institute Economic Review* 84, 84–96.

[131] Targeted exceptions to party autonomy are discussed in more detail in the following chapter of this book.

[132] See Lombardo (n 5) 320–21; Paterson (n 97) 146–47.

This thesis can only hold water if the ownership of shares is equated with ownership of the company. The notion that owners of shares are indeed the owners of companies is, in fact, the dominant thesis. It is reflected in both economic and legal literature, which focus on the agency problem between 'owners' and managers. Indeed it is also reflected in basic British company law textbooks.[133] However, it is submitted that the equation of share ownership with the ownership of the company is exaggerated. At best, it is an equation that should be qualified on the basis of the fact that the ownership of the company is not absolute. At worst, it is indicative of a predilection for a particular economic model and of a slight, but significant, misunderstanding of the legal nature of share ownership. Notwithstanding the etymology of the term, a share is not a portion of ownership but 'an interest in the company . . . measured by a sum of money, for the purpose of liability in the first place, and of interest in the second'.[134] It is a corporate security that entitles the holder to particular limited rights.[135] The holder of a share cannot use and abuse the company's assets at will but can only enjoy rights thereto in accordance with rules regulating matters such as the declaration of dividends by the board of directors.[136] It is only the share itself that can notionally be used and abused freely, and even that limited right of ownership is restricted by laws and internal company regulations. Further, any statement about share-ownership requires refinement, since different classes of shares accord different rights to their bearers. In order for shares as a whole to be treated in tandem, it must be presumed that the bearers of shares to which limited rights are attached have voluntarily limited their rights, and that the said rights would otherwise be identical to those of bearers of ordinary voting shares.

In economic theory the thesis of shareholder ownership is unsettled. Every factor of production is 'owned' by a stakeholder in the firm. In the first place, it can be argued that the company is economically owned by creditors to the same degree as it can be argued that shareholders are owners, although this is not legally tenable in the normal course of affairs: 'Options theory teaches us that once a firm issues debt (as almost all firms do), it makes just as much sense to say that the debtholders "own" the right to the corporation's cash flow but have sold a call option to the shareholder.'[137] Further, besides those who have a call upon the company's assets, there exist investors of 'human capital' such as workers: 'ownership of capital should not be confused with ownership of the firm. Each factor in a firm is owned by somebody'[138] The risk borne by the manager or worker is firm-specific whereas the shareholders may reduce their financial vulnerability by investing in a balanced portfolio that limits dependence on the profitability of a single company.[139]

[133] See eg D French, S Mayson and C Ryan, *Mayson French and Ryan on Company Law,* 27th edn (Oxford, Oxford University Press, 2010) 4.

[134] *Borland's Trustee v Steel Brothers & Co Ltd* [1901] 1 Ch 279.

[135] Stout (n 72) 1191.

[136] ibid; *Macaura v Northern Assurance Company* [1925] AC 619.

[137] Stout (n 72) 1192.

[138] E Fama, 'Agency Problems and the theory of the firm' (1980) *Journal of Political Economy* 288, 290.

[139] ibid 291.

Accordingly, the investment of human capital may outweigh the a priori investment of monies. To some theorists, the investment of human capital warrants an acknowledgment of the ownership of a factor of production that is vital to the company.[140] The firm-specific investment is far greater for stakeholders who forgo the opportunity to acquire transferable skills through their commitment to a particular company. If it is conceded that different factors of production constitute a firm and that ownership is therefore extended beyond shareholders, it is no longer tenable to argue that shareholders' ownership rights should warrant the governance of a company for the exclusive benefit of shareholders' or the empowerment of shareholders to determine a company's governing law.

Finally, it is not legally sound to assume that ownership should justify party autonomy whether or not the company is legally or economically the property of shareholders. Even if one were to conclude that shareholders do own companies, one would still need to evaluate the quality of that ownership for the purposes of private international law theory. Ownership comprises the right to use, abuse and to enjoy the fruits of the thing owned, within certain limits prescribed by the law. It does not comprise an entitlement to determine which law should govern the very same ownership rights. Nor does it include the right to determine the entire range of conditions that limit the enjoyment of that property or the manner in which it might be transferred or disposed of. In the case of immovable property, it is the situation of that property that is the determinant factor – ownership does not confer the right to determine the governing law over acts which affect rights *in rem* over the property.[141] The fact of ownership alone cannot entitle the owner to determine the law that governs a thing in any conceivable circumstance. Indeed, the property rights of shareholders are restricted in private international law also in respect of the shares themselves. Shareholders may not directly prescribe the law which is applicable to their shares. Rather, it is the *lex situs* which will apply to shares.[142] Since the *lex situs* is associated with the place of incorporation of the issuing company, the governing law of a share may not be changed without a change in the governing law of the company.[143] It follows that, on balance, the property argument can strengthen the party autonomy approach from a conflicts perspective, but it cannot settle the matter.

Still, property rights may justify a liberal model of choice of corporate law if one includes control in the equation. Hart explains that 'Given that a contract will not specify all aspects of asset usage in every contingency . . . the owner of the asset has *residual control rights* over that asset: the right to decide all usages in any way not inconsistent with a prior contract, custom or law' [emphasis retained].[144] It follows that 'control over nonhuman assets leads to control over human assets'.[145] However,

[140] ibid. See also Freeman (n 120) 67; Alkhafaji (n 122) 153; Blair (n 118) 63.

[141] Rome I Regulation art 4(c).

[142] *Macmillan Inc v Bishopgate Investment Trust plc and others (No 3)* [1996] 1 WLR 387.

[143] For further discussion of the nature of the *lex situs* rule, see M Ooi, *Shares and Other Securities in the Conflict of Laws* (Oxford, Oxford University Press 2003) 13–20.

[144] O Hart, *Firms, Contracts and Financial Structure* (Oxford, Oxford University Press, 1995) 30.

[145] ibid 58.

for the purposes of transnational law, this argument is circular. It is based on the premise that control of non-human assets is vested in the 'owners' of those assets. This is not the case in every jurisdiction. Where control of non-human assets is shared, as in the co-determination model, one could just as easily argue that control of human assets is shared. Accordingly, the logic of Hart's approach cannot be applied in the context of choice of corporate law.

2.4.4 Efficiency: Choice of the Best Law

This lack of unanimity in corporate theory is borne out in national rules regarding the permissibility of shareholder autonomy in selecting a company's governing law. Those states that limit choice are not averse to party autonomy as a contractual principle, and they uphold that principle in transnational contract law, with few exceptions.[146] Their resistance to party autonomy in corporate law can therefore be explained in terms of their subscription to an alternative view of the corporate form, rather than adversity to contractual liberty – a view that identifies complexity in corporate law and that proposes to account for said complexity in the conflict of laws.[147] However, a third economic argument for party autonomy proposes that it is more efficient: (i) to limit decision-making processes to shareholders, and (ii) to grant them absolute freedom of choice.

The first arguable claim emanates from corporate legal theory and relates to the internal organisation of the company. Because there is a cost in negotiation when compared to direction through authority, it is more efficient to limit the elements that influence the decision-making process. The centralisation of oversight and management is therefore viewed as an essential factor of team production.[148] In view of the discussion in the above sub-sections, it is clear that the matter of decisional efficiency is most cogent if the company is deemed to be only an instrument of profit. In a transnational context, this suggests that the decision-making processes which states prescribe that companies must adopt are a means to an end, rather than an end in themselves – that states do not attach an intrinsic value to the system of governance, rather than the results of good governance. In practice it appears that states do in fact attach intrinsic value to decision-making processes, and are moved to adopt, and retain processes because of domestic political concerns rather than efficiency.[149] What is more, the cogency of the argument depends on whether there is a single prevalent notion of the goals that the corporate form is intended to achieve. However, even if one accepts the profit-making purpose of companies, it remains arguable that team production 'requires cooperative non-opportunistic behavior'.[150] This would require decision-making processes that

[146] Stein (n 64) 1334.

[147] C Azzolini, 'Problemi Relativi alle Persone Giuridiche nella Riforma del Diritto Internazionale Privato' (1993) *Rivista di Diritto Internazionale Privato e Processuale* 893, 905.

[148] Alchian and Demsetz (n 105) 788.

[149] Hansmann and Kraakman (n 96) 446.

[150] Bowie (n 123) 111.

include stakeholders in a manner that ensures procedural democracy.[151] In this construct, a consensual approach to decision-making is preferred to centralisation. Legislative imagination to date would suggest that the best approach to addressing procedural justice in a transnational context is to allow some decision-making to be made through the political choices of states.

Party autonomy must be shown to select laws that are efficient and that may meet the needs of all corporate constituencies. The thesis that efficient rules governing corporate choice of law will benefit all constituencies relies on broad economic considerations that are not internal to a single company. By way of example, if consideration for the welfare of workers is not a matter of concern for corporate law, efficiency in the market must compensate for any loss suffered by workers. The assumption is that the loss of employment in one company is part of the organic development of an efficient market. Inefficiencies are weeded out and replaced by more efficient or more adaptable alternatives. Thus, loss of employment is compensated for by the availability of employment elsewhere. This economic truism requires further consideration, particularly in a growing geographic market such as the EU. The fact of the matter is that workers who are made redundant often suffer wage reductions when they find new employment.[152] Moreover, when one considers the European market, the assumption of internal efficiency in the job market is little more than an assumption. The free movement of persons that is meant to provide fluidity and efficiency in an EU-wide market has not yet been realised, because blue collar workers are not readily mobile, whether for economic, cultural or linguistic and educational reasons. The absence of a uniform EU-wide market is recognised in other areas of law such as regional development aid. There is no reason why this should not also be the case in addressing market failures in the corporate form. Accordingly, a choice of law regime that touts efficiency as a justification for allowing, or indeed requiring, the disregard of workers' rights is based on a premise that is, arguably, false.

The second aspect is that it is efficient on a macro level to allow incorporators to select laws and to thereby instigate competition between legal systems to provide corporations with the most efficient laws. In other words, a market for incorporations is considered to be positive because it causes legislators to optimise laws and eliminate unnecessary costs. Neither of these economic matters has a direct bearing on the nature of the company; rather, the extent to which they are cogent for the purposes of private international law is dependent on what the purpose of companies actually is deemed to be as a matter of transnational law.

As regards the matter of competition between legal systems, the potential benefits are dependent on the assumption of a race to the top, rather than a race to the bottom. The argument for a race to the top proceeds as follows: competition is 'a neutral and technical process which serves no particular end, other than the goal of efficiency.'[153] Indeed, Maduro suggests that legal competition is not only

[151] ibid.

[152] Blair (n 118) 156.

[153] Deakin (n 91) 440–41.

efficient, but that mutual recognition enables states to realise new deliberative moments because the polity in each state is instigated to change rules which had been retained for lack of initiative.[154] However, this presumes that legal competition is comparable to competition in the market for goods. Deakin suggests, persuasively it is submitted, that 'Legal rules, by contrast, and in particular legislative ones, are seen as serving political goals, which are often redistributive in nature, and so likely to be highly contested.'[155] Accordingly, a judgment of the efficiency of choice of corporate law depends on political judgment. That which the shareholder primacy model deems to be the top may well be the same as what the stakeholder model deems to be the bottom. Efficiency for the purposes of the generation of profit may come at the cost of employee welfare, creditor protection or the community at large. For this reason, it is pertinent to situate consideration of efficiency in the context of a discussion regarding the nature of the firm. On this basis, it is impossible to judge whether competition in corporate law achieves desirable efficiencies. It is, perhaps, better to consider which efficiencies a plurilegal system might wish to further, and which political choices are deemed worthy of protection.

2.4.5 Efficiency: Legal Certainty

It is uncontroversial that the conflict of corporate laws should establish the closest connection between a company and its governing law without thereby creating a cumbersome process of discovery that leads to uncertainty and the costs associated therewith. However, the sub-discipline of the conflict of corporate laws is perhaps atypical, in that proponents of both the leading theories claim that their preferred approach enhances legal certainty and that the other approach is detrimental to it.[156] The discussion hereunder illustrates that disagreement between advocates of the two schools of thought stems from a different understanding of the very nature of legal certainty and the sphere in which certainty is to be furthered and evaluated – whether legal certainty is best achieved by facilitating the discovery of the governing law on a transnational level, or whether it is achieved through uniformity of laws within a geographical space.

The incorporation theory is said to further certainty because it establishes a one-stop check in order to establish the legal existence of a corporation and its governing law. This check is free of legalisms and simply involves ascertaining that a formal administrative act has been completed in a given jurisdiction – one need merely look to where the formal act of the creation of the company was purportedly completed

[154] MP Maduro, 'So Close and Yet so Far: the Paradoxes of Mutual Recognition' (2007) *Journal of European Public Policy* 814, 816.

[155] Deakin (n 91) 441.

[156] In contrast, the major schisms in European doctrinal debate, such as the pitting of *lis alibi pendens* against *forum non conveniens*, stem from a disagreement regarding the balance to be struck between legal certainty and the furtherance of justice, and indeed the extent to which legal certainty implicitly serves the ends of justice.

in order to find the answer to both the question of the corporation's formal existence and the question of its governing law.[157] The law of the place of incorporation will regulate the full spectrum of matters relating to the corporation, including its internal organisation and external capacity.[158] The simple virtues and practical advantages of the incorporation theory have been described as self-evident, from a practical rather than a theoretical perspective.[159] Indeed, theorists who are sceptical of the virtues of the incorporation theory will readily admit that the theory furthers certainty: 'The exclusive supremacy of the law of incorporation may be suggested as the only rule of certainty and easy application.'[160]

The counter-argument is that the benefit of predictability is not available where companies that operate predominantly in a single jurisdiction may be governed by a plurality of laws. The presence of a multitude of applicable laws within a single jurisdiction may lead to added costs of discovery of the law applicable to a company, as well as the necessity of counsel regarding the content of those laws. The benefits of an accommodating legal regime are mitigated by the costs incurred by third parties.

Advocates of the real seat theory propose that legal certainty is achieved by reassuring stakeholders that all corporations that have their management centre in a given jurisdiction are subject to the same rules.[161] The goal of attaining certainty is informed by the assumption that justice is best served in the context of societal goods, as opposed to the expectations, legitimate or otherwise, of the parties to the corporate contract. The intended beneficiaries of legal certainty as construed by the real seat doctrine are therefore not only the immediate contracting parties, but every stakeholder that interacts with the company. The underlying assumption is that companies will conduct business principally in the jurisdiction in which their central office is established.[162] Accordingly, when transacting business with a company having its seat in a given territory, without the need of discovering the provisions of a foreign law, contracting parties will be aware of the capacity of the company's representatives to bind the company; creditors and suppliers will be reasonably aware of the minimum capital requirements and disclosure obligations applicable to a company; stakeholders will be aware of the rights and obligations of management, and to whom management owes fiduciary obligations; workers will be certain of their right to participation and representation within the corporate structures; the surrounding community will be aware of the extent of corporate social responsibility requirements in the decision-making process within the firm;

[157] Rammeloo (n 1) 14; RR Drury, 'The Regulation and Recognition of Foreign Corporations: Responses to the "Delaware Syndrome"' (1998) *Cambridge Law Journal* 165, 168–69; Latty (n 82) 139–40.

[158] Drury (n 157) 169.

[159] E Rabel, *The Conflict of Laws: A Comparative Study* vol II, 2nd edn (University of Michigan, 1960) 31–32.

[160] Latty (n 82) 139.

[161] Ebke (2002) (n 10) 1027–28.

[162] WG Ringe, 'The European Company Statute in the Context of Freedom of Establishment' (2007) *Journal of Corporate Law Studies* 185, 198.

diligent stakeholders will be able to envisage the effects of regulatory action on all of the above with reference to but one legislative authority, rather than needing to follow developments in an unlimited plurality of states.[163] Legal certainty as construed in the real seat doctrine refers to the ease of discovery of all of the rights and obligations incumbent on a company, as opposed to the determination of the governing law, which is then followed by a process of discovery of the said rights and obligations. The benefit of legal certainty as construed in the real seat doctrine extends to the minimisation of costs. Where market actors interact principally with corporations incorporated under the law of their own jurisdiction, they do not incur the risk of the potentially unknown capacity of the foreign company and its officers. Hence lower costs through the elimination of the necessity of foreign legal counsel.

The view that the real seat doctrine enhances certainty is cogent in the context of inward-looking private international law regimes that view the discipline as a purely municipal system without due regard to the extraterritorial effects of private international law. That view is divorced from both the realities and the aspirations of international and regional trade. Given that the aims of regional integration include the enhancement of cross-border trade, and given that international trade also aspires to the removal of barriers in order to improve efficiency, legal certainty within a single jurisdiction cannot realistically refer to only one legal system. When a company that has its centre of management in state A conducts business in state B, the benefits of the real seat doctrine are largely irrelevant because there is no fathomable reason why market actors in state B should be any more aware of the rights and obligations arising from the law of state A than they are of the rights and obligations obtaining under the laws of a third state. When considered in the context of transnational business transactions, the real seat doctrine is therefore divorced from the benefits that exist where the hypothesis is limited to trade conducted in a single jurisdiction. Thus the theoretical cogency of the real seat doctrine is limited to its application in the majority of cases where companies engage in business in one jurisdiction. However, in the growing minority of cases of companies that engage in business transnationally, the doctrine's claim to increasing certainty cannot be made with reference to the benefits of the application of one law in one jurisdiction. Accordingly, from the perspective of legal certainty, the doctrine is built on anachronisms that are likely to become more accentuated over time. It must be emphasised that this is more so when one considers that it is the intention of the European Union, with the express agreement of every Member State, to further integrate markets and encourage companies to engage in cross-border trade.

Further, when one recalls that the real seat theory is but one of a plurality of doctrines that coexist in the transnational sphere, the theory's claim to enhancing certainty is even less convincing. The real seat theory would not only enhance but also virtually ensure legal certainty in a context where it is applied by all states –

[163] See Ebke (2004) (n 3) 817; Rammeloo (n 1) 14.

where it is a jurisdictional rule that does not encounter conflicts of conflict of laws norms. If that were the case, no state would charter a company that did not have its seat in its territory, there would be no question of the potential applicability of another governing law, and certainty would thereby be guaranteed. By way of example, there is no difficulty as between Germany and Italy, since neither state will incorporate a company that has its seat outside its territory, because their conflicts doctrines require that every company incorporated under their laws has its seat in their respective territories. The picture begins to muddy when the real seat theory encounters an incorporation state that allows companies incorporated under its laws to be resident in another jurisdiction. Thus, under traditional national laws, where a company that has its seat in Germany is incorporated under English law, both states would claim jurisdiction to regulate the internal affairs of the said company, and there would be an irreducible conflict of conflicts norms. The company would be validly constituted under English law, but would not have legal personality under German law. In addition, every incorporation state, and every state that applies the incorporation theory to companies having their seat outside its territory, would recognise the company. Thus the company would be validly constituted in the eyes of most states, but not in the eyes of the state in which the seat is situated. Of course, by the same measure, the incorporation doctrine cannot be said to increase certainty when faced with a state that applies the real seat doctrine and refuses to recognise the prescriptive jurisdiction of the state of incorporation.

In order to evaluate the relative merits of the theories, the question to be posited must therefore relate to the extent of ease of determination of the governing law in the event of a conflict of conflict of laws, as opposed to the full import of the governing law in the context of a single jurisdiction. In the present discussion, legal certainty is understood to refer to certainty of outcome – in the context of conflicts of corporate law, certainty must necessarily include the ease of ascertainment of the law by which the corporation will be governed. It implies certainty as to the results of a legal relationship. This should not be confused with the meaning of legal certainty when applied to a purely internal matter. In the latter case certainty refers to expectations regarding the effects of a set of rules that will apply within that jurisdiction. It is respectfully submitted that proponents of the real seat theory often betray a misunderstanding of the notion of certainty – the conflict of laws implicitly admits that laws are not uniform, and that different results will ensue depending on which law is applied. The problems associated with the potential for disharmony within a given jurisdiction must not be confused with uncertainty as to the identity of the governing law.

In the context of certainty of outcome, the real seat theory poses legalistic questions that are not capable of simple resolution. The means of determining the seat of a company under the real seat theory presents symptoms of the practical pitfalls of doctrines based on a factual connection, as opposed to a juridical one.[164] By way

[164] See Rammeloo (n 1) 14–15.

of example, one's citizenship may be determined in a relatively straightforward manner, whereas one's habitual residence is discovered through deeper investigation. Thus whereas habitual residence is accepted as a more appropriate connecting factor than citizenship for adjudicatory jurisdictional purposes, this is most certainly not because habitual residence is more readily determined. Similarly, in order to ascertain where a company has its seat one must engage in the discovery of facts, as opposed to the simpler discovery of a formal juridical relationship. The seat of a company is not to be construed as the place that is merely nominally designated as the company's management centre.[165] Consider the example of a company that is incorporated in Liechtenstein, has its registered office in Liechtenstein, but in fact has management decisions taken in Germany. In *Liechtenstein AG* it was held that 'the place where the management office and the organs representing the company are engaged in business is the place where fundamental decisions of the management and control office are taken and effectively carried out'.[166] Accordingly, companies may not evade the application of the law of the factual control centre by setting up fictitious headquarters in a jurisdiction other than that in which the management and control are in fact carried out. From a theoretical perspective, this adds to the cogency of the real seat model as a factual connecting factor that levels the playing field within a jurisdiction. However, the practicalities are tenuous. How is one to define a central office? In a digital age in which borders are less relevant, how is one to determine where decisions are taken?[167] Perhaps more fundamentally, there is no evidence that the third parties that the theory seeks to protect have any non-legalistic means to determine that a central office is situated in a particular jurisdiction: a particularly large branch office might give the appearance of being a central office, whereas the fundamental decisions affecting a business may plausibly be taken in a tiny studio apartment.

Notwithstanding the foregoing, the penalties for non-compliance with the requirements of the real seat theory may be such as to be coercive of practical implementation on a voluntary basis. This can be illustrated with reference to the example of incorporators who are aware of their rights and obligations under the law of the jurisdiction in which they are based, as the law will presume that they are, and indeed as they are likely to be if provided proper legal counsel. In such circumstances, prudent promoters of companies will only seek incorporation in a jurisdiction other than that of the companies' seat if they are willing to endure the possibility of the companies being deemed to be unincorporated, with the consequence of personal liability for the companies' debts.[168] For any legitimate business concern, the magnitude of the penalty is likely to outweigh the benefits of incorporation in a more accommodating jurisdiction. Evidence of the efficacy of voluntary compliance with the real seat theory is to be found in the emigration

[165] *Liechtenstein AG* BGH 21 March 1986, BGHZ 97, 269 trans per Rammeloo (n 1) 179.
[166] ibid.
[167] P Vlas, *Rechtspersonen in het international privaatrecht* (Deventer, Kluwer, 1982) 8 per Rammeloo (n 1) 17.
[168] See Rammeloo (n 1) 11.

of companies to the United Kingdom from real seat states following the *Centros* line of judgments. While the benefits of incorporation in the United Kingdom were available prior to the judgments of the ECJ, those benefits were only availed of en masse following liberalisation occasioned by judgments that declared the penalties for non-compliance incompatible with the Treaty.[169] It can therefore be stated with some certainty that prior to *Centros,* an appetite for more accommodating laws was offset by costs in the majority of cases. Thus the lack of certainty that arises from a conflict of conflicts norms was largely theoretical because the penalties that are built into the real seat doctrine make certain that companies having their seat in a jurisdiction will comply with the requirement of incorporation thereat.

In the final analysis, it cannot be said that the real seat theory is detrimental to transnational legal certainty. However, it must be emphasised that the theory's claim to furthering certainty is more true of the municipal sphere than it is in the context of integrated markets where the laws of several states interact as a matter of course.

2.4.5.1 Outreach Statutes

The certainty provided by the incorporation model is limited in practice because the theory is not always applied uniformly. The following chapter of this book shows that states that apply the incorporation theory as a general rule often depart from the rule under particular circumstances. They so do by employing outreach statutes – mandatory rules – that apply elements of their own laws to companies that they recognise as validly incorporated under foreign law and validly governed by foreign law for most respects and purposes. The uncertainty caused by outreach clauses may be of two types: (i) uncertainty throughout the life of the company in respect of which law is to be applied to certain matters; and (ii) one-off uncertainty of outcome in view of the claim to applicability of a law other than the law of incorporation in foreseeable circumstances.

An example of the latter type is to be found in article 159 of the Swiss Private International Law Code of 1987, which is discussed in section 3.2.5 below. This article provides that 'when the operations of a company created under a foreign law are carried out in or from Switzerland, the liability of the persons acting in the name of such company is governed by Swiss law.'[170] Laws such as this are open to criticism on the grounds that they harm certainty and are inherently contradictory on a number of levels. Firstly, no distinction is made between a company that purports to be a Swiss company and one that is overt about its status as a foreign company. This departure from the incorporation theory is contradictory, in that the law does not set out only to curtail situations where a company is fraudulently incorporated outside Switzerland in order to evade Swiss law, as appears to have

[169] See Becht, Mayer and Wagner (n 16) 242.

[170] trans per B Dutoit, *Commentaire de la loi fédérale du 18 décembre 1987* (Frankfurt-sur-le-Main, Helbing und Lichtenhahn, 1996) 429.

been intended.[171] Secondly, no distinction is made between foreign remedies that are more favourable to third parties and those that are less favourable than those provided under Swiss law. Given that third parties are as likely to be aware of the powers of the company's organs under the relevant foreign law as they are of the remedies provided by the said law, it is perfectly plausible that they may expect the representatives of the company to submit to the potentially greater penalty provided under foreign law. Thirdly, the foreign company will have to be approximated to a Swiss corporate form in order to determine the relevant rights and responsibilities. This is a matter that requires costly judicial exploration of the facts of each case, and therefore provides ample room for uncertainty in a system that otherwise sets out to guarantee predictability. Fourthly, the persons acting in the name of the company are only liable if the law governing the Swiss corporate form to which the company is approximated provides for such responsibility.[172] Accordingly, this may lead to a scenario where representatives of a company may escape liability entirely and third parties will therefore be rendered entirely unprotected, whereas they would have been protected had the governing law of the company been applied. Fifthly, and most importantly, provisions of this sort invite forum shopping. The result of a dispute may be vastly different if the court seised is a Swiss court bound by Swiss private international law, or if the court seised is that of the state of incorporation. Accordingly, such provisions may suggest that a jurisdiction is serious about a specific area of law, but they serve to introduce uncertainty in that very same area of law by virtue of the fact of the possible application of different laws.

A clear example of an outreach statute which may cause continuous uncertainty is the California Corporations Code. The outreach provisions of that statute are applicable where a threshold is crossed of 50 per cent of the corporation's real and tangible property, its payrolls and its sales, and the residence of the holders of 50 per cent of its voting securities are situated in California's territorial space.[173] It goes without saying that these connecting factors are fluid, and if figures hover around the 50 per cent mark whereby they would trigger the application of California law, the question of whether or not Californian law would purportedly be applicable could make some aspects of the governance of a company impossible to administer. The uncertainty arising from the potential application of laws emanating from a plurality of states is most striking when one considers the incumbency of two obligations that are mutually exclusive.[174] In such situations, decision-makers are forced to choose between breaching one law or another. In sum, the unilateral use of outreach clauses cannot possibly be efficient because it imposes the cost of non-compliance on companies and their officers.

[171] ibid 430.
[172] ibid.
[173] California Corporations Code § 2115 (a).
[174] See DeMott (n 5) 172–79; AE Anton and PR Beaumont, *Private International Law: A treatise from the standpoint of Scots law*, 2nd edn (W Green, Edinburgh, 1990) 703.

2.5 Conclusions

In view of the foregoing, it can be stated with some certainty that economic theory provides only qualified support for the furtherance of party autonomy in transnational corporate law. Economic theory reveals that the nature and purpose of the corporate form can be understood in fundamentally different ways. Commonalities such as a profit-making purpose do exist in all the noteworthy theories. Yet there are fundamental differences both in terms of what goods are to be taken into account, and the way in which those goods are to be achieved and redistributed. Those divergences are reflected in national corporate laws, which also differ considerably regarding the place of different stakeholders in the company. The effect of party autonomy is the erosion of those features of substantive law that discourage the incorporators' demand for the legal product on offer. The change does not occur because of a shift in political or societal values that would ideally accompany legal reform, or because of a desire to improve national laws in pursuit of the common good. Nor does the change occur because a comparative exercise leads legislators to the conclusion that foreign norms could be borrowed to improve the legislation of the receiving state. Rather change is induced by fiscal policies that set out to maintain competitiveness in the market for incorporations. Those policies are demand-motivated and are designed to accommodate the aspirations of incorporators by altering the supply side for their benefit.[175]

In the context of discussion of corporate legal theory, it has been astutely observed that the economic theory that considers the entrepreneur to be the central figure in the firm has not only served to explain but has also consolidated a particular Anglo-American view of the company.[176] A similar phenomenon can be discerned in the conflict of corporate laws camp – economic analyses of the firm cited in conflicts literature often express a view which is but one of many, as though that one view were a matter of economic dogma. By premising discussion on the central role of the entrepreneur, it appears to follow logically that shareholders should enjoy unlimited choice of law. But this approach does not account for the fact that there exist different views of what a company actually is in economic terms. Moreover, it is possible to surmise different implications from any given economic theory, resulting in diverse regulatory approaches. The theoretical deficiency noted in corporate legal theory is accentuated in transnational law because states adopt different models of company law, and they reflect those choices in private international law norms which protect or further the model of their choice. This is illustrated further in the next chapter, which highlights the manner in which states set out to protect corporate law choices through the private international law of companies.

[175] See Becht, Mayer and Wagner (n 16) 252.
[176] Paterson (n 97) 144.

3

The Plural Aims of Conflict of Corporate Laws

3.1 Introduction

In the previous chapter it was argued that, despite the intuitive appeal of party autonomy, the underpinnings of the theory in choice of corporate law are imperfect. This chapter identifies limitations to party autonomy in private international law of companies, as well as the policy concerns which motivate states to adopt such limitations. The restrictions that are cited below serve to highlight the multifarious interests which move states to express a preference for a particular choice of corporate law regime. Particular reference is made to targeted exceptions to the incorporation theory which, by virtue of their exceptional nature, are illustrative of the assorted goals of corporate choice of law regimes. In addition, this chapter includes a brief overview of divergences in European corporate law which have emerged since the judgment in *Centros*.[1] These examples serve to illustrate developments in national laws which might have been afforded protection through private international law, had this remained possible. It should be noted, however, that this chapter does not purport to constitute a scientific survey or an exhaustive list of exceptions. The illustrative examples serve merely to highlight restrictions in transnational law which correspond with a broad array of stakeholder interests identified in corporate legal theory. In the final analysis it is argued that choice of law norms are dependent on the expression of preferences by states rather than any universally applicable principle.

Prior to addressing substantive limitations to party autonomy, this introductory section identifies broad themes concerning theoretical connections between recognition theories and states' corporate law policies. This discussion completes the theoretical setting prior to discussion of the place of party autonomy in European law, which follows in Chapters 4 and 5.

[1] Case C-212/97 *Centros Ltd v Erhvervs-og Selskabsstyrelsen* [1999] ECR I-01459.

3.1.1 The Real Seat Theory

In the case of states that employ the real seat theory, the connection between corporate law policy and choice of law principle is implicit. The real seat theory is intended to establish the closest connection between a corporation and the jurisdiction in which that corporation 'lives',[2] as well as to guard against the encroachment of foreign laws.[3] Thus it is the entirety of the corporate law and policy of real seat states that is protected. This is the very essence of the theory which was established with the purpose of guarding against the avoidance of the law of the state in which a company is situated.[4]

The manner in which some real seat countries apply that theory offers further compelling evidence that the rationale for limiting party autonomy is intimately connected to corporate law goals. By way of example, Italian law provides that companies are regulated by the law of the state of incorporation as a general rule – hence the designation of Italy as a state which applies the incorporation theory by some commentators.[5] However, where the administrative seat or principal activity of the company is situated in Italy, Italian law purports to govern the company, notwithstanding that the constitution of the company was perfected in another jurisdiction.[6] Where Italian regulatory interests are directly affected, that is where the administrative seat or the principal object of the company is within Italy's territorial jurisdiction, the real seat theory will trump the incorporation theory. The penalty for non-compliance with the requirement of conforming to Italian law and the formalities of registration in terms of Italian company law is the unlimited liability of persons acting on behalf of the company.[7] Accordingly, in contrast to the Swiss system upon which the Italian code is based,[8] Italian law is not permissive of incorporation outside its jurisdiction where the management or activities of the company are situated in Italy. In every case, as of the moment that the company's seat or centre of activities is to be found on Italian territory, the foreign company will be subject to all the requirements of Italian law, including the requirement of registration.[9]

[2] D Coester-Waltjen, 'German Conflict Rules and the Multinational Enterprise' (1976) *Georgia Journal of International and Comparative Law* 197, 206.

[3] See eg B Angelette, 'The Revolution that Never Came and the Revolution Coming – *De Lasteyrie du Salliant, Marks & Spencer, Sevic Systems* and the Changing Corporate Law in Europe' (2006) *Virginia Law Review* 1189, 1193–94.

[4] ibid.

[5] See eg T Ballarino and A Bonomi, 'The Italian Statute on Private International Law of 1995' (2000) *Yearbook of Private International Law* 99, 116–17.

[6] L 31 maggio 1995, n 218 art 25; See T Ballarino, *Diritto Internazionale Privato,* 3rd edn (Napoli, Simone, 2006) 54–55. Prior to the litigation in *Cartesio* (Case C-210/06 *Cartesio Oktató és Szolgáltató bt* [2008] ECR I-9641), Hungarian law adopted an identical approach: B Pasa, GA Benacchio and L Orme (tr), *The Harmonization of Civil and Commercial Law in Europe* (Budapest, Central European University Press, 2005) 280.

[7] L 31 maggio 1995, n 218 art 25; Ballarino (n 6) 54–55.

[8] S Rammeloo, *Corporations in Private International Law: A European Perspective* (Oxford, Oxford University Press, 2001) 223.

[9] A Santa Maria, 'Problemi attinenti al diritto internazionale privato e processuale delle società' (1987) *Rivista delle Società* 1473, 1487–89.

The Italian approach highlights states' regulatory interests in the conflict of corporate laws. Party autonomy is not rejected in itself but is denied in the state's territorial sphere because of the role that corporations may play in the socio-economic governance of their territory. Autonomy is rejected because the contractual covenants made by the incorporators are not only prescriptive amongst themselves but also have the effect of prescribing conditions which regulate third parties who interact with the corporation and have a stake in its governance. States therefore intervene to limit the extent of the prescriptive rights of incorporators and assume the role of arbiters of the competing claims to the goods and liabilities emanating from the corporate form.

However, because the real seat theory requires the application of the entirety of a state's corporate law, one cannot identify specific policy motivations, save to the extent that it is arguable that real seat states tend to be less permissive in both their substantive and transnational laws.[10] It is from targeted exceptions in incorporation states that one can identify more incontrovertible connections between private international law and corporate law policies.

3.1.2 The Incorporation Theory

The nexus between substantive and conflicts legislation in incorporation states is equally discernible. States that adopt a contractual view of the company tend also to be liberal in the conditions under which they approach the governing law of companies.[11] The incorporation doctrine is founded on the principle that the connection to be established between a company and a state is simply the will of the incorporators. In formal terms, this is expressed as the place where the act of incorporation is completed. There is no need for physical presence in a territory or any personal connection with a state – the act of incorporation suffices to create the necessary connection between the company and its governing law. Of itself, this says a great deal about the private international law of companies, in that it confirms that divergence in transnational law stems from a different view of the nature and purpose of companies. However, what is more revealing is that incorporation states seldom apply their governing law doctrine without exception. The mandatory rules that are enforced by these states in respect of certain foreign corporations highlight those areas of corporate law that are deemed to be so important as to override the autonomy of incorporators to select a governing law. This deviation from principle constitutes compelling evidence that the governing law of companies is rarely determined in a truly libertarian fashion, and that a purely contractarian approach to corporate choice of law is therefore quite removed from

[10] J Dine, *The Governance of Corporate Groups* (Cambridge, Cambridge University Press, 2000) 67; RR Drury, 'The Regulation and Recognition of Foreign Corporations: Responses to the Delaware Syndrome' (1998) *Cambridge Law Journal* 165, 182–83; WF Ebke, 'The "Real Seat" Doctrine in the Conflict of Laws' (2002) *The International Lawyer* 1015, 1027–29.

[11] ibid.

the reality of corporate choice of law principle. The existence of targeted exceptions to liberal doctrine is, of course, symptomatic of the fact that states differ on the goals of corporate law, and balance rights and obligations within a company in different ways.

This chapter therefore focuses principally on areas of corporate law that are subject to specific protection, particularly in states which adopt the incorporation doctrine. Each selected law highlights a targeted exception to the principle of incorporators' autonomy in selecting a governing law where a legislative preference for protective principle over party autonomy is demonstrated. These examples serve to highlight the fact that party autonomy is not an absolute good, and that it is necessary to account for the political consensus that has led to specified areas of law being favoured over a principle of general application. It must be emphasised that the analysis hereunder does not purport to set out a comprehensive compendium of protective conflict of corporate laws, but merely one that is representative of the matters that legislators may take into account when establishing a cross-border corporate laws regime. Each section also highlights the corporate law policy motivations for the exceptions to otherwise liberal doctrine.

3.2 Targeted Protective Mechanisms

3.2.1 Shareholders' Rights

3.2.1.1 Principles

In the preceding chapter the shareholders' place in the contractual paradigm was addressed with only limited reference to wider social and economic concerns. This section sets out an analysis of the rights and obligations of shareholders quite apart from contractual theory. Rather, the focus here is on the policy motivations of a socio-economic nature that underpin protective conflict of laws norms. The rationale for the protection of shareholders in municipal and transnational law stems, at least in part, from the emergence of dispersed share-ownership and the attendant change in the popularly recognised profile of shareholders. It is no longer true of all shareholders that they are well-financed entrepreneurs, or indeed that they are either well-financed or entrepreneurs by profession. An emergent shareholding class transcends the divide between blue and white-collar workers and constitutes a hybrid social subset having distinct class interests.[12] Indeed, workers' ownership of shares in companies blurs the division between labour and capital and renders workers equal members of a shareholding class that has a quantifiable stake in the ownership of the major assets that drive large economies.[13]

[12] H Hansmann and R Kraakman, 'The End of History for Corporate Law' (2001) *Georgetown Law Journal* 439, 451–53.

[13] ibid.

This is broadly in keeping with the original goals of corporate law. The introduction of limited liability was intended to democratise access to enterprise by allowing the investment of capital without the risk of personal financial ruin.[14]

However, a substantial contingent of the broad class of shareholders invests monies in a spirit that is similar to the risk-averse spirit with which it deposits monies in banks, rather than out of entrepreneurial zeal.[15] In times of ordinary performance, markets in shares are perceived as low-risk, high-interest alternatives to banking, whether that investment is made through direct purchase of shares or through investment in funds which consist of a portfolio of shares and other securities. To the minds of some shareholders, the share market therefore doubles up as a savings account:

> [In economic terms,] direct share ownership – the traditional focus of legal scholarship – constitutes only one among a wide range of *competing* savings and investment media, so that instead of there being separate markets for deposit accounts, life policies, unit trusts and so on, *there is what is in effect a single market for personal investment* [emphasis added].[16]

Accordingly, the protection of shareholders is necessary to resolve a broad agency problem involving a swathe of personal savings. The emergence of a shareholder class in most jurisdictions necessitates protection of non-controlling shareholders. To this end, political pressures are successfully brought to bear on legislators to adapt corporate law to protect shareholders' investments.[17]

Shareholder protection is, of course, also expedient from the perspective of the attraction of capital. This too renders the manner in which shareholders are treated in private international law a matter of macroeconomic governance, rather than a mere private matter. Indeed, states' efforts to protect shareholders are intended to create an environment that is conducive to attracting investment in a market in shares.

At the heart of the problem of shareholder protection is the fact that shareholders invest trust in the directorship of the company on the basis of limited information, which in turn allows them only limited potential to influence the decisions of directors,[18] or indeed to decide who those directors might be.[19] What is more, shareholders whose investment is not extensive are rationally apathetic because the cost of participation in corporate governance often outweighs the potential benefits.[20]

[14] For an account of the introduction of limited liability in its historical context, see D Loftus, 'Capital and Community: Limited Liability and Attempts to Democratize the Market in Mid-Nineteenth-Century England' (2002) 45 *Victorian Studies* 93, 93–120.

[15] See AC Page and RB Ferguson, *Investor Protection* (London, Weidenfeld and Nicolson, 1992) 4–5.

[16] ibid 10–11.

[17] Hansmann and Kraakman (n 12) 452.

[18] SM Bainbridge, 'Director Primacy and Shareholder Disempowerment' (2006) *Harvard Law Review* 1735, 1745.

[19] LA Bebchuk, 'The Case for Increasing Shareholder Power' (2005) *Harvard Law Review* 833, 851–56.

[20] ibid. For a qualified view of rational apathy, see Bebchuk (n 19) 891; R Romano, 'Answering the Wrong Question: The Tenuous Case for Mandatory Corporate Laws' (1989) *Columbia Law Review* 1599, 1611. Bebchuk and Romano argue that institutional shareholders are more sophisticated and better informed and are therefore not rationally apathetic. Bainbridge, correctly it is submitted,

The asymmetry of information, which is problematic from a contractual perspective, is also problematic from the perspective of participative and representative governance. As such there is a structural problem concerning the governance of a socio-economic vehicle. Corporate laws set out to ensure that shareholders maintain an appropriate degree of influence over the management of companies. Yet the rational apathy of shareholders, coupled with their disparate goals,[21] arguably renders directors of large corporations unaccountable to those who have the legal right to appoint and remove them.[22]

In view of these structural vulnerabilities, the private international law rules of several states contain provisions which protect shareholders' rights from being undermined by a foreign governing law that is not sufficiently protective. This is best illustrated with reference to the mandatory rules which are applied to formally foreign corporations in states that employ the incorporation theory as a general rule. The targeted departure from the incorporation theory is a testament to the central importance that shareholders are given as holders of inalienable substantive rights. Effectively, this protects the shareholders from their own folly where the governing law does not safeguard their rights to the requisite standards of the state that purports to protect them against a lax governing law.

3.2.1.2 The California Corporations Code

A number of states in the United States of America employ outreach legislation in order to protect shareholders who are resident in their territory, or arguably merely to exercise jurisdiction over their residents. These legislative measures persist notwithstanding that it is not clear that certain mandatory rules, referred to as outreach clauses, are constitutionally permissible.[23] Chapter 21 of California's Corporations Code (hereafter in this sub-section referred to as the 'Code') seeks to regulate corporations that are incorporated in a state other than California and that enter into repeated and successive transactions in California.[24] The outreach clauses apply when more than half of the foreign corporation's voting securities are held by persons with California addresses, provided that over 50 per cent of the corporation's real and tangible property, its payrolls and its sales are also situated in California in that year.[25]

The state of California purports to exercise prescriptive jurisdiction over a great swathe of matters where Californian law considers the company to be sufficiently connected to its jurisdiction.[26] A significant portion of the outreach clauses are intended to protect Californian shareholders from abusive choices of foreign

disagrees on the basis of the same cost-benefit analysis as is applicable to all rational shareholders: Bainbridge (n 18) 1751–52.

[21] See Bainbridge (n 18) 1745–46.

[22] Bebchuk (n 19) 851–56.

[23] DA DeMott, 'Perspectives on Choice of Law for Corporate Internal Affairs' (1985) *Law and Contemporary Problems* 161, 183–97.

[24] California Corporations Code § 2115.

[25] ibid.

[26] ibid.

law.[27] Applicable provisions of California law include the degree of scrutiny which shareholders may exercise over directors, including rights to elect and remove directors, as well as provisions concerning access to documents.[28] Protection of minority shareholders is also provided for through the application of local law concerning qualified majority voting and the rights of dissenting shareholders.[29]

While the 'extraterritorial' application of California law generally requires the coincidence of a number of connecting factors, the Code also provides a real seat test in respect of a limited number of its provisions. A corporation that satisfies the real seat test is 'a foreign corporation having its principal executive office in this state or customarily holding meetings of its board in this state.'[30] The provisions of the Code that are triggered by the real seat test concern the duty to report to shareholders by way of annual reports,[31] and the shareholders' right to obtain the names and particulars of other shareholders of the company.[32] This enhances the potential for shareholders to canvas each other and to thereby influence the governance of formally foreign corporations. It is perhaps surprising that shareholder protection should be singled out as a matter that requires the application of outreach clauses where operational headquarters are present in California, as opposed to the general rule which requires residence of the majority of shareholders in that state. The peculiar use of connecting factors does not, however, detract from the fact that California law emphasises the need for shareholder protection in preference to the free election of a governing law.

3.2.1.3 The New York Business Corporation Code

The New York Business Corporation Code also addresses the informational balance between shareholders and directors through claims to limited jurisdiction over pseudo-foreign corporations. Asymmetry of information is not only dealt with by realigning the informational balance, but also through the imposition of obligations upon the holder of the information. New York sets out to protect its residents from an informational imbalance through (arguably aggressive) outreach clauses that are imposed upon foreign corporations.[33] Section 1315 of the Business Corporation Code provides that any New York resident who is a shareholder of a foreign corporation shall have the right to examine the corporation's record of shareholders.[34] Further, the state of New York adopts an approach based on 'doing business' jurisdiction, whereby corporations that do business in New York are subject to its law in respect of shareholders' inspection rights and directors' liability for neglecting or violating certain duties.

[27] ibid.
[28] ibid.
[29] ibid.
[30] ibid § 1501(g), § 1600(d).
[31] ibid § 1501.
[32] ibid § 1600.
[33] See DeMott (n 23) 165.
[34] New York Business Corporation Law § 1315.

3.2.1.4 The EU Company Law Directives

In contrast to California and New York, national laws in Europe do not use the residence or nationality of shareholders as a connecting factor in the ordinary course of the determination of the governing law of a corporation. In states that adhere to the real seat theory, the nationality, residence or domicile of shareholders is not considered to be a relevant factor. In Europe, shareholders are generally only considered to be relevant in the determination of the applicable law to the extent that the law will recognise the autonomous act of choosing a state in which to incorporate a company or in which to situate the management centre of the corporation. In *Centros* the Danish government did refer to the nationality of shareholders as a connection to its jurisdiction,[35] but in reality this had the reverse goal to that evidenced in the actions of California and New York – the Danish government wished to impose obligations upon the shareholders in view of their nationality and residence, whereas the broad intention in California and New York is to protect residents who hold shares in foreign companies.

The judgments in *Centros* and *Inspire Art*[36] provide that European Union Member States must recognise companies incorporated under the laws of other Member States, and that they may not superimpose provisions of their own laws on such pseudo-foreign corporations having their operational headquarters in their territories. However, the legislation of the Union recognises the necessity of limited transnational protection of minority shareholders, although this is not such as to permit the bifurcation of the governing law of a company.

Article 4(2) of the Cross-Border Merger Directive[37] permits specific provision for the protection of minority shareholders:

> A Member State may, in the case of companies participating in a cross-border merger and governed by its law, adopt provisions designed to ensure appropriate protection for minority members who have opposed the cross-border merger.

It is worth reiterating that the directive does not permit the extraterritorial application of the law of a Member State of one of the merging companies to the merged company in matters relating to the protection of shareholders. Rather, Member States may prescribe higher standards of minority shareholder protection in the run-up to a cross-border merger than would be applied if the merger were internal. Thus, by way of exception to the rule that shareholders are subject to the covenants in corporate statutes as subsequently amended, the directive affords Member States additional leeway in the protection of minority shareholders where the latter's rights and obligations are to be altered drastically.

[35] *Centros* (n 1) para 16.

[36] Case C-167/01 *Kamer van Koophandel en Fabrieken voor Amsterdam v Inspire Art Ltd* [2003] ECR I-10155.

[37] Directive (EC) 2005/56 of the European Parliament and of the Council of 26 October 2005 on cross-border mergers of limited liability companies [2005] OJ L310/1.

The Directive on Shareholders' Rights[38] also makes specific provision for the transnational protection of shareholders in listed companies. The directive does not allow a Member State other than the state of incorporation to alter the balance of power envisaged by the governing law of the company.[39] The obligation, and indeed the right, to protect shareholders residing outwith the state in which the company is registered is incumbent on the state in which the company is in fact registered.[40] In recognition of the difficulty that shareholders face in exercising their rights transnationally, the directive merely provides that the Member States shall adopt laws to facilitate shareholders' access to information and participation in listed companies.[41]

Accordingly, notwithstanding that there is only limited exception to the principle of autonomy in the selection of a company's governing law, it is evident that EU law recognises the need to protect non-controlling shareholders in transnational law.

3.2.2 The Limits of Shareholders' Liability

3.2.2.1 Principles

The legal fiction of corporate legal personality and the concession of limited liability are not granted unconditionally by any state. The laws of most states envisage conditions under which shareholders may be liable for the acts of the company or where they may be liable for their own acts qua shareholders, and those of the company. In the ordinary course of a company's existence the governing law of the company governs these acts. Nevertheless, there is a principled argument that private international law should contain provision for the liability of shareholders where the application of foreign law is inappropriate or insufficient.

The most drastic method is to deny the existence of the corporate veil altogether – that is, to deny that the company is properly incorporated as a separate legal person.[42] This mechanism is employed to rectify the incorporation of a company in a state other than that of its real seat, rather than superimposing local law on a duly recognised pseudo-foreign corporation. The company may be denied recognition altogether, or it may be assimilated with an entity provided in local law which should, but might not be, an entity that is closely associated with the entity that the incorporators sought to set up under foreign law. In either case the shareholders may be rendered liable for all of the company's debts, either because no separate legal person is recognised or because the legal person which is superimposed is more akin to a commercial partnership that does not provide the benefit

[38] Directive (EC) 2007/36 of the European Parliament and of the Council of 11 July 2007 on the exercise of certain rights of shareholders in listed companies [2007] OJ L184/17.

[39] Art 1(2).

[40] ibid.

[41] Arts 3–14.

[42] Rammeloo (n 8) 11.

of limited liability to its members. The denial of the intended legal personality of a company is not by way of exception to liberal conflicts theory, but is intended to further a broad protective policy by applying the governing law of the state of the company's real seat.

The application of local law to the liability of shareholders of pseudo-foreign companies is also in evidence in some incorporation states. Historically, California extended the liability of Californian shareholders to Californian creditors where shareholder liability would have been excluded under the law of the state of incorporation.[43] Remnants of this approach to shareholder liability remain in section 506 of the California Corporations Code. This section regulates the liability of shareholders of pseudo-foreign corporations who receive an unlawful distribution.[44] This operates as a capital maintenance provision that protects creditors from the alienation of corporate funds. Proposals to extend shareholders' liability for the debts of pseudo-foreign corporations by way of exception were entertained in the original draft of the Swiss Private International Law Code, a code which otherwise adopted the incorporation theory even in its original formulation.[45] That draft provided that persons controlling or directing pseudo-foreign corporations would be responsible for the corporation's debts.[46] In the event the legislator rejected this proposal since it was deemed to run counter to Switzerland's status as an international commercial hub.[47] Despite the eventual rejection of the said proposal, it is noteworthy that the status of pseudo-foreign corporations is such as to justify consideration of the extension of liability beyond the extent of unpaid shares.

3.2.2.2 Corporate Shareholders

Changes to the profile of shareholders through the emergence of corporate groups and increased participation of institutional investors in the market for shares[48] provide a principled case for corporate shareholders to be treated differently from individual shareholders. The societal reality of modern corporations is not the same as that in which corporate law was born and originally flourished.[49] Limited liability was intended to function in a market environment where the corporation deals with all third parties at arm's length.[50] Arm's-length dealing allows market actors to be

[43] B Gustin, 'What Law Governs Liability of Shareholders for Corporate Debts' (1914) *Harvard Law Review* 575, 576.

[44] California Corporations Code § 2115(b).

[45] See P Reymond, 'Les personnes morales et les sociétés dans le nouveau droit international privé suisse' in F Dessemontet (ed), *Le nouveau droit international privé suisse. Travaux des journées d'études organiseés par le Centre de droit de l'entreprise les 9 et 10 octobre 1987, à l'Université de Lausanne* (Lausanne, Cedidic, 1988) 143, 190.

[46] ibid.

[47] ibid.

[48] CM Bruner, 'The Enduring Ambivalence of Corporate Law' (2008) *Alabama Law Review* 1385, 1432–33.

[49] See PI Blumberg, 'The Corporate Entity in an Era of Multinational Corporations' (1990) *Delaware Journal of Corporate Law* 283, 285.

[50] K Hofstetter, 'Parent Responsibility for Subsidiary Corporations: Evaluating European Trends' (1990) *International and Comparative Law Quarterly* 576, 576.

compensated, at market value, for the cost of the limitation of liability.[51] However, the emergence of corporate groups recasts the traditional paradigm of individual ownership of shares, and economic reality does not conform to the view of corporations as separate entities.[52] Corporate groups stultify the functioning of the market because the inclusion of further artificial legal structures quashes the notion of the independent corporation that the law intended.[53] What is more, corporate groups are often multi-layered structures in which most members of the group are owned by other corporations in a complex web designed to make the most efficient use of the legal benefits of separate legal personality.[54] In the place of individual shareholders being protected from bankruptcy through the limitation of liability, we now have multiple parts of an enterprise being protected from the liability of related parts. In a multinational setting, the protection afforded by the corporate veil is enforced further by the addition of a 'jurisdictional veil' which may protect parent companies from the tortious and contractual liabilities of their foreign subsidiaries.[55] In view of the foregoing, there is a principled argument that it should be easier to pierce the veil of incorporation of foreign companies that form part of corporate groups, than of foreign companies that stand alone.[56] This principle is in fact given effect to varying degrees in the law and practice of several states, including the United States, the United Kingdom, France, Italy and Germany.[57] Notwithstanding the reality of the widespread use of corporate groups, the private international law of the EU treats members of corporate groups as separate entities. It does not account for the intimate connection between a subsidiary and its parent, and there has been little progress towards a unified approach to the treatment of groups.[58]

[51] See SE Woodward, 'Limited Liability in the Theory of the Firm' in DA Wittman (ed), *Economic Analysis of the Law: Selected Readings* (Oxford, Blackwell, 2003) 153.

[52] Blumberg (n 49) 285; J McLean, 'The Transnational Corporation in History: Lessons for Today?' (2004) *Indiana Law Journal* 363, 376.

[53] Hofstetter (n 50) 576.

[54] SK Miller, 'Piercing the Corporate Veil Among Affiliated Companies in the European Community and in the U.S.: a Comparative Analysis of U.S., German, and U.K. Veil-Piercing Approaches' (1998) *American Business Law Journal* 73, 129–32.

[55] P Muchlinski, 'Corporations in International Litigation: Problems of Jurisdiction and the United Kingdom Asbestos Cases' (2001) *International and Comparative Law Quarterly* 1, 16–17.

[56] Parent companies are rendered liable for the debts of their subsidiaries where the existence of an intimate connection between companies is deemed more important than the separate legal personality of the constituent corporations in a group. The greater ease of veil-piercing limits the extent to which companies may benefit from multiple-insulation from liability. This is justified on the basis that complex structures may give third parties a mistaken impression of the capital structure of the group. The liquidity of the company that is actually being traded with might easily be confused with the reputed liquidity of its parent company, another related company, or the entire group of companies. Accordingly, the separation of capital from risk through the establishment of weakly capitalised trading companies is a widespread practice which legislators sometimes curtail. See J Armour, G Hertig and H Kanda, 'Transactions with Creditors' in R Kraakman and others (eds), *The Anatomy of Corporate Law: A Comparative and Functional Approach,* 2nd edn (Oxford, Oxford University Press, 2009) 140–41; M Andenas and F Wooldridge, *European Comparative Company Law* (Cambridge, Cambridge University Press, 2009) 448–90.

[57] ibid.

[58] Art 5(5) of the Brussels I Regulation provides that a company may, in matters other than those concerning its internal affairs, be sued 'as regards a dispute arising out of the operations of a branch, agency or other establishment, in the courts for the place in which the branch, agency or other establishment is

The laws of the Member States of the EU vary in their approach to groups of companies. At one extreme, the UK Companies Act and the judgments of the UK courts err on the side of upholding the separate personality of the constituent parts of a group of companies. The general reluctance to pierce the veil is, however, punctuated by some notable exceptions where the courts took the view that a corporate group is in fact a single economic entity, and where it has been treated as such rather than as a number of separate persons.[59] The exceptions to the principle of separate legal personality have been of both a substantive and a procedural nature. It is submitted that the judgment in *Lubbe et al v Cape Industries*[60] illustrates the manner in which an English court will not hesitate to disregard foreign law in assessing whether or not it may assume jurisdiction. In his seminal paper on corporations in international litigation, Muchlinski frames the problem as one of adjudicatory jurisdiction.[61] However, it is submitted that the litigation also highlights problems of prescriptive jurisdiction and, albeit indirectly, extends the prescriptive jurisdictional reach of the state of incorporation of the parent company to matters that fall within the ambit of the governing law of the foreign subsidiary.

situated.' If the parent company chooses to carry on business in its own name it will therefore be subjected to the jurisdiction of a foreign court. If it carries on business through a subsidiary, the distinct personality of the subsidiary will relieve the parent company of foreign jurisdiction. This is a logical consequence of the distinct legal personality of the parent and subsidiary. However, in effect it allows companies to insulate themselves from the jurisdiction on the grounds that a different business vehicle has been adopted in order to accrue an identical benefit – whether the company sets up a branch or a subsidiary, it intends to enjoy the fruits of the enterprise – in the case of a branch, directly through profits, and in the case of a subsidiary, through dividends. The parent–subsidiary relationship is therefore rewarded notwithstanding that the business model is virtually identical to the establishment of a branch. The absence of jurisdiction over a parent company in one forum does not exclude suit in the forum of the parent company's domicile. However, it does emphasise the structural favour that is given to the establishment of separate legal personality. The fact of jurisdiction by virtue of the presence of a branch or agency but not by virtue of the presence of a subsidiary highlights the unfairness of the mechanisms that European private international law employs, at least in respect of jurisdiction.

This doctrinal stringency is relaxed slightly by the judgment in Case 218/86 *SAR Schotte GmbH v Parfums Rothschild Sarl* [1987] ECR 4905. In this case a German parent company was held to be an establishment of a subsidiary French company in whose name it conducted negotiations, with which it shared identical management, and which had an identical name. The judgment will equally apply in a situation where the subsidiary company acts on behalf of its parent. However, this is limited to circumstances where one group company acts as though it were a branch of another group company, rather than where it acts on its own behalf: J Fawcett and JM Carruthers, *Cheshire, North and Fawcett Private International Law,* 14th edn (Oxford, Oxford University Press, 2008) 260; WA Allwood, 'Article 5(5): meaning of "branch, agency or other establishment"' (1988) *European Law Review* 213, 215.

The EU has made some progress in its treatment of groups of companies through directives that require Member States to adopt laws whereby group accounts must be compiled and disclosed: Council Directive (EEC) 1983/349 based on art 54(3)(g) of the Treaty on consolidated accounts [1983] OJ L193/1. This has the advantage of allowing prudent businessman to properly evaluate their relationships with group companies and to contract with them accordingly. However, in the context of the issues affecting groups of companies, this may be little more than an aesthetic exercise, given that the jurisdictional rules and veil-piercing regulation remain oblivious to the existence of corporations that form part of a single economic entity. The failure to adopt a directive on the piercing of the corporate veil leaves the liability of corporate shareholders to be regulated by market forces and/or the Member States.

[59] See eg *DHN Food Distributors v Tower Hamlets LBC* [1976] 1 WLR 852 (Lord Denning).

[60] *Lubbe et al v Cape Industries plc* [1997] 4 All ER 335.

[61] Muchlinski (n 55) 1.

The Court disregarded the extent to which the foreign governing law of a subsidiary of an English company would render the parent company liable for the tortious acts of its subsidiary. In that case, an English company was sued for payment of damages arising from the tortious acts of its South African subsidiaries whereby the subsidiary companies' employees suffered asbestos poisoning. Having satisfied itself that there was in fact a relationship of control between the English parent and foreign subsidiary, the English Court explored whether there was a causal link between the acts of the parent company and the damages suffered by the employees of its foreign subsidiaries. The House of Lords did not, however, address the question of whether the law of a foreign subsidiary provided for liability of the parent company. It did not address the question of whether South African law provided that the shareholders of a South African company may be liable for the tortious acts of the said company. The Court did not question whether the veil of incorporation, which was prescribed by a foreign corporate law, would protect a shareholder from local law. Instead, English conflict rules were applied to determine tortious liability of an English company for the acts of its subsidiaries. This does not directly stultify the incorporation doctrine, since the Court did not apply English company law to the piercing of the foreign company's veil – the English Court did not set out to displace a foreign internal law of a foreign company. However, it indirectly applied principles of English tort law to the piercing of the veil of a foreign corporation. In effect it was deemed to be self-evident that the duty of care that is provided in English tort law should override the corporate law of the subsidiary's place of incorporation. The net effect is that an English court will ignore the law of the place of incorporation of a foreign subsidiary and treat the entire corporate group as an economic unit that is subject to English substantive and conflicts law.

In contrast, several continental states, most notably Germany,[62] are more inclined to view corporate groups as a single entity and to subject the parent company to liability for the debts of its subsidiaries. This is the case whether the group is multinational, or based in a single jurisdiction.[63] Of course it should also be noted that the real seat theory renders it more difficult to set up a multinational enterprise that is managed in Germany, since residual rules of German law prescribe that any company that has its management centre in Germany must be governed by German law. In order for the enterprise to include companies that are incorporated in jurisdictions other than Germany, the foreign companies must not have their centre of management in Germany. Accordingly, the requisite degree of control over the subsidiary is not likely to be as patent as in the case of a group of companies that are managed and controlled virtually simultaneously. Nevertheless, the connection between a parent and a subsidiary may be established by virtue of ownership itself, without the need to establish a degree of effective control or coordination of activities. Further, the effect of the *Centros-Inspire Art* line of judgments is likely to result in more German companies setting up subsidiaries that are managed in Germany

[62] Andenas and Wooldridge (n 56) 451–78.
[63] ibid 460.

but governed by foreign law. It is submitted that this will likely bring to the fore the differences between national laws on the piercing of the corporate veil. Given that the doctrinal differences between the Member States have prevented the adoption of a European Directive,[64] it is highly likely that the legislative lacuna in European private international law will also be left to be patched up by the ECJ.

3.2.3 Creditor Protection

3.2.3.1 Principles

Because every person that transacts with a company, whether as an employee, a supplier of goods or services or as a supplier of cash flow in the form of loans, becomes a creditor of the company for a given time, creditors are the only non-shareholder constituency that is protected by the company law of every state.[65] The protection of creditors is a universally accepted means to offset the risk posed by the concession of the limitation of shareholders' liability.[66] This notwithstanding that the price mechanism arguably compensates for the risk of limited liability since those who contract with the company will impute limited liability as a cost that the company will be charged for.[67] Indeed, such is the central place of creditors in corporate law that Hansmann and Kraakman argue that creditors are in fact beneficiaries of limited liability, since ring-fencing the company's funds protects the company from the shareholders' personal creditors.[68] Still, limited liability poses a risk to creditors, and states do prescribe obligations upon corporations in order to limit the risk that limited liability imposes on persons that transact with the company and thereby invest some reliance upon its financial wellbeing.[69]

Creditor protection is most commonly associated with capital requirements that establish the minimum net assets that the company must hold and that limit the extent to which the company may distribute its assets.[70] States employ a variety of techniques to ensure that creditors are safeguarded from lax foreign laws by virtue of protective conflict of laws rules. The approach of the real seat theory is to require that all corporations that have their management centre in a territory comply with local law – the very origins of the real seat theory are in fact to be found in the desire of states to protect local stakeholders, including creditors, from

[64] ibid 449; Pasa, Benacchio and Orme (n 6) 370 .

[65] G Hertig and H Kanda, 'Creditor Protection' in R Kraakman and others (eds), *The Anatomy of Corporate Law: A Comparative and Functional Approach* (Oxford, Oxford University Press, 2004) 71.

[66] Limited liability transfers any risk that exceeds the limits of the liability of investors of capital to third parties, namely the creditors of the company. Accordingly, the limitation of shareholders' liability operates to increase the liability of each creditor, whether he or she transacts with the corporation habitually or merely on a one-off basis: Woodward (n 51) 153.

[67] Woodward (n 51) 153.

[68] Limitation of liability eliminates the cost of monitoring the shareholders' financial interests when creditors set out to evaluate the liquidity of a company: H Hansmann and R Kraakman, 'The Essential Role of Organizational Law' (2000) *Yale Law Journal* 387, 399–403.

[69] Hertig and Kanda (n 65) 71.

[70] L Enriques and M Gelter, 'Regulatory Competition in European Company Law and Creditor Protection' (2006) *European Business Organization Law Review* 417, 422–28.

foreign laws. This ensures equivalence for all relevant corporations and predictability to all potential creditors.[71] Alternatively, the targeted approach of various incorporation countries may achieve the same result by splitting the governing law through the application of mandatory creditor protection rules.

In Europe, the transnational treatment of minimum capital requirements has to date been inconsistent. The protection of creditors through the establishment of minimum capital requirements has been affected both by positive harmonisation in the shape of the company law directives,[72] as well as through negative harmonisation by means of the European Court of Justice's indirect dismantling of protective private international law rules. On the one hand, article 6 of the Second Company Law Directive provides that public companies shall have a minimum subscribed share capital of not less than 25,000 euros.[73] This provision bound states such as the United Kingdom to establish requirements that had not hitherto existed.[74] On the other hand, there is no European minimum capital requirement for private companies. Since some Member States require that private companies have a legally established minimum capital while others do not, the *Centros* line of judgments that liberalised competition for incorporations caused a haemorrhaging of incorporations to the United Kingdom, where there is no legal minimum capital requirement for private companies.[75] This has arguably given rise to some 'defensive regulatory competition' aimed at safeguarding against losing incorporations of private companies to Member States that have lower minimum capital requirements or none at all:[76]

> Anecdotal evidence from the websites of company formation agents is strongly suggestive that the driver of regulatory arbitrage by entrepreneurs is clearly the restrictive capital adequacy and maintenance requirements of many continental jurisdictions.[77]

As a result, France, Spain and Germany have rolled back capital requirements,[78] and the Netherlands considered doing so.[79] In France the declared reasons for the

[71] See Ebke (n 10) 1027–29.

[72] Council Directive (EEC) 1977/91 on coordination of safeguards which, for the protection of the interests of members and others, are required by Member States of companies within the meaning of the second paragraph of Article 58 of the Treaty, in respect of the formation of public limited liability companies and the maintenance and alteration of their capital, with a view to making such safeguards equivalent [1977] OJ L26/1.

[73] ibid.

[74] See PL Davies, *Gower and Davies' Principles of Modern Company Law*, 8th edn (Oxford, Oxford University Press, 2008) 259; Pasa, Benacchio and Orme (n 6) 310.

[75] M Becht, C Mayer and HF Wagner, 'Where do Firms Incorporate?' (2008) *Journal of Corporate Finance* 241, 242.

[76] Enriques and Gelter (n 70) 424.

[77] J Armour, 'Legal Capital: An Outdated Concept?' (2006) *European Business Organization Law Review* 5, 26.

[78] ibid; Loi n° 2003-721 du 1 août 2003 pour l'initiative économique; Gesetzes zur Modernisierung des GmbH-Rechts und zur Bekämpfung von Missbräuchen (MoMiG). See M Miola, 'Legal Capital and Limited Liability Companies: The European Perspective' (2005) *European Company and Financial Law Review* 413, 445; Becht, Mayer and Wagner (n 75) 243.

[79] The Dutch Ministry of Justice http://english.justitie.nl/currenttopics/pressreleases/archives2006/-Simplified-Formation-of-BVs-for-Smaller-companies-and-Start-up-Businesses.aspx; see Becht, Mayer and Wagner (n 75) 243.

removal of this requirement are a desire to remove barriers to the market, the arbitrariness of a legal minimum capital and the inefficacy of this method of creditor protection.[80] As a matter of fact, by downwardly revising minimum capital requirements for private companies, France has successfully curtailed the movement of incorporations to the United Kingdom.[81] However, because the European legislator has acted to establish minimum capital requirements for public companies, the regulatory competition instigated by *Centros* has not eradicated protection of creditors in transnational law entirely.

3.2.3.2 Transnational Creditor Protection in Practice

The litigation in *Centros* itself provides a clear illustration of creditor protection by way of exception from the incorporation theory.[82] The issues at stake in *Centros* highlight the extent to which some states attach importance to their chosen methods of limiting the risk that limited liability poses to creditors. In that matter two Danish citizens had established a company in the United Kingdom. The company then applied for permission to set up a branch in Denmark, as European Union law gives every company properly incorporated in the UK the undisputed right to do. This notwithstanding, the Danish authorities refused to allow the branch to be registered, on the grounds that the company did not trade in Britain and was in fact attempting to set up its primary establishment in Denmark in circumvention of Danish minimum capital requirements, rather than merely setting up a branch as its secondary establishment.[83] Denmark therefore went to great lengths to limit a European right because it viewed the avoidance of its minimum capital requirements as a matter that merited those efforts. It is worth reiterating that it did so notwithstanding its adherence to the incorporation theory. Despite Denmark's adherence to the shareholder-centric incorporation theory, the avoidance of its minimum capital requirements was sufficiently important for the administrators of her corporate policy to pursue this case in reference proceedings before the European Court of Justice. The ensuing controversy highlights the fact that protective state action against the autonomous decisions of incorporators is not solely the province of countries that adopt the real seat theory. Jurisdictions that are otherwise liberal in their recognition of foreign incorporations may from time to time go to great lengths to apply the substantive rules on the protection of corporate creditors.

A more typical method of affording protection to creditors is through the imposition of mandatory rules on corporations which are otherwise governed by foreign law and recognised as foreign corporations. There are two classes of situations where the state in which the company has its management centre will apply its creditor protection legislation in preference to the purported governing law of the

[80] Projet de Loi Pour l'Initiative Économique www.assemblee-nationale.fr/12/pdf/projets/pl0507.pdf 5–6.

[81] Becht, Mayer and Wagner (n 75) 252.

[82] *Centros* (n 1).

[83] *Centros* (n 1) para 16.

corporation: (i) the application of rules to pseudo-foreign corporations, and (ii) the application of creditor protection rules to companies which result from a merger, and at least one of which was previously connected to the relevant state by virtue of its previous governing law:

(i) Despite the Netherlands' adherence to the incorporation theory, the law provides a system of protection which effectively renders her conflicts rules a hybrid between the incorporation and real seat theories.[84] However, since the judgment of the ECJ in *Inspire Art*[85] the Netherlands has restricted the scope of the outreach clauses in respect of pro-forma foreign companies to non-EU/EEA companies.[86] In respect of such companies, although the corporation remains governed by foreign law generally, it must conform to Dutch minimum capital and reporting requirements if its seat is situated in the Netherlands.[87] The rationale for the application of Dutch law in preference to foreign law is reminiscent of arguments put forward in support of the real seat theory, namely that corporations which have their seat in Dutch territory should be placed on a level playing field, whether they are incorporated in the Netherlands or elsewhere.[88]

(ii) The European Cross-Border Merger Directive[89] provides for the furnishing of information to creditors in the event that a company is to be transformed into a foreign company.[90] The EU Directive, which is addressed in more depth in section 4.4.1, also allows Member States to enact legislation in order to protect creditors in the event that a company is to be merged with a foreign company.[91] In a similar vein, Swiss federal law provides that a Swiss company may change its governing law, provided that creditors are notified that they must state their claims against the company,[92] and that adjudicatory jurisdiction to satisfy these claims will remain in Switzerland.[93]

3.2.4 Employees

There is a marked ideological divide among states and theorists regarding the position of employees in the governance of corporations. Those who believe that corporate directors are bound to pursue profit to the exclusion of socially driven

[84] Rammeloo (n 8) 105.
[85] *Inspire Art* (n 36).
[86] XE Kramer, 'Dutch Private International Law – Overview 2002-2006' (2007) Erasmus Universiteit Rotterdam http://hdl.handle.net/1765/9232, 6–7.
[87] Andenas and Wooldridge (n 56) 96.
[88] ibid. Rammeloo (n 8) 104–8.
[89] Directive of the European Parliament and of the Council (EC) 2005/56 on cross-border mergers of limited liability companies (the Cross-Border Merger Directive) [2005] OJ L310/1.
[90] ibid arts 6–7.
[91] ibid art 4.
[92] Loi fédérale du 18 décembre 1987 art 163.
[93] ibid art 164; see F Guillaume, 'The Law Governing Companies in Swiss Private International Law' (2004) *Yearbook of Private International Law* 251, 280.

goals view workers as extraneous to the core structures of the company.[94] Others take the view that workers are not merely factors of production that the company contracts with, but rather that they are investors in the company, since they make a firm-specific investment of skills. The investment is of a different nature to shareholders' capital investment, in part because it cannot be quantified with precision in every case and a *quid pro quo* is therefore not readily calculable.[95] Yet it is an investment nevertheless and it is one that is fundamental to the functioning of a firm. There is therefore an argument that employees should be privy to the decision-making process in the company as stakeholders in its governance. There are three principal views of the worker's place in corporate law:

(i) At one end of the spectrum workers are not viewed as subjects of corporate law. Corporate law governs the relations between management and shareholders and the company; it does account for creditors, but not specifically for workers, except to the extent that they may also be creditors. The ultimate goal is the maximisation of shareholder wealth. It is principally argued that non-shareholder constituencies should not be of any concern to company law, but that if they were of concern, that the shareholder value model best serves them. The pursuit of profit facilitates financial success of shareholders which will filter through to other constituencies organically rather than through conscious decisions which detract from the goal of profitability.[96] Employment law, employment contracts and collective agreements are the appropriate means to determine the position of workers vis-à-vis the company, rather than any mechanism internal to the corporation;[97]

(ii) The median position adopted in the United Kingdom still sets out to maximise shareholder wealth. However, in the enlightened shareholder value model, the maximisation of shareholder wealth is not the only consideration that directors must take into account in their decision-making. Whereas the principal duty is 'the success of the company for the benefit of members as a whole', directors must also, as far as possible, have regard to other considerations, including the interests of the company's employees.[98]

[94] The view that the investment made by workers is extraneous to the core of the firm is reflected in Coase's theory where he explains that the entrepreneur employs workers in order to maximise efficiencies for his own purposes and 'can always revert to the open market if he fails to [thereby acquire factors of production at a lower price]'. R Coase, 'The Nature of the Firm' (1937) *Economica* 386, 392. This view was most famously stated in Milton Friedman's famed article in the *New York Times Magazine*, the title of which succinctly explains his argument: M Friedman, 'The Social Responsibility of Business Is to Increase Its Profits' *New York Times Magazine* (New York, 13 September 1970) 32–33.

[95] M Blair, *Wealth Creation and Wealth Sharing: A Colloquium on Corporate Governance and Investments in Human Capital* (Washington DC, Brookings Institute, 1996) 10 per J Paterson, 'The Company Law Review in the UK and the Question of Scope: Theoretical Concerns, Practical Constraints and Possible Directions' in R Cobbaut and J Lenoble (eds), *Corporate Governance. An Institutional Approach* (Netherlands, Kluwer Law International, 2003) 156.

[96] See Hansmann and Kraakman (n 12) 450–51. Hansmann and Kraakman do not propose a shareholder-oriented model out of antipathy towards employees, but because they are of the view that this model is more efficient and therefore generates more industry and wealth.

[97] ibid 440–42.

[98] Companies Act 2006 s 172.

(iii) Elsewhere, such as in Germany, it is thought that workers should have a say in the governance of the company through the appointment of employee representatives on the board of directors of the corporation. Legal instruments which are extraneous to the firm are considered insufficient to place the worker at the heart of the corporate form. Notwithstanding that international competitive pressures are brought to bear upon this model of corporate governance, these States go to great lengths to preserve this social model of the company, arguably for political reasons of purely domestic concern.[99]

The latter two positions may both be attributed to the state's recognition of the investment of firm-specific human capital. Workers are the only non-shareholder constituency that any company law protects through direct representation on the board of directors of a company.[100] This occurs despite the fact that, theoretically, every other constituency is capable of protection through direct representation on the board.[101] Jurisdictions that provide for worker representation therefore appear to attach great importance to the place of workers in the governance of the company. The representation of workers evidences a social model of the company wherein representation and participation of workers is preferred to a free rein for shareholders and management. In contrast, states whose corporate law focuses on maximising shareholder value take the view that, if employees are indeed to be protected by corporate law itself, the pursuit of profit for shareholders serves all corporate constituents – a company that makes profits can continue to employ workers and to pay their wages. It is then for employment law to redress any imbalance of power suffered by employees.

It does not appear that states that include employees in the corporate decision-making process protect that ideological stance in their conflict of corporate laws rules through targeted measures. However, this does not constitute evidence that workers are not given due consideration in the conflict of corporate laws. Rather, those states that include workers in governance structures employ the broad-brush real seat approach to protect the entirety of their corporate law. Germany is perhaps the clearest such example. Prior to the *Centros* line of judgments, the protective nature of the real seat doctrine had ensured that Germany could safeguard its model of worker co-determination.[102] The judgments of the ECJ concerning freedom of establishment have severely limited the possibility of using private international law to safeguard co-determination norms. It is therefore no surprise that the judgment in *Centros* has attracted such extraordinary academic attention in Germany, even when compared to other Member States that adhere

[99] Hansmann and Kraakman (n 12) 446.

[100] H Hansmann and R Kraakman, 'The Basic Governance Structure' in Kraakman and others (n 65) 61.

[101] ibid.

[102] JC Dammann 'The future of codetermination after *Centros*: Will German corporate law move closer to the U.S. model?' (2003) *Fordham Journal of Corporate and Financial Law* 607, 610–12; Ebke (n 10) 1028.

to the real seat theory but do not prescribe worker co-determination in their substantive company law.[103]

In addition, to national broad-brush measures, EU private international law of companies contains targeted exceptions to liberal choices of law.[104] These measures are addressed in the next chapter of this book.

3.2.5 Accountability of Directors

The discussion of legal certainty in the previous chapter exposed the pitfalls of extraterritorial imposition of obligations on directors who are already subject to the law under which the company is constituted. One will recall that the imposition of additional, and differing, obligations may expose directors to irreducible conflicts of obligations. Notwithstanding these difficulties, some laws do in fact extend prescriptive jurisdiction to the directors of formally foreign corporations. The private international law of several jurisdictions sets out to correct a perceived imbalance which often emerges in the relations between shareholders and directors. Often, the duties and liabilities of directors under the law of incorporation are modified through outreach clauses in the laws of the jurisdiction in which the corporation has its seat.

In response to the migration of corporations to Delaware, California imposes obligations on directors of pseudo-foreign corporations binding them to abide by the standard of care expected of directors of California companies.[105] This suggests that corporations that are based in California cannot be fully foreign and must be managed according to the standards that are prescribed by the representatives of the Californian polity. A pseudo-foreign corporation may be born of the law of Delaware but it cannot live exclusively according to those laws – California deems that corporation to be so intimately linked to its jurisdiction that it must set the standards by which the directors, as the governors of the corporate nexus of relationships, must abide.

It is perhaps more striking that Swiss law would provide exceptions to the incorporation theory in order to impose greater liability on directors. Switzerland has otherwise been so unwavering in its application of the incorporation theory that it deemed it expedient to reject the *fraude à la loi* exception which previously had reined in pseudo-foreign corporations.[106] Article 159 of the Swiss Private International Law Code of 1987 provides that 'when the operations of a company created under a foreign law are carried out in or from Switzerland, the liability of

[103] See WF Ebke '*Centros* – Some Realities and Some Mysteries' (2000) *The American Journal of International Law* 623, 623–25; WH Roth, 'From *Centros* to *Ueberseering*: Free Movement of Companies, Private International Law, and Community Law' (2003) *International and Comparative Law Quarterly* 177, 177–80.

[104] Directive 2005/56/EC of the European Parliament and of the Council of 26 October 2005 on cross-border mergers of limited liability companies [2005] OJ L310/1.

[105] California Corporations Code § 2115 (b).

[106] *Chilon Valeurs Inc c. Financial Construction Company Inc* ATF 117 II 497 cons 5 and 6 per B Dutoit, *Commentaire de la loi fédérale du 18 décembre 1987* (Frankfurt-sur-le-Main, Helbing und Lichtenhahn, 1996) 420.

the persons acting in the name of such company is governed by Swiss law.'[107] This provision creates a peculiar situation in which foreign law will determine the powers of the company,[108] while Swiss law will govern any abuse of the powers bestowed by that foreign law.[109] The purpose of this departure from the incorporation theory is the curtailment of abuse where the carrying on of operations in or from Switzerland gives the appearance that a foreign company is in fact a Swiss company. This is intended to afford third parties the pertinent level of protection where the relevant foreign legal system is lax in this respect.[110] This anomalous system of conflicts rules evidences a strong policy bias in favour of promoting an open economic system that is simultaneously protective of the foreign investment that the adoption of the incorporation doctrine was intended to encourage. Given that Swiss law is otherwise notable for its strict adherence to the incorporation theory, the theoretical anomaly in Swiss law highlights the importance of the regulation of the governors of corporations as a matter of national economic concern.

3.3 Enduring Divergence in Corporate Law, and Potential Exceptions in Private International Law

As corporate laws continue to evolve and to respond to political development, new divergences inevitably emerge. Innovation in corporate law is particularly susceptible to avoidance since, by definition, the most innovative states are initially the only states whose laws contain certain provisions. Where the innovations are not overtly designed to achieve efficiencies for corporate decision-makers, or where benefits are not universally accepted, one might expect companies to migrate to other jurisdictions. Given the intimate connection between corporate policy and conflict of laws, states might seek to limit avoidance of novel laws through the imposition of elements of local law on formally foreign legal persons. This section contains a selection of examples of laws which enshrine policies of such importance as to merit exception to contractual freedom.

One such example is the gender equality laws which are emerging in a number of European states. As noted in section 1.7 of this book, a number of European states have adopted laws to bring about equal representation of each gender in the boards of certain companies.[111] The relevant laws are intended to instigate broad

[107] trans per Dutoit (n 106) 429.

[108] Switzerland Private International Law Code of 1987 art 154.

[109] See Rammeloo (n 8) 168.

[110] Dutoit (n 106) 429.

[111] S Terjesen and V Singh, 'Female Presence on Corporate Boards: A Multi-Country Study of Environmental Context' (2008) *Journal of Business Ethics* 55, 62. Belcher suggests that, in the absence of corporate legislation, there is qualified potential for gender equality to be addressed through sex discrimination law: A Belcher, 'Board Diversity: Can Sex Discrimination Law Help?' (2005) *Northern Ireland Legal Quarterly* 356, 362–72. However, Villiers argues, correctly it is submitted, that it is better to resolve matters at the core of corporate law than to compensate for the shortcomings of corporate

changes in the governance of economic policy within the territories of those states. In view of the *Centros* line of judgments, these states have not been able to accompany substantive changes with protective conflict rules. This may reduce the effectiveness of the relevant laws if promoters of companies choose to avoid gender equality legislation by establishing a company under other laws.[112] One might therefore speculate that states would have included outreach clauses in their gender equality laws had this been permissible under European law. What is more, as political sensibilities evolve, it is probable that positive discrimination on the basis of matters such as ethnicity or disability will also be addressed in corporate law. These too may be thwarted by the possibility of importing laws from other states in preference to the less accommodating local law.

Further potential divergence may emerge in the treatment of involuntary creditors. Corporate activity may affect individuals and communities with which companies do not have any contractual relationship. The limited liability that contractual stakeholders may impute into their pricing also affects persons who could not have bargained against the cost of limitation of liability. Of particular note are claims in tort against under-capitalised companies, including subsidiaries of major parent companies. Examples of damage to individuals and communities abound, including the 2010 oil spill in the Gulf of Mexico, and asbestos poisoning in the *Cape* cases.[113] By definition, there is a local interest in such matters. Astute corporate groups keep valuable assets in non-trading holding companies, well away from their riskier operations. They thereby effectively ring-fence funds and limit their tortious liability to the extent of the capital invested in the risky venture, that is potentially under-capitalised. This renders the involuntary creditor particularly vulnerable, since there is no *ex ante* possibility of bringing holding companies in as guarantors for a tortious claim: 'Put differently, to the extent that the corporate form insulates shareholders from tort damages or fines, shareholders are free to opt out of the laws that control the negative externalities of production, including product liability law, environmental law, and tort law generally.'[114]

While the possibility of opting out of tortious liability is true of the internal law of most states, it is even more so where incorporators have the option of selecting the governing law of the corporation. A variety of methods to insulate non-contractual creditors have been recommended by corporate law scholars. These include indirect methods such as capital maintenance requirements, and direct methods such as compulsory insurance, the piercing of the corporate veil in the event of an unsatisfied obligation in tort, and priority in bankruptcy claims.[115]

law *ex post facto*: C Villiers, 'Achieving Gender Balance in the Board Room: Is it Time for Legislative Action in the UK?' (2010) *Legal Studies* 533, 533–57.

112 Villiers (n 111).

113 *Lubbe et al v Cape Industries plc* [1997] 4 All ER 335.

114 Hertig and Kanda (n 65) 76–77.

115 See generally H Hansmann and R Kraakman, 'Toward Unlimited Shareholder Liability for Corporate Torts' (1991) *Yale Law Journal* 1879; DW Leebron, 'Limited Liability, Tort Victims and Creditors' (1991) *Columbia Law Review* 1565; D Kershaw, *Company Law in Context* (Oxford, Oxford University Press, 2009) 714.

However, significantly, most states do not adopt any strategy to directly protect involuntary creditors. If innovators do emerge, freedom of choice of corporate law would allow companies to opt out of the costs of their non-contractual obligations. Involuntary stakeholders who have no a priori means to protect themselves against non-contractual losses that they had no means to foresee may therefore be prejudiced by unfavourable choices of corporate law.

3.4 Conclusions

The discussion in this chapter demonstrates that states which apply the incorporation theory often make exceptions to their acceptance of a foreign governing law. One might not be surprised to find that real seat countries attempt to exercise control over foreign corporations. However, there is an ideological inconsistency in the application of local rules to foreign corporations in incorporation countries. It is submitted that the preponderance of these rules in incorporation countries reaffirms the place of stakeholder protection as a central tenet of the private international law norms of most jurisdictions. The exception to the liberal contractual approach of the incorporation theory betrays the fact that party autonomy is just one of many considerations that may be taken into account in determining the appropriate connecting factors between a company and a legal system.

The examples cited above do not reveal consistency in the extraterritorial application of specific areas of corporate law. By way of example, one state may be inclined to impose its minimum capital requirements but not its shareholder protection, whereas the reverse is true in another state. The above analysis therefore illustrates that it is impossible to identify a universally applicable model through which to limit party autonomy. Rather, it is clear that each relevant state has a unique view of the manner in which the conflict of laws should operate, and the parameters within which promoters of companies are free to select a company's governing law.

That noted, the pervasiveness of protective conflicts rules does not of itself disprove the thesis that incorporators should be afforded the liberty to select the governing law of a company through the act of incorporation; there is no overriding need for absoluteness in the application of a philosophy, for the philosophy itself to hold water. It could well be argued that the exceptions to the theory are pollutants, which legislators should strive to eliminate. A theory is no less perfect simply because it is applied imperfectly. Nevertheless, the imperfection of application reflects the fact that there exist a variety of interests that states deem to arise from the corporate form. Those interests are not limited to the shareholders' needs and wants, despite the fact that the stated aims of the legislator may be restricted to the furtherance of the autonomy of shareholders. States select interests which they deem to require protection from the encroachment of foreign norms. The selection of specific areas of corporate law indicates that the manner in which the governing law of companies is determined is not a matter of neutral private international law theory. Rather, the governing law of companies is applied within the constraints of the corporate law policy of the jurisdiction in question.

4

Party Autonomy in European Law

4.1 Introduction

The foregoing chapters illustrated that party autonomy in transnational corporate law cannot be deemed to be an absolute good. This is because the theory of party autonomy in corporate law is partially unsound, it is controversial and is seldom unqualified in State practice. As such, it is for legislators to express a preference in favour of party autonomy or otherwise. This chapter sets out to identify whether EU law expresses a preference for contractual freedom of promoters of companies, and, if so, the extent to which it does so.

The most obviously relevant Treaty articles are articles 49 and 54 TFEU (articles 43 and 48 EC) which cumulatively provide for freedom of establishment for companies.[1] Article 293 EC, which has been repealed by the Treaty of Lisbon, is also relevant, in that it has helped to shape the case law of the ECJ.[2] This article empowered Member States to enter into negotiations to legislate the private international law of companies. The repeal of article 293 EC does not remove the basis for harmonisation of the private international law of companies since article 81 TFEU (article 65 EC) provides a broad basis for the adoption of measures concerning private international law. In cross-border situations, particularly where necessary for the proper functioning of the internal market, the European Parliament and the Council may adopt legislation concerning 'the compatibility of the rules applicable in the member states concerning conflict of laws and of jurisdiction'.[3] However, these articles are not the principal focus of discussion in this chapter, because their content is unclear, their treatment by the Court is equally so, and one can therefore glean few incontrovertible insights. In addition, articles 49 and 54 TFEU and article 293 EC are worthy of separate discussion in the next chapter of this book, since their inconsistent interpretation by the Court is of itself a matter of concern. Nevertheless, one should recall at the outset that the ECJ's *Centros* line of judgments grants promoters of companies a great degree of autonomy to select the law that will govern their company on the basis of the Court's interpretation

[1] Freedom of corporate establishment is subject to some conditions that have been poorly defined by the Court of Justice. The conditions will be discussed in more detail in the next chapter of this book.

[2] Art 293 EC has been relevant in the ECJ's reasoning in several cases, including the most recent relevant judgment in Case C-210/06 *Cartesio Oktató és Szolgáltató bt* [2008] ECR I-9641.

[3] Art 81(2)(c) TFEU.

of articles 49 and 54 TFEU (articles 43 and 48 EC).[4] In addition, obiter dicta in *Cartesio* indicate that the Court is sympathetic to a right to reincorporation without winding up and reconstituting a company.[5] These matters are addressed only briefly in this chapter in the context of a discussion of the constitutional status of party autonomy.

Rather, this chapter takes an aerial view of the law of the internal market, and then focuses on article 50(2)(g) (article 44(2)(g) EC), which provides that harmonisation of company law is to provide the basis for corporate freedom of establishment. The company law directives promulgated under the authority of article 50 are also addressed, as is the treatment of choice of corporate law in the regulation of supranational European business vehicles. In the final analysis, it is concluded that in its present state, EU law adopts an ambivalent approach to party autonomy.

4.2 The Constitutional Treatment of Party Autonomy

It was found in Chapter 2 that analogies with European contract law lead to the conclusion that, as a matter of contractual principle, party autonomy may fall to be restricted in transnational corporate law. The reasoning in that chapter might appear to pre-empt a discussion of the constitutional status of party autonomy, in that it illustrates a priori that party autonomy is indeed capable of restriction. Nevertheless, it is self-evident that capacity for restriction does not of itself undo a rule. It therefore remains pertinent to consider whether there exists a basic norm of EU law which expresses a preference for party autonomy. If so, are there any exceptions, and are there any constitutional limits to any such exceptions? In other words, can it be said that EU law provides that the governing law of every relationship may be determined by the parties, save in the event that the law provides otherwise? If so, does the law provide otherwise in the case of corporate law, and what might be the consequences of the general presumption in respect of the exception?

It is arguable that party autonomy is central to the philosophy underlying the foundation of the European Union. In the neo-liberal construct, the European economic constitution expresses a preference for divesting public institutions of control over private action. The fundamental freedoms are viewed as self-executing rules of such constitutional value as to be central not only to an economic project, but to the very political goals of a post-totalitarian Europe in which individual

[4] Case C-212/97 *Centros Ltd v Erhvervs-og Selskabsstyrelsen* [1999] ECR I-01459; Case C-208/00 *Überseering BV v Nordic Construction Company Baumanagement GmbH* (NCC) [2002] ECR I-9919; Case C-167/01 *Kamer van Koophandel en Fabrieken voor Amsterdam v Inspire Art Ltd* [2003] ECR I-10155; Case C-411/03 *Sevic Systems AG* [2005] ECR I-10805.

[5] *Cartesio* (n 2) paras 110–12.

autonomy acts as a guarantee against the possible excesses of the State.[6] If it can be shown that the autonomy of individual actors is a central constitutional principle, the argument for unlimited choice of corporate law will surely be difficult to rebut. Nevertheless, it is submitted that such broad statements of principle do not represent the constitutional history of the Union appropriately. It is truer of Europe's history that integration was intended to avoid conflict between nation states.[7] As such, party autonomy in the context of the fundamental freedoms can be seen as a functional instrument of integration, rather than a shield against totalitarianism which merits vigorous protection. Accordingly, if there is indeed a presumption in favour of party autonomy, it is to be found in a more modest reading of the fundamental freedoms.

Yet party autonomy, and mutual recognition, which is its corollary, remains a chosen mode of governance within the European Union,[8] or at least an instrument that allows 'choice of governance.'[9] The fundamental freedoms create a presumption that where parties choose the law of a Member State, this choice is to be respected, save in the event that the public interest necessitates the application of overriding mandatory requirements.[10] In private international law terms, this establishes a rebuttable presumption that Member States should recognise the legality of that which is legally sanctioned under the laws of other Member States. This is motivated, at least in part, by economic considerations. Mutual recognition enables the optimum allocation of resources by allowing labour and capital to be deployed where they are needed, thus allowing the optimum return on enterprise.[11] It also serves as a tool for the establishment of the internal market, since it eliminates the cost to multinational enterprises of conforming to multiple laws.[12] In addition, mutual recognition is economically preferable to the use of objective connecting, factors which cause uncertainty by requiring compliance with complicated factual tests.[13] This is not to say that party autonomy is guaranteed by the Treaty without qualification: 'What is guaranteed . . . is that restrictions and exclusions of party-autonomy are brought within the scope of the Court's scrutiny and

[6] See MP Maduro, *We The Court: The European Court of Justice and the European Economic Constitution. A Critical Reading of Article 30 of the EC Treaty* (Oxford, Hart Publishing, 1998) 126–29; W Sauter and H Schepel, *State and Market in European Union Law: The Public and Private Spheres of the Internal Market before the EU Courts* (Cambridge, Cambridge University Press, 2009) 13–15.

[7] R Schuman, 'The Schuman Declaration of 9 May 1950' in AG Harryvan and J van der Harst (eds), *Documents on European Union* (London, Macmillan, 1997) 61–63.

[8] SK Schmidt, 'Mutual recognition as a new mode of governance' (2007) *Journal of European Public Policy* 667, 667–68; MP Maduro, 'So close and yet so far: the paradoxes of mutual recognition' (2007) *Journal of European Public Policy* 814, 815.

[9] JP Trachtman, 'Embedding mutual recognition at the WTO' (2007) *Journal of European Public Policy* 780, 783.

[10] J Israël, *European Cross-Border Insolvency Regulation: A Study of Regulation 1346/2000 on Insolvency Proceedings in the Light of a Paradigm of Co-operation and a* Comitas Europaea (Intersentia, Oxford 2005) 125–26.

[11] PC Müller-Graff, 'Basic Freedoms – Extending Party Autonomy Across Borders' in S Grundmann, W Kerber and S Weatherill (eds), *Party Autonomy and the Role of Information in the Internal Market* (Berlin, de Gruyter, 2001) 134–35.

[12] Schmidt (n 8) 671–72.

[13] Israël (n 10) 125.

the need for justification.'[14] Yet, the rigour that is exercised in scrutinising restrictions to party autonomy tends to outweigh the Court's sympathy for Member States' justifications.[15] This is evident in the Court's judgments concerning freedom of corporate establishment which allow Member States only limited scrutiny of choices of corporate law.[16]

Indeed, following initial reluctance in the judgment in *Daily Mail* to find that freedom of establishment granted a directly effective right to corporations to establish themselves in any Member State,[17] the Court has consistently found that incorporation in one Member State is to be respected throughout the Union.[18] The Court's analysis has seldom explicitly cited party autonomy. However, AG La Pergola's Opinion in *Centros* defined freedom of establishment and its constitutional setting in the following terms:

> The right of establishment is essential to the achievement of the objectives set in the Treaty, the purpose of which is to guarantee to all Community citizens alike the freedom to engage in business activities through the instruments provided by national law, thus giving them the chance to enter the market, irrespective of the motives that may actually have prompted the person concerned. In other words, it is the opportunity to exercise business activities that is protected, and with it the contractual freedom to make use of the instruments provided for that purpose in the legal systems of the Member States.[19]

From this it followed that 'in the absence of harmonisation, competition among rules must be allowed free play in corporate matters'.[20] AG La Pergola's Opinion is a forceful, overt statement which suggests that party autonomy should be placed at the heart of European law. However, the Court's judgment did not address party autonomy and regulatory competition at all.[21] A company's intention to

[14] ibid 127.

[15] A Johnston and P Syrpis, 'Regulatory competition in European company law after *Cartesio*' (2009) *European Law Review* 378, 388–89; see Case C-55/94 *Reinhard Gebhard v Consiglio dell'Ordine degli Avvocati e Procuratori di Milano* [1995] ECR I-4565 para 37.

[16] *Centros* (n 4); *Überseering* (n 4); *Inspire Art* (n 4); *Sevic Systems* (n 4); *Cartesio* (n 2). Further evidence of the Court's sympathy for claims that the Member States have restricted the fundamental freedoms is to be found in such cases as C-438/05 *International Transport Workers' Federation v Viking Line ABP* [2007] ECR I-10779 and C-341/05 *Laval un Partneri Ltd v Svenska Byggnadsarbetareforbundet* [2007] ECR I-11767. Here, the implication of the Court's findings was that even the most fundamental of social rights are to be subjected to a strict test of proportionality if the said social rights restricted the exercise of economic freedoms. See generally J Malmberg and T Sigeman, 'Industrial Actions and EU Economic Freedoms: the Autonomous Collective Bargaining Model Curtailed by the European Court of Justice' (2008) *Common Market Law Review* 1115, 1115–46; P Syrpis and T Novitz, 'Political and Social Rights in Conflict: Political and Judicial Approaches to their Reconciliation' (2008) *European Law Review* 411, 411–26; A Hinarejos, 'Laval and Viking: the Right to Collective Action Versus Fundamental Freedoms' (2008) *Human Rights Law Review* 714, 714–29.

[17] Case 81/87 *The Queen v HM Treasury and Commissioners of Inland Revenue, ex p Daily Mail and General Trust plc* [1988] ECR 5483 para 21.

[18] *Centros* (n 4); *Überseering* (n 4); *Inspire Art* (n 4); *Cartesio* (n 2).

[19] *Centros* (n 4) para 20 (AG La Pergola).

[20] ibid.

[21] See Johnston and Syrpis (n 15), 395–96; M Gestri, 'Mutuo Riconoscimento delle Società Comunitarie, Norme di Conflitto Nazionali e Frode alla Legge: il caso *Centros*' (2000) *Rivista di Diritto Internazionale* 71, 90.

transfer its seat, or the absence of such intention, was only cited later as part of the rationale to distinguish the facts in *Daily Mail*[22] from the liberalising judgments in subsequent cases.[23] Party autonomy was thus part of the justification for a departure from precedent and the removal of barriers to freedom of establishment. Yet it must be noted that the statements of the Court regarding party autonomy have the character of obiter dicta and do not reveal a sustained analysis of that principle in the context of corporate law. The principal, and enduring, distinction remains the notion that a Member State is free to regulate companies established under its own laws, but must recognise companies incorporated abroad and must also recognise the full extent of the law governing that company.[24] This has the effect of placing some limitation on autonomy. Once a company is established under the laws of a Member State, it must comply with the substantive and private international law of that state, even if the said laws restrict the company's autonomy to select its factual location.[25] Autonomy is therefore not a central or pervasive principle, and the secondary nature of the principle is reflected both in the absence of any sustained engagement with the princple, and in the ECJ's upholding of national laws that restrict corporate emigration.[26]

Regardless of the paucity of analysis of party autonomy in the Court's judgments, by favouring mutual recognition of companies, the ECJ has implicitly furthered autonomy. In *Centros*[27] the ECJ found that Member States must recognise companies incorporated in other Member States, regardless of where the companies' operational headquarters are situated. The judgment in *Centros* did not cite the above-quoted AG's analysis insofar as regulatory competition is concerned, but the effect was identical in decisively moving European choice of corporate law in a direction that maximised regulatory competition and that consequently limited the role of states in connecting a company to a jurisdiction.[28] Subsequent judgments in *Überseering*[29] and *Inspire Art*[30] built upon the *Centros* doctrine, the latter judgment adding that Member States could not adopt outreach clauses that impose obligations upon pseudo-foreign corporations or their officers in addition to those imposed by the law of the Member State of incorporation.[31] Promoters of companies are therefore free to select a governing law of their company, virtually without restriction. Moreover, in *Sevic Systems* it was found that companies could not be precluded from merging across borders.[32] This allowed companies the autonomy to escape the shackles of a national legal system without

[22] *Daily Mail* (n 17).
[23] *Überseering* (n 4) para 62.
[24] *Cartesio* (n 2) para 122.
[25] ibid para 110.
[26] ibid.
[27] *Centros* (n 4).
[28] See Johnston and Syrpis (n 15) 395–96.
[29] *Überseering* (n 4).
[30] *Inspire Art* (n 4).
[31] ibid para 101.
[32] *Sevic Systems* (n 4).

the need for winding up.[33] Finally, the Court's most recent relevant judgment, *Cartesio*, provided that corporate emigration could not be restricted in the event that it was intended that a company's governing law would be changed in the process.[34] The Court has not yet addressed the question of reincorporation independently of a physical seat transfer, but the thrust of the Court's judgments is certainly favourable to party autonomy.

This is symptomatic of the Court's teleological approach, which looks to further the broader aims of legislation, rather than concerning itself excessively with the *lex specialis* at issue. The approach to choice of corporate law fits well with the Court's approach to private international law of companies, as illustrated in the judgment in *Powell Duffryn* concerning a prorogation clause in a company statute.[35] Despite finding that 'a resolution adopted by a majority at a meeting of a company . . . in principle resists inclusion in any contractual classification',[36] AG Tesauro concluded that the theoretical difficulty should not hinder the resolution of the facts of the case.[37] The AG's view, which was endorsed by the Court, was motivated by an over-arching desire to further the aims of the Brussels I Regulation and to prevent multiple grounds of jurisdiction.[38] Thus, despite an understanding of the finer details of corporate law and conflicts of corporate laws,[39] an integration-driven Court was inclined to safeguard party autonomy in choice of adjudicatory jurisdiction to further a broad legislative goal. Similarly, the Court has been more inclined to further integration than to concern itself with the finer details of the Treaty's treatment of autonomy in respect of the governing law of companies.

4.3 The Origins and Purpose of Article 50

As noted above, the discussion in this chapter focuses on article 50(2)(g) TFEU (article 44(2)(g) EC) which provides a Treaty basis for harmonisation, as well as the directives promulgated under the authority of the said article. Article 50 provides that, in order to attain freedom of establishment, the European Parliament and the Council shall adopt directives 'coordinating to the necessary extent the safeguards which, for the protection of the interests of members and others, are

[33] See MM Siems, '*Sevic:* Beyond Cross-Border Mergers' (2007) *European Business Organization Law Review* 307, 312–13; MM Siems, 'The European Directive on Cross-Border Mergers: An International Model?' (2005) *Columbia Journal of European Law* 167, 179–81; LL Hansen, 'Merger, Moving and Division Across National Borders – When Case Law Breaks through Barriers and Overtakes Directives' (2007) *European Business Law Review* 181, 196–98; FM Mucciarelli, 'Company "Emigration" and EC Freedom of Establishment: *Daily Mail* Revisited' (2008) *European Business Organization Law Review* 267, 276–77

[34] *Cartesio* (n 2) paras 110–12.

[35] Case C-214/89 *Powell Duffryn v Petereit* [1992] ECR I-9337.

[36] *Powell Duffryn* (n 35) para 4 (AG Tesauro).

[37] ibid.

[38] *Powell Duffryn* (n 35) para 20.

[39] ibid paras 10 and 16.

required by Member States of companies or firms . . . with a view to making such safeguards equivalent throughout the Union'.[40]

This does not of itself say a great deal about party autonomy in European corporate law. However, it does suggest that the Union's foundational law foresees that the contractual covenants which establish a company should be limited by state law. Article 50(2)(g) constitutes recognition of multi-party interests in corporate law – the requirement of safeguards of equivalent standard can only mean that some safeguards are in fact to be put or kept in place. Indeed, by equalisation of standards one must perforce understand that there is an implicit requirement of the raising of lower standards of protection. In addition, the Treaty requirement of harmonisation illustrates that European law did not intend that market forces should be the principal driver for the approximation of legal standards. Rather, it was intended that the directives of the EU lawmaker should provide that impetus. As such, European law expresses a preference for legislative limitation of party autonomy, albeit without necessarily denying autonomy altogether.

The historical motivation for the inclusion of the provision is also revealing. Article 50(2)(g) was included in the EEC Treaty at the insistence of the French government in order to protect against the encroachment of companies from Member States that offered lower standards of protection – particularly the Netherlands at the time.[41] The reasons for France's apprehension were twofold. There was a rational concern that foreign companies would gain a competitive advantage over companies which were subject to higher standards of stakeholder protection.[42] In this guise, it is clear that the Union's founders viewed the corporate form as an essential vehicle for the establishment of the internal market,[43] and that it was their intention to create a level competitive playing field as the basis of corporate mobility[44] without sacrificing the standards of protection established in some Member States. Yet the principal concern of the French government was that companies which had their seat in France would opt for incorporation in the Netherlands and take advantage of the internal market by subsequently setting up secondary establishments in other Member States.[45] Thus harmonisation of

[40] The original French text refers to 'les intérêts tant des associés que des tiers', which might have been more faithfully translated as 'the interests of members and third parties'. The reference to third parties is noteworthy in that it indicates a dichotomy between shareholders, who have contractual interests that are internal to the firm, and third parties to whom some undefined fiduciary obligation may be owed.

[41] S Grundmann, 'The Structure of European Company Law: From Crisis to Boom' (2004) *European Business Organisation Law Review* 601, 605; CWA Timmermans 'Company Law as Ius Commune?' (2002) Walter van Gerven Lecture, Leuven Centre for a Common Law of Europe www.law.kuleuven.ac.be/ccle/pdf/wvg1.pdf 5.

[42] Grundmann (n 41) 605.

[43] The importance attached to the harmonisation of company law is highlighted by the fact that company law was the first area of private law falling within the ambit of civil codes to be harmonised in the Union. Indeed, company law remains the area of private law that is, arguably, the most intensely harmonised, save for competition law: Grundmann (n 41) 605.

[44] TH Tröber, 'Choice of Jurisdiction in European Corporate Law – Perspectives of European Corporate Governance' (2005) *European Business Organization Law Review* 3, 57.

[45] Timmermans (n 41) 5; J Wouters, 'European Company Law: *Quo Vadis*?' (2000) *Common Market Law Review* 257, 269–70.

company law was predicated on a desire to guard vigorously against the emergence of a European Delaware.[46] It is noteworthy that fear of Delawarisation was not entirely rational at a time when the real seat theory limited, or indeed excluded, party autonomy.[47] Still, this does not diminish the relevance of article 50(2)(g) from a conflicts perspective. Rather, the reverse is true. Article 50(2)(g) is significant from a schematic perspective, since it highlights the extent to which the Union's founders set out to restrict party autonomy. In addition to existing national private international law measures, harmonisation of substantive law was intended as a further defence against undesired effects of economic integration which could impinge upon state control over the content of corporate law.

Article 50 as it was originally construed is to be contrasted with the manner in which it has developed as an instrument for the establishment of an internal market in which common standards would facilitate trade.[48] Both the Commission and academic commentators have suggested that harmonisation is an instrument of EU industrial policy intended to facilitate the granting of credit to corporations whose form was unfamiliar to lenders, and therefore posed an additional risk and barrier.[49] This is borne out by the content of a plurality of company law directives that harmonise accounting standards and capital maintenance requirements.[50] Thus, from its origins as a safeguard against Delawarisation, the provision became an instrument of market integration, and this with the consent of the Member States as expressed in their assent to secondary legislation. Nevertheless, this revised interpretation of article 50(2)(g), which has in fact become the predominant interpretation, does not greatly alter the status of party autonomy. It remains true that party autonomy and regulatory competition are not deemed to be so desirable in Treaty law as to be unrestricted. Limits to the Union's competence to legislate are established in article 5 TEU, which requires that the Union act in accordance with the principles of proportionality and subsidiarity, and in the case law of the ECJ which elaborates these limits. Although restrictions to the EU's law-making capacity are not extensive in practice, the fact of their existence suggests that harmonisation is 'only intended for the abolition, or at least reduction, of

[46] ibid.

[47] Timmermans (n 41) 5; Wouters (n 45) 283–84.

[48] In support of the view that art 50(2)(g) TFEU is intended to facilitate integration by making national corporate laws relatively homogenous, see B Pasa, GA Benacchio and L Orme (tr), *The Harmonization of Civil and Commercial Law in Europe* (Budapest, Central European University Press, 2005) 264–72, and Wouters (n 45) 289–90.

[49] See Wouters (n 45) 268–72.

[50] Council Directive (EEC) 1968/151 of 9 March 1968 on coordination of safeguards which, for the protection of the interests of members and others, are required by Member States of companies within the meaning of the second paragraph of Article 58 of the Treaty, with a view to making such safeguards equivalent throughout the Community [1968] OJ L065/8; Council Directive (EEC) 1977/91 of 13 December 1976 on the coordination of safeguards which, for the protection of the interests of members and others, are required by Member States of companies within the meaning of the second paragraph of Article 58 of the Treaty, in respect of the formation of public limited liability companies and the maintenance and alteration of their capital, with a view to making such safeguards equivalent [1977] OJ L026/1.

disparities which cause barriers to free movement'.[51] It follows that some autonomy is envisaged in the general scheme of the basic law of the EU. Still, there remains an implicit rejection of absolute autonomy. This is so regardless of whether harmonisation is intended to facilitate market penetration by foreign corporations, as the revised view would suggest, or if it is also – and indeed principally – intended for the purpose of the protection of stakeholders, as a textual reading of article 50(2)(g) would suggest. What is more, article 3 TEU envisages the establishment of an internal market which is based, inter alia, on a 'highly competitive social market economy'. The precise meaning of these terms is unclear, and their justiciability suspect. However, reference to a social market economy, competitive or otherwise, constitutes a further rejection of absolute autonomy.

In addition, the industrial policy motivation for harmonisation negates the principal justification for party autonomy, namely that party autonomy instigates a race to the top. The central argument made by proponents of a race to the top is that market actors will select the most efficient law,[52] or the law which is most attuned to their specific needs.[53] Presumably, this should be a law that will inspire confidence in lenders and thereby grant companies access to credit. By electing to employ harmonisation to facilitate the granting of credit, EU law implicitly suggests that free market mechanisms are not sufficient, or are at best inferior to legislative intervention. Accordingly, even in its most pro-entrepreneurial guise, EU legislation denies the basic tenets of free competition for corporate charters and opts instead for a degree of legislative intervention. Thus, even if, for the sake of the argument, one were to set aside the multi-party motivations for the harmonisation of corporate law, it remains true that article 50(2)(g) demonstrates only limited faith in market mechanisms as a means to improve corporate law in the Member States.

4.3.1 Article 50(2)(g) after *Centros*

If article 50(2)(g) was significant to a discussion of party autonomy from the date of the EEC's inception, its significance is magnified in a post-*Centros* environment where promoters of companies are free to elect a governing law which is more convenient than the law of the company's real seat. Since the Member States' private international law norms which limit party autonomy are now virtually neutralised, EU-wide harmonisation of substantive and conflicts norms becomes the only instrument which can mitigate the effects of party autonomy.

If Delawarisation does occur and is deemed undesirable by a sufficient plurality of Member States, the haemorrhage of incorporations to states with lower standards of stakeholder protection could be mitigated by compulsorily raising

[51] Wouters (n 45) 289–90.

[52] A Ogus, 'Competition Between National Legal Systems: A Contribution of Economic Analysis to Comparative Law' (1999) *International and Comparative Law Quarterly* 405, 405–09.

[53] CM Tiebout, 'A Pure Theory of Local Expenditures' (1956) *Journal of Political Economy* 416, 416–24.

standards throughout the Union. The adoption of company law directives requires only a qualified majority in the Council of Ministers and a simple majority in the European Parliament.[54] Accordingly, a Member State that abuses the autonomy granted to promoters of companies may in fact be brought to change its laws in a manner that is acceptable to the majority of the Member States, whether it is acceptable to the would-be European Delaware or otherwise.

Nevertheless, *Centros*, *Inspire Art* and *Cartesio* arguably remove one of the principal justifications for harmonisation, namely that of the establishment of a level competitive playing field that is free of artificial distortion.[55] The collective effect of the judgments is to allow almost absolute freedom of choice of law through incorporation and reincorporation under the full extent of a chosen law. The one caveat is that mutual recognition does not require Member States to incorporate companies which have their headquarters in another Member State.[56] Accordingly, the national laws of a state that employs the real seat theory will not be available to a company unless it situates its headquarters in that state.[57] Still, this is unlikely to have much impact on legal competition because real seat states do not tend to have permissive laws.[58] As such, the judgments realign the basis upon which freedom of establishment, and indeed substantive harmonisation, could be achieved. Prior to the Court's rulings, it was clear that regulation was the chosen vehicle for the establishment of parity between corporations emanating from different Member States.[59] However, following the deregulating judgments in *Centros*, *Inspire Art* and *Cartesio*, it is no longer necessary to establish parity between different company laws – since entrepreneurs are afforded unfettered choice of law, nationals of each Member States are placed on a level pegging. If the industrial policy goals of harmonisation have in fact been achieved, mutual recognition could suffice to create a level playing field.

The goal of affording equivalent protection is arguably also achieved by opening up a market for incorporations and thereby allowing incorporators to avail themselves of any of the Member States' laws. Through mutual recognition and the possibility of reincorporation, convergence of corporate laws is predicted. This is already borne out in practice by post-*Centros* amendments to some national laws.[60]

[54] TFEU art 50(2(g) and art 294.

[55] See Tröber (n 44) 57; L Enriques, 'Company Law Harmonization Reconsidered: What Role for the EC?' in SM Bartman (ed), *European Company Law in Accelerated Progress* (The Hague, Kluwer, 2006) 59, 69.

[56] *Cartesio* (n 2) paras 110–13.

[57] ibid 110.

[58] J Dine, *The Governance of Corporate Groups* (Cambridge, Cambridge University Press, 2000) 67; RR Drury, 'The Regulation and Recognition of Foreign Corporations: Responses to the Delaware Syndrome' (1998) *Cambridge Law Journal* 165, 182–83; Ebke 2002 (n 10) 1027–29.

[59] See TE Abeltshauser, 'Towards a European Constitution of the Firm – Problems and Perspectives' (1990) *Michigan Journal of International Law* 1235, 1246–50.

[60] Gesetzes zur Modernisierung des GmbH-Rechts und zur Bekämpfung von Missbräuchen (MoMiG) art 5a(1); Loi n°2003–721 du 1 août 2003 pour l'initiative économique art 1; the Dutch Ministry of Justice http://english.justitie.nl/currenttopics/pressreleases/archives2006/-Simplified-Formation-of-BVs-for-Smaller-companies-and-Start-up-Businesses.aspx. For academic commentary see: J Armour, 'Legal Capital: An Outdated Concept?' (2006) *European Business Organization Law Review* 5,

Further market-driven harmonisation of standards of protection is likely. The question would then be whether the laws of the Member States would converge after a race to the top or one to the bottom, or indeed a race to nowhere in particular.[61] If the race is not to the top, it is difficult to argue that mutual recognition could fulfil the requirement of equivalent protection in article 50(2)(g). It is implicit that article 50 calls for equality through raising or maintenance of standards of stakeholder protection. Party autonomy is unlikely to hasten the raising of standards.

Freedom of choice creates a market in which corporate decision-makers in different Member States have more or less equal access to laws containing diverging safeguards. As such it is no longer possible for freedom of establishment to be achieved through legislative equalisation of safeguards, as prescribed by the Community's founders. The harmonisation process, thus divested of its role as the instrument of choice for the attainment of parity, is left only with the possibility of preserving minimum standards throughout the Union and preventing or mitigating a race to the bottom. The said process is therefore an instrument for states to limit the scope and effects of regulatory competition and to preserve elements of their corporate governance traditions, as well as an instrument for the Union as a whole to benefit from the social and economic benefits of good corporate governance. The legislative process has thus been denied part of its functional purpose through the intercession of the judicial branch of the Union.

Freedom of establishment as construed by the ECJ may therefore limit the efficacy of future efforts by Member States to react quickly to threats, real or perceived, to corporate governance in their jurisdictions given the possible resistance of a blocking minority in the Council. The possibility of the existence of such a blocking minority is compounded by freedom of incorporation, since some Member States may make a strategic decision to position themselves as a European Delaware. That this has not happened to date should be of little comfort going forward. The only Member State which, to date, has been well-placed to become a European Delaware, namely the United Kingdom, has voluntarily raised corporate law standards because it has a thriving corporate market of its own which affects its own socio-economic affairs. It is submitted, however, that the smaller Member States from the eastern and Mediterranean enlargements of 2004 and 2008 may be better placed to Delawarise Europe in future. At present those Member States must continue to convey the message that their legislation is sound, in order to attract investment and earn respect as emerging markets. Once that message has been successfully conveyed and consolidated, there is every possibility that regulators will seek to lead a market for incorporations in much the same way

26; M Miola, 'Legal Capital and Limited Liability Companies: The European Perspective' (2005) *European Company and Financial Law Review* 413, 445; M Becht, C Mayer and F Wagner, 'Where do Firms Incorporate? Deregulation and the cost of entry' (2008) *Journal of Corporate Finance* 241, 252.

[61] See generally WW Bratton, 'Corporate Law's Race to Nowhere in Particular' (1994) *Toronto Law Journal* 401.

as Malta and Cyprus, the Union's smallest Member States, are global leaders in ship registration.[62]

The goal of harmonisation brings into sharp contrast the conflicting goals of uniformity in the results to be attained through the transposition of directives on the one hand, and the autonomy of promoters and regulatory competition furthered by the Court on the other. This is not to say that the two goals are mutually exclusive. First, the harmonisation process is not intended or amenable to lead to the unification of company law – the vast majority of company laws remain untouched by the harmonising directives and therefore remain subject to free competition between regulators. Secondly, it is in the very nature of directives that states are empowered to retain their own legal systems and to accommodate the result to be achieved by the instrument of harmonisation through the form and methods that are most consistent with each legal system.[63] Thus the transposition of each directive will have divergent effects in the host company law systems, because its transposition will act either as a pollutant or an enriching factor to varying extents in each system.[64] The result of the transposition of directives will also vary because Member States are free to adopt or retain standards that are higher than the minimum established by a directive. Thirdly, regulatory competition allows room for voluntary harmonisation through the imitation and fine-tuning of 'foreign' legal solutions and innovations that are discovered following independent experimentation. Nonetheless, the establishment of minimum standards in specific areas denies the possibility of the fullest degree of competition between legal systems. The rationale for the curtailment of competition is of course explained with reference to article 50 TFEU, specifically the goal of the establishment of an internal market in which unfair advantages are not readily available, and where there is a level playing field in which competition is not distorted. Accordingly, it appears that the Member States have never overtly opted for the establishment of an internal market with regulatory competition in corporate law at its core, although they have not succeeded in limiting regulatory competition to the extent that some may have wished. The legislators of the Union preferred to establish a level playing field by means that did not encroach on the socio-economic standards that they had established in their territories before they voluntarily limited their own sovereignty.

Article 50(2)(g) is now illustrative of the shortcomings of the EU's legislative processes when compared to the industry of the Court of Justice. It represents a

[62] In 2004 Malta had the world's seventh largest merchant fleet and Cyprus the world's ninth largest. Greece is the only Member State that surpasses these microstates in terms of gross tonnage, having the world's fourth largest fleet: *Lloyd's Register Fairplay data,* 2006 per L French, 'Introduction' in Stephenson Harwood, *Shipping Finance,* 3rd edn (London, Euromoney Institutional Investor, 2006) 7. Similarly, following its accession in 2004, Malta has established itself as a centre for the provision of cross-border gambling services in the EU: see J Borg Barthet, 'Online Gambling and the Further Displacement of State Regulation: A Note on *PMU v Zeturf* (2008) *International and Comparative Law Quarterly* 417, 417–26.

[63] TFEU art 288.

[64] See eg G Tuebner, 'Legal Irritants: Good Faith in British Law or How Unifying Law Ends Up in New Divergences' (1998) *Modern Law Review* 11, 11–32.

reminder of the goals that the Union's legislator unsuccessfully set out to achieve, and the manner in which the Court has rendered that task more difficult. The Community's founders intended that a significant degree of convergence of substantive corporate law would ensue, as a quid pro quo for the granting of access to markets. This has not yet materialised. The Court has introduced a notion of party autonomy that contrasts with the cautious approach preferred by the legislator. Indeed, through the *Centros* line of judgments, article 50(2)(g) is rendered less likely to produce any substantive harmonisation. The impetus to advance a process that had already lost momentum is more wanting in a regulatory environment where it is in the interest of some states to resist harmonisation that would limit their competitive advantage in attracting incorporations.

4.4 The Substantive Effects of Harmonisation on Party Autonomy

The directives which have been adopted and implemented successfully have ensured the following, among other matters: (i) minimum standards of creditor protection through the adoption of minimum capital requirements[65] and disclosure obligations,[66] (ii) a minimum of worker representation and participation,[67] (iii) stipulating conditions governing mergers and divisions of companies,[68] and (iv) the protection of certain shareholder rights.[69] However, the directives have not harmonised the core ideological features of the company laws of the Member States. The Fifth Directive concerning the structure, powers and obligations of public companies has never become law despite the Commission's best efforts in the seventies, eighties and nineties. As such, the harmonisation programme falls

[65] Council Directive (EEC) 1977/91 of 13 December 1976 on the coordination of safeguards which, for the protection of the interests of members and others, are required by Member States of companies within the meaning of the second paragraph of Article 58 of the Treaty, in respect of the formation of public limited liability companies and the maintenance and alteration of their capital, with a view to making such safeguards equivalent [1977] OJ L026/1.

[66] Council Directive (EEC) 1968/151 of 9 March 1968 on co-ordination of safeguards which, for the protection of the interests of members and others, are required by Member States of companies within the meaning of the second paragraph of Article 58 of the Treaty, with a view to making such safeguards equivalent throughout the Community [1968] OJ L065/8.

[67] Directive (EC) 2009/38 of the European Parliament and of the Council of 6 May 2009 on the establishment of a European Works Council or a procedure in Community-scale undertakings and Community-scale groups of undertakings for the purposes of informing and consulting employees (recast) [2009] OJ L122/28. The directive will come into force on 5 June 2011 and will replace Council Directive (EC) 1994/45 on the establishment of a European Works Council or a procedure in Community-scale undertakings and Community-scale groups of undertakings for the purposes of informing and consulting employees [1994] OJ L254.

[68] Directive of the European Parliament and of the Council (EC) 2005/56 on cross-border mergers of limited liability companies (the Cross-Border Merger Directive) [2005] OJ L310/1.

[69] Directive 2007/36/EC of the European Parliament and of the Council of 11 July 2007 on the exercise of certain rights of shareholders in listed companies [2007] OJ L184/17.

short of the expectations of advocates of a greater unification in European company law whose proposals would further circumscribe party autonomy. The successes of the programme can therefore be described as 'trivial' in the context of the more ambitious goals embraced in the failed directives.[70] Member States are not yet in agreement regarding the goods to be achieved by the corporate form, or the means by which those goods are achieved. They have disagreed in particular on the place of the worker within corporate governance systems, specifically on whether employment relations should be addressed within corporate law or exclusively by employment law.[71] They have also failed to agree on whether a company is better administered and directed by a single board or a two-tier system.[72]

This might logically lead one to a conclusion that party autonomy should be limited where the Member States fail to agree on a common way forward. Given that the equalisation of safeguards remains unfulfilled on a pan-European level, and given the scheme of the Treaty, which reflects a preference for the permanence of safeguards in corporate law, extending freedom of choice would appear to be the less logical approach. However, following *Centros*, promoters of companies are at liberty to select a governing law from a diverse catalogue of company laws. In this scenario, the failure to agree on a common legislative template, which was caused by the jealous guarding of national norms, paradoxically becomes permissive of party autonomy that will serve to undermine those very norms that are jealously guarded.

Notwithstanding the cogency of an argument in favour of limiting party autonomy through legislation, the procedure for the adoption and transposition of directives severely limits the practical application of the principle. First, the requirement of agreement among a qualified majority of Member States in Council renders the process laborious. Even if the Union's institutions were to adopt legislation in an extraordinarily swift manner, there would remain the matter of 27 Member States transposing the relevant directives into national law, a process that may vary widely in the Member States and that is dependent on the peculiarities of each legislative system and the temporal political realities to which they are all subjected. In this context, it may be unrealistic to expect harmonisation alone to prevent the emergence of a European Delaware. Indeed, where the EU has faced challenges to corporate governance of a pan-European scale that required concerted action, harmonisation alone has failed to raise standards and to thereby limit private ordering that would bypass those higher standards. By way of example, the legislative reaction of the United States to the Enron crisis has been far swifter, more far-reaching and unorthodox than that of the EU to such challenges.[73] However, it

[70] See generally L Enriques, 'EC Company Law Directives and Regulations: How Trivial Are They?' (2006) *University of Pennsylvania Journal of International Economic Law* 1, 1–75.

[71] Pasa, Benacchio and Orme (n 48) 364–68.

[72] ibid 365–66.

[73] By way of example, the EU's rules on oversight of statutory audits are less prescriptive than those in the Sarbanes-Oxley Act: PT Muchlinski, 'Enron and Beyond: Multinational Corporate Groups and the Internationalization of Governance and Disclosure Regimes' (2005) *Connecticut Law Review*, 725, 748–49. For a chronology of the reactions to Enron and other corporate scandals in Europe and the United States, see P Davies, 'Enron and Corporate Governance in the UK and the European Community' in J Armour and JA McCahery (eds), *After Enron: Improving Corporate Law and Modernising Securities*

is also true that Commission proposals often induce or inspire Member States to adopt legislation prior to the enactment of European laws. In the wake of the Enron crisis and US reforms in response thereto, the Commission's reactions in the form of a policy agenda was expeditiously followed by several Member States,[74] albeit in their independent prescriptive capacity rather than as a matter of European obligation. Yet it is also patent that the expeditious response of a plurality of Member States is insufficient where private ordering allows promoters to elect a governing law of a state which has been less expeditious, or which has resisted pressure from the Commission and other Member States.

The remainder of this chapter considers the extent to which secondary legislation furthers or restricts private ordering.

4.4.1 The Cross-Border Merger Directive

The principal aim of the Cross-Border Merger Directive[75] is to provide a statutory basis to allow the merging of companies established under the laws of different Member States.[76] The directive was finalised contemporaneously with the litigation in *Sevic Systems*,[77] where the Court of Justice found that the right to a cross-border merger emanated directly from articles 49 and 54 TFEU (articles 43 and 48 EC). The Court's judgment attached few enforceable conditions to the facility to transfer a company's seat.[78] The legislation prescribes procedures to be followed in order for the directly effective Treaty right to be enjoyed and as such serves both to facilitate and to delimit engagement in cross-border mergers.

In practical terms, cross-border mergers also permit the two-stage reincorporation of companies under a different governing law. This is achieved by establishing a subsidiary in another jurisdiction and then employing a reverse vertical merger whereby the subsidiary absorbs the parent company.[79] Accordingly, in addition to the declared goal of facilitating the concentration of the activities of companies from different Member States, the directive allows companies to change their governing law from that of one Member State to another. It therefore provides existing companies with a means – indeed their only reliable means[80] – to transform

Regulation in Europe and the US (Oxford, Hart, 2006), 415–21; KJ Hopt, 'Modern Company and Capital Market Problems: Improving European Corporate Governance After Enron' in Armour and McCahery (ibid) 446–50.

[74] Enriques (n 70) 20.

[75] Directive of the European Parliament and of the Council (EC) 2005/56 on cross-border mergers of limited liability companies (the Cross-Border Merger Directive) [2005] OJ L310/1.

[76] ibid recitals 1–2.

[77] *Sevic Systems* (n 4).

[78] ibid para 28.

[79] See Siems (2007) (n 33) 312–13; Siems (2005) (n 33) 179–81; Hansen (n 33) 196–98; Mucciarelli (n 33) 276–77.

[80] The Commission halted the process towards the adoption of the proposed Fourteenth Company Law Directive on Cross-Border Seat Transfers: Commission (EC), 'Impact Assessment on the Directive on the cross-border transfer of registered office' SEC (2007) 1707, 12 December 2007, 25; C McCreevy, 'Speech 07/441: Company Law and Corporate Governance Today' (2007) http://europa.eu/rapid/

themselves into companies governed by a different law without the need for dissolution. The long-standing employment of this method of cross-border seat transfers in the United States of America must perforce lead one to the conclusion that this side-effect of the directive was foreseeable.[81] If it was not an intended consequence, it most certainly was not a by-product that was deemed to be so undesirable as to be impeded. Accordingly, the directive evidences the legislator's concession of further rights to companies and their management in preference to the exercise of control by the Member States.

The possibility of using a cross-border merger to change a company's governing law stems from the fact that the merging companies may select the governing law of the resulting merged company.[82] This evidences a strong preference for party autonomy both in respect of companies resulting from conventional mergers, and in respect of companies that might employ cross-border mergers for the purpose of reincorporation. Nevertheless, the freedom to select a governing law remains limited by the private international law of some Member States. In the present state of EU law, Member States may continue to require the permanence within their territory of both the registered office and the operational headquarters of companies established under their laws.[83] A company may therefore be denied the possibility of changing its governing law to that of a 'real seat' Member State because the potentially prohibitive cost of transferring its headquarters may have to be incurred in addition to the administrative costs. However, this limitation is principally theoretical rather than practical – empirical evidence concerning post-*Centros* incorporations of pseudo-foreign corporations suggests that real seat states are likely to experience net emigration through reincorporations, since their company law regimes are less attractive to promoters of companies.[84] Although, theoretically, the market for reincorporation may prove to be different to that for primary establishment, it is highly unlikely that this will be the case, given that both incorporation and reincorporation are driven by the same efficiency considerations. One can therefore safely assume that the 'real seat' barrier to autonomy poses little practical difficulty.

In addition to the above restrictions on party autonomy, the directive itself limits choice insofar as employee participation is concerned.[85] As a general rule,

pressReleasesAction.do?reference=SPEECH/07/441&format=DOC&aged=1&language=EN&guiLanguage=en. The Court of Justice found that there existed a right to cross-border seat transfers and change in governing law only where this was permitted under the laws of the state to which the company wished to transfer: *Cartesio* (n 2) paras 111–13.

[81] See JC Dammann, 'Freedom of Choice in European Corporate Law' (2004) *Yale Journal of International Law* 477, 489–90.

[82] Art 5(a).

[83] *Cartesio* (n 2) para 110.

[84] See generally Becht, Mayer and Wagner (n 60).

[85] This is by way of deference to the concerns of Member States that view employees as internal to the governance of a firm – employee participation constituted the principal obstacle to the adoption of the directive. See M Pannier, 'The EU Cross Border Merger Directive – A New Dimension for Employee Participation and Company Restructuring' (2005) *European Business Organisation Law Review* 1424, 1424.

the law of the merged company's registered office will also govern employee participation.[86] However, the legislator expresses a preference for the limitation of autonomy where the standards of employee participation under the laws of the merged company are lower than the standards obtaining under the laws of one of the companies dissolved by the merger. In the latter event the merged company shall be subject to the higher standard enshrined in the otherwise redundant governing law. The bifurcation of the company's governing law is subject to a somewhat complicated formula that requires the discovery of the laws of each Member State involved in the merger, as well as the factual circumstances of each merging company. In order for the law of the company's registered office to be supplanted, one of the merging companies must have had an average of in excess of 500 employees in the six months preceding the merger, and must have been operating under an employee participation system.[87] If that condition is satisfied, the law of the Member State of the registered office will be set aside in two scenarios. First, if it is shown that there is a proportionately lower level of employee participation in the 'administrative or supervisory organ or their committees or of the management group which covers the profit units of the company' than was the case in one of the merging companies.[88] Secondly, the law of the registered office will be set aside if the governing law of one of the merging companies afforded participation rights to employees of the company who are situated in a third Member State, and the law of the registered office does not afford equivalent rights.[89]

Yet the directive again defers to the autonomous will of the parties by empowering employees and the company to provide for alternative arrangements to the default rules.[90] In this respect, it must be emphasised that party autonomy is to be construed widely in the sense that private actors may displace the default rules that are promulgated by the state. The parties are not only the companies and their incorporators, but also include employees – indeed, the autonomy of the merging companies is curtailed by the autonomous will of the employees. What is more, it is arguable that it is the employees' autonomy which is in fact furthered by the relevant provisions, given that it is only the latter who would be inclined to make use of the effective vetoing powers that both parties have in respect of an agreement to displace more protective employee participation rules.

Although the degree of autonomy afforded to the parties to the merger reflects some preference for the autonomous will of incorporators to supersede more formal connecting factors, such as the real seat of a company, it is incorrect to surmise that the directive constitutes an expression of the Union's legislators' resolve in favour of freedom of incorporation. That resolve clearly does not exist, as is evidenced by the default bifurcation of the merged company's governing law in order to safeguard the employee participation rules obtaining in some Member States.

[86] Art 16(1).
[87] Art 16(2).
[88] Art 16(2)(a).
[89] Art 16(2)(b).
[90] Art 16(4)(b).

In sum, the Member States have expressly relinquished control over the factors which connect a company to a governing law only limitedly. They have done so in a manner that excludes employee participation norms because of the regard with which some Member States view employee participation, and because of the disparate views regarding the place of employees in the corporate laws of the 27 Member States.

In addition, given the particular risks associated with a cross-border merger, the directive empowers Member States to make specific provision 'to ensure appropriate protection for minority members who have opposed the cross-border merger.'[91] Minority shareholders may therefore be granted an exit route in the event that they are prejudiced by the merger. This is in addition to the protection of creditors, which was discussed in section 3.2.3 of this book.

4.4.2 The Works Council Directive

The Works Council Directive[92] is not promulgated under the authority of article 50(2)(g), but it is nevertheless relevant to the present discussion in view of its impact on transnational corporate governance and its limitation of autonomy to opt out of employee participation laws. The directive provides that Member States must establish procedures whereby community-scale undertakings are to inform and consult with their employees.[93] Community-scale undertakings are undertakings that have at least 150 employees in at least two Member States and more than 1,000 employees in total within the Union.[94] Accordingly, employees of large companies that have a significant employment base in more than one Member State have the right to participate in the company's decision-making processes. The directive reflects a pre-*Centros* environment in which the German corporate model was being put forward throughout the Union.

Notwithstanding the pan-European requirement to introduce procedures for employee participation, private ordering of the extent of said participation is far from excluded by the directive. The legislation does not provide that the relevant procedures for employee participation should form part of the company's internal structures. In a post-*Centros* environment, the directive therefore creates a further anomaly as between companies which fall to be governed by European laws, and those which are governed only by national laws. Because the directive only addresses community-scale undertakings, it does not harmonise laws regarding

[91] Art 4(2).

[92] Directive (EC) 2009/38 of the European Parliament and of the Council of 6 May 2009 on the establishment of a European Works Council or a procedure in Community-scale undertakings and Community-scale groups of undertakings for the purposes of informing and consulting employees (recast) [2009] OJ L122/28. The directive entered into force on 5 June 2011, replacing Council Directive (EC) 1994/45 on the establishment of a European Works Council or a procedure in Community-scale undertakings and Community-scale groups of undertakings for the purposes of informing and consulting employees [1994] OJ L254.

[93] Art 1.

[94] Art 2(a).

companies that do not satisfy the requirements of the definition of a community-scale undertaking. Accordingly, promoters of companies remain free to opt out of the laws of Member States that view their own companies as social vehicles. By way of example, the directive does not address companies incorporated in the United Kingdom and having their employment base entirely in Germany – employees of these companies do not have a European right to consultation and participation. This creates a somewhat anomalous scenario whereby community-wide undertakings that employ 150 workers in Germany place employees within the decision-making framework, as is the norm in Germany, whereas a company that has its entire workforce in Germany but is incorporated in another Member State would not be required to do so. It is only through employment law that Germany retains prescriptive jurisdiction. The German connection to the latter pseudo-foreign company is far more intimate, yet the German view of the social construct of a corporation is inapplicable to it. Accordingly, the German view of the firm is transposed to a limited extent in a European setting, but it is not necessarily applicable in a purely German setting since incorporation, or indeed reincorporation, in another Member State allows promoters of companies to dispense with employee participation altogether for so long as their companies' dimensions do not satisfy the directive's definition. The Works Council Directive therefore creates a landscape of employee rights in Europe which lacks philosophical cohesion.

Moreover, the directive provides a far higher threshold of employees in order to trigger the requirement of worker participation, when compared to the 50 employees required for German co-determination legislation to be activated.[95] Accordingly, party autonomy remains a potent instrument for avoidance of national laws that may be burdensome from an entrepreneur's perspective. In the absence of agreement on the form and purpose of corporations that would allow for the unification of laws through European regulations,[96] the approximation of laws through positive harmonisation cannot fully set off the dismantling of protective measures occasioned by the ECJ's judgments.

In the absence of specific protection for employees through conflict of laws regulations of general application, companies may readily avoid employee participation in enterprises that do not qualify as 'community-scale undertakings' in terms of the directive – incorporators of companies can hardly be expected to share corporate decision-making power by choosing to incorporate under a governing law that adopts a holistic view of the company where they are provided the option of retaining control in other jurisdictions. Although workers' rights to participate in corporate decision-making have been enhanced, the measures that have been adopted to date have not placed workers at the heart of corporate law throughout Europe. The aggregate effect of the negative and positive harmonisation therefore remains that

[95] L Enriques, H Hansmann and R Kraakman, 'The Basic Governance Structure: minority Shareholders and Non-Shareholder Constituencies' in R Kraakman and others (eds), *The Anatomy of Corporate Law. A Comparative and Functional Approach,* 2nd edn (Oxford, Oxford University Press, 2009) 100–1.

[96] See C Barnard and S Deakin, 'Reinventing the European Corporation? Corporate governance, social policy and the single market' (2002) *Industrial Relations Journal* 484, 485–86.

the removal of barriers places workers outside the fold of corporate law in jurisdictions that had been able to prevent this through the application of the real seat theory.

4.4.3 The Directives that Never Were, and a New Basis for Harmonisation

The success of the harmonisation process has on several occasions been stalled by a lack of agreement among the Member States. The directives that have failed to be adopted are the proposed Fifth, Ninth and Fourteenth Company Law Directives. The Fifth[97] and Ninth[98] Directives have long been removed from the Commission's legislative agenda, whereas the Fourteenth may yet see the light of day.

The Fifth Directive concerned the powers, obligations and structure of public companies. The earliest draft, that of 1972, faced severe criticism from a majority of Member States, most particularly the United Kingdom and Ireland.[99] The original draft would have harmonised the Member States' laws in accordance with the corporate governance tradition of Germany, specifically by requiring a two-tier board and employee participation.[100] Subsequent drafts of the directive allowed more flexibility and departed from the erstwhile strict adherence to the German model. Thus it had become patent that an approach to harmonisation that sought to impose the corporate governance philosophy of one state upon all others was doomed to failure. However, the compromises achieved did not suffice to overcome the difficulties that several Member States had in restructuring their corporate governance systems in accordance with a single European model.[101] The Fifth Directive was eventually shelved and the compromises transposed in the European Company Statute.[102] The latter instrument does not alter the corporate governance of the company laws of the Member States but creates a European regime for a European company. As such, the Member States were not required to adopt a legal instrument that realigned the manner in which companies are governed in a purely domestic setting. The principle of subsidiarity was therefore upheld without sacrificing harmonisation in matters of undeniably transnational character.

The Ninth Directive concerning the conduct of groups of companies also closely followed the German model, perhaps because Germany remains the only Member State to have comprehensive legislation concerning groups of companies.[103] That

[97] Draft Fifth Directive on the structure of public limited companies and the powers and obligations of their Organs [1972] OJ C131.

[98] Draft Ninth Directive on links between undertakings and in particular on groups. Not published.

[99] See for a contemporary discussion, CM Schmitthoff, 'Company Structure and Employee Participation in the EEC – the British Attitude' (1976) *International and Comparative Law Quarterly* 611, 611–20; Pasa, Benacchio and Orme (n 48) 365.

[100] Pasa, Benacchio and Orme (n 48) 365–66.

[101] ibid 365–67.

[102] ibid 367.

[103] ibid 368–71.

directive has also failed to command sufficient support to be adopted. One might speculate that the reason for lack of approval was again the association with the laws of a single Member State. A more precise explanation would be that the draft directive introduced a regime with which the vast majority of market-actors in the Union were unfamiliar, and one that was rigid, to boot.[104] Although the directive remains in limbo, a number of Member States have transposed German law into their domestic law in a manner that is typical of the widespread transplantation of laws.[105] However, it is quite apparent that the wholesale adoption of national legislation on a European level will encounter resistance, whether for political reasons or because of genuine difficulties with the adoption of foreign concepts that are so alien as to be incapable of seamless reception.

However, it is the latest episode of failure of positive harmonisation that is most poignant. The unceremonious removal from the Union's legislative agenda of the proposed Fourteenth Company Law Directive on the cross-border transfer of a company's seat highlights the tensions between the thrusts of negative and positive harmonisation. In explaining the Commission's decision not to use its legislative initiative to submit a proposal for a directive, the Commissioner for the Internal Market made the following statement:

> our preparatory work has led me to the conclusion that we should not rush forward with legislation. If we are to propose legislation, we must be sure there is a reasonable chance of a result with added value for business. The economic case is not as obvious or as clear-cut as it may seem and Member States currently follow very different approaches to which they are strongly attached.
>
> Moreover, the Court of Justice will soon take a decision in a case that could provide us with new insights on the current legal situation in Europe. As you know, the Court has already in the past delivered fundamental judgments in the area of company mobility. I am therefore convinced that we should wait for the outcome of this case which is likely to bring more clarity into this complicated matter. We expect the judgment to be delivered in the autumn of this year.[106]

The Commissioner cites three reasons for halting the project, namely questionable economic necessity, resistance from the Member States, and the then-pending litigation in *Cartesio*.[107] The economic argument must be dismissed, because there can be little doubt that the employment of the Societas Europaea and the use of cross-border mergers as a means to transfer a company's seat involve costs in addition to a change in a company's operational headquarters.[108] Secondly, the Commissioner's political arguments are not convincing when considered in the context of legal arguments made before the Court of Justice. In *Cartesio* the Commission argued in its submissions that barriers to seat transfers constitute an

[104] ibid 370.

[105] M Andenas and F Wooldridge, *European Comparative Company Law* (Cambridge, Cambridge University Press, 2009) 448–49.

[106] McCreevy (n 80).

[107] *Cartesio* (n 2).

[108] GJ Vossestein, 'Transfer of the Registered Office: The European Commission's Decision not to Submit a Proposal for a Directive' (2008) *Utrecht Law Review* 53, 59–60.

unjustified and costly curtailment of freedom of establishment.[109] It would therefore appear that the Commission has simply taken the view that negative harmonisation is a tool that is more easily employed than positive harmonisation because it does away with the necessity of negotiation among the Member States, some of which are opposed to the process. One can certainly understand that there is no point in legislating for a matter that the law already provides for, and there can be no doubt that the law is that which the judicial branch interprets it to be from time to time. However, there is also a political undercurrent, namely that the judicial branch is taking the law in a direction that several Member States would resist if they were given the opportunity to adopt, and indeed adapt, legislation on the basis of a Commission proposal. It can therefore be surmised that the Commission had adopted the line of least resistance – rather than encountering the resistance of the Member States, the goal of attaining mobility of companies and regulatory competition in Europe was, the Commission surmised, more easily attained through a judicial branch with whom the Commission appeared confident of having a unity of purpose, or at least a unity of understanding of the meaning of the law. As a matter of fact, had the AG's Opinion in *Cartesio* been endorsed in the Court's judgment, there would have been no need for a directive, and the transferability of a company's seat would be a matter of right at primary EU law. In addition, negative harmonisation has historically attached fewer conditions to the liberalisation of company law than has positive harmonisation. The Court's judgments have not attached such conditions as the coincidence of the registered office and the main office, or transitional stakeholder protection measures. Article 10(2) of the draft directive provides that Member States may refuse to register a transfer of the company's head office if the registered office is not situated in that state. The residual conflicts rules were therefore left intact in the Commission's proposal. Thus, while the Commission's apparent election to go the route of negative harmonisation may be viewed as the abdication of the legislative organs' prescriptive competence, had it been as successful as expected it could equally have been viewed as a political victory for the institution having legislative initiative in its efforts to achieve unconditional liberalisation. In the event, the judgment in *Cartesio* did not endorse the views of the Commission and the Advocate General, and the Commission swiftly effected another U-turn on the necessity of regulation.[110]

[109] AG Maduro in *Cartesio* (n 2) paras 24 and 31.

[110] Commission (EC), 'An area of freedom, security and justice serving the citizen' (Communication) COM (09) 262 final, 14.

4.5 Supranational Business Vehicles

4.5.1 Introduction

The introduction of supranational business vehicles constitutes an implicit admission of party autonomy. EU law offers promoters of companies a choice as between national corporate forms and European ones. It admits the possibility of selecting a corporate form other than the national corporate forms which the conflicts rules of a Member State would otherwise designate. Accordingly, while the general thrust of harmonisation of national laws reflects a preference for limiting choice as between national company laws, this is partly compensated for through supranational vehicles which are created through the collective accord of the Member States as expressed in European laws.

It is pertinent, however, to identify the quality of the autonomy that is implicitly provided to promoters of companies. The extent to which supranational companies can truly be considered to give promoters a free choice is open to question on two fronts: (i) does the quality of convenience in employing European corporate forms compare well to national corporations? And (ii) perhaps most important of all, what is the effect on party autonomy of the private international law provisions which govern these business vehicles and the content of their governing laws?

4.5.2 The Societas Europaea (SE)

The Regulation on the Statute for a European Company (SE),[111] establishes a public company of a supranational character. The adoption of the Regulation constitutes a significant step in the development of the disciplines of European company law and conflict of company laws alike. Unlike the harmonising directives, there is no specific Treaty basis for the adoption of the SE statute by the Union. Rather the legal basis is article 352 TFEU (article 308 EC) which empowers the Council acting unanimously to adopt legislation where it is necessary for the attainment of the goals of the Treaty.[112] The SE is therefore not constitutionally bound to the multipartite approach to corporate law of article 50(2)(g) (article 44(2)(g) EC). However, the autonomy to select the SE as a company's legal form was the fruit of 40 years of compromise between Member States[113] and the resulting form reflects the concerns of Member States that wished to avoid excesses of party autonomy, particularly insofar as employee participation is concerned.[114]

[111] Council Regulation (EC) 2157/2001 on the statute for a European company (SE) [2001] OJ L294/1.

[112] SE Regulation 2157/2001 recitals 28–29.

[113] See S Lombardo and P Pasotti, 'The *Societas Europaea*: a Network Economics Approach' (2004) *European Company and Financial Law Review* 169, 171–72.

[114] Council Directive (EC) 2001/86 supplementing the Statute for a European company with regard to the involvement of employees [2001] OJ L284/22.

The SE was intended to resolve several issues of mobility and recognition of companies in the EU by creating a business vehicle that emanates in part from European law and that is capable of transferring its seat without the requirement of dissolution and reincorporation. This notwithstanding, the impact of the SE on the regulatory landscape of the Union's company laws is limited. Divergences among the Member States regarding the details of the European company law project impede the attainment of a truly united notion of the company which would displace national company laws and conflict of corporate law norms in favour of a unitary European instrument. The SE is therefore not truly a product of transnational law, in that it is not governed by a European company code. The business vehicle is only available to incorporators under limited circumstances and can scarcely be described as a widely available alternative vehicle to those that are available under the company laws of the Member States.[115] As such, the impact of the SE in resolving substantive and transnational law issues must be considered within the limited context of the business vehicle's practical utility.

The private international law aspects of the SE have been described as 'Solomonic'[116] in that the Regulation adopts the transferability of a company's seat without winding up from the incorporation doctrine,[117] and from the real seat theory the determination of the governing law with reference to the location of the company's registered office, which is to be situated in the Member State of the company's head office.[118] The Regulation prohibits the separate transfer of the registered office and the head office. The penalty for non-compliance is the liquidation of the company.[119] Thus the net effect of the conflict of corporate laws provisions is to permit the transferability of the company's seat, and consequently the possibility to change its governing law, but limitedly to situations where the physical place where management decisions are taken is also transferred. While it can be argued that the choice of connecting factor is in fact a hybrid between the real seat and incorporation doctrines because the registered office is the explicitly selected connecting factor,[120] the necessity of coincidence between the registered and real seats of the company renders the real seat theory applicable in terms of determining the applicable law.

The choice of the real seat as the appropriate connecting factor for the purposes of the SE's governing law speaks volumes in the context of the judgments of the ECJ concerning the recognition of companies incorporated under the laws of the Member States. The Regulation adopts the real seat theory in respect of the governing law of European companies for precisely the reasons that the ECJ rejected as justifications for limitations to freedom of establishment in respect of the company laws of the Member States, namely that the connection to the jurisdiction of

[115] Art 2.

[116] WG Ringe, 'The European Company Statute in the Context of Freedom of Establishment' (2007) *Journal of Corporate Law Studies* 185, 188.

[117] Art 7.

[118] Art 8.

[119] Art 64(2).

[120] See Ringe (n 116) 189–90.

the centre of the company's principal economic activities protects stakeholders and reduces information costs in discovering the provisions of foreign law.[121] There is therefore a principled argument that the secondary legislation establishing the SE contravenes the primary legislation of the Union in that article 7 of the Regulation, which binds an SE to the law of its seat, impinges upon the freedom of establishment guaranteed by the Treaty.[122] This argument presupposes that the judicial interpretation of the primary legislation is in fact cogent. It is submitted that the better view is that the Member States did not intend freedom of establishment to include freedom of incorporation, and that the judgments of the ECJ are in fact an example of judicial activism that redefines the Treaty rather than resolving its lacunae.[123] Had it been the intention of the Member States to create a legal vehicle that afforded freedom of choice to incorporators, the SE Regulation would surely have enshrined that principle through the adoption of the incorporation doctrine. The Member States did just the opposite, and expressed the intention to limit the extent to which incorporators may pick and choose legal systems. Accordingly, it can be surmised that there has been absolutely no occasion on which the Member States expressed a desire to divest themselves of all authority to prescribe the manner in which corporations that are most closely connected with their respective jurisdictions will function. There can therefore be little doubt that there is a tension between the intentions of the Member States and the ECJ's interpretation of the laws promulgated by or with the assent of the same Member States.

The take-up of SEs has not been a resounding success by any measure, as incorporators appear to be more inclined to opt for corporate forms available under the laws of the Member States. This may be attributed to the costs of establishment and compliance, a lack of familiarity with this corporate form in both the business and legal community, and a cultural and psychological hesitance to employ a corporate form that diverges from the corporate cultures of the Member States.[124] Minimum capital requirements of €120,000 also pose a major obstacle to the SE

[121] Ringe (n 116) 196–97.

[122] ibid 191–98. However, Timmermans suggests that, following the judgment in *Cartesio*, it is clear that the Treaty enables Member States to select connecting factors as they see fit. By the same measure, the EU legislator must also be at liberty to select any connecting factor: C Timmermans, 'Impact of EU Law on International Company Law' (2010) *European Review of Private Law* 549, 557.

[123] For a criticism of the ECJ's activist approach see eg T Hartley, 'The European Court, judicial objectivity and the constitution of the European Union' (1996) *Law Quarterly Review* 95, 95–109; H Rasmussen, *On Law and Policy in the European Court of Justice* (Kluwer, Lancaster 1986) 10–13; KJ Alter, 'Who Are the "Masters of the Treaty"?: European Governments and the European Court of Justice' (1998) *International Organization* 121, 121–47. For a more nuanced view of judicial activism, see JHH Weiler, 'A Quiet Revolution: The European Court of Justice and its Interlocutors' (1994) *Comparative Political Studies* 510, 510–34; J Bengoetxea, N MacCormick and L Moral Soriano, 'Integration and Integrity in the Legal Reasoning of the European Court of Justice' in G de Búrca and JHH Weiler (eds), *The European Court of Justice* (Oxford, Oxford University Press, 2001) 43–85. For a view which is supportive of the ECJ's approach, see eg A Arnull, 'The European Court and Judicial Objectivity: a Reply to Professor Hartley' (1996) *Law Quarterly Review* 411, 411–23.

[124] See WJ Bratton, JA McCahery and EPM Vermeulen, 'How Does Corporate Mobility Affect Law Making? A Comparative Analysis' (2008) ECGI Law Working Paper No 91/2008 http://ssrn.com/abstract=1086667, 15–16.

becoming a preferred business vehicle, particularly for small and medium enterprises or start-up businesses. Businesses of these dimensions must therefore continue to depend on the corporate forms available exclusively under the laws of the Member States until they acquire the critical mass to convert their corporations into an SE. In the event that they wish to benefit from corporate mobility and transfer their seat to another jurisdiction, it appears that it may be easier to do so by taking advantage of the developments in the case law concerning freedom of establishment, provided that they also change their governing law where necessary.[125] As AG Maduro noted in his Opinion in *Cartesio*, 'for small and medium-sized companies, an intra-Community transfer of operational headquarters may be a simple and effective form of taking up genuine economic activities in another Member State without having to face the costs and the administrative burdens inherent in first having to wind up the company in its country of origin and then having to resurrect it completely in the Member State of destination.'[126] A seat transfer would relieve SMEs of the costs and administrative burdens of setting up an SE and complying with the continuing administrative requirements in order to keep the company in good standing, as stipulated in the Regulation.

An ancillary drawback is the fact that article 2 of the Regulation provides that the SE is not available to natural persons but may only be formed by companies already incorporated under the laws of a Member State. From a business perspective this adds further administrative and financial barriers to the establishment of SEs. From a purely legal-theoretical perspective, the requirement of the involvement of Member States' corporate laws denies the business vehicle the truly supranational character that would have rendered its genesis a watershed in the harmonisation, or indeed the unification, of European corporate laws.

Since the adoption of the SE statute, there has been a noted increase in extraterritorial incorporations following *Centros*, but there has not been a rush to use the SE.[127] Incorporators who have been granted a wide choice of corporate laws have opted for the lower standards offered by Member States such as the United Kingdom, rather than the form that the Union's legislators deemed to be the appropriate vehicle.[128] When granted freedom of choice among the laws of the Member States and those of the EU, incorporators have logically been more inclined to adopt an accommodating foreign corporate form, rather than a less accommodating, but also unfamiliar, European vehicle.

The SE's dependence upon the laws of the Member States bears witness to the fact that, contrary to the views of Hansmann and Kraakman,[129] the end of history of corporate law is not nigh. Rather, the SE preserves the laws of the Member States and

[125] *Cartesio* (n 2) paras 110–13.

[126] *Cartesio* (n 2) para 31 (AG Maduro).

[127] In the first five years in which the SE was available there were only 176 incorporations of SEs: H Eidenmüller, A Engert and L Hornuf, 'How Does the Market react to the Societas Europaea?' (2010) *European Business Organization Law Review* 35, 37.

[128] See generally Becht, Mayer and Wagner (n 60).

[129] H Hansmann and R Kraakman, 'The End of History for Corporate Law' (2001) *Georgetown Law Journal* 439.

their divergences, and cannot exist without the said divergent laws. Consequently the SE should be viewed not quite as an alternate business vehicle, but, more importantly, as a further failed attempt to resolve some of the remaining problems in the private international law of the EU and its Member States.

4.5.3 The Societas Privata Europaea (SPE)

In June of 2008 the Commission formally signalled its intention to introduce legislation governing European small and medium sized enterprises. A Commission Communication ambitiously refers to a 'Small Business Act' for Europe.[130] The legislative centrepiece of the Commission's action plan is the proposed statute for a European private company (Societas Privata Europaea – SPE).[131] After a period in which the proposed statute was left in abeyance due to disagreement regarding the seat of an SPE, employee participation, and capital requirements, the Council reached political agreement regarding an amended draft in May 2011.[132] The Commission's original Explanatory Memorandum noted that over 99 per cent of companies in the EU are private companies, but that only 8 per cent of them conduct cross-border trade.[133] The proposal for an SPE statute is intended as part of a package to facilitate exploitation of the internal market by SMEs and to thereby stimulate entrepreneurship in the Union. The proposed SPE marks a departure from the flawed notion that the generation of wealth in the Union requires vehicles such as the SE having a scale that is commensurate to the scale of the internal market, a notion that in the past led to an extensive body of law governing public companies to the exclusion of smaller enterprises.[134]

To characterise SPEs purely as an instrument for the furtherance of small and medium enterprises would, however, be a mistake. The setting up of a private company, while typically a matter for closely held small businesses, may equally be of value to larger enterprises which, by way of example, might wish to set up an informal and relatively inexpensive business vehicle for joint ventures, or that wish to benefit from fewer formalities and fewer obligations towards non-shareholder constituencies.[135] In fact, lobbying from business organisations is recognised as one of the reasons that have led to the proposal of the SPE statute. The motivation was, at least in part, to facilitate the cross-border establishment of subsidiary companies by public companies.[136] Indeed, discussions conducted by the drafters of

[130] Commission (EC), '"Think Small First": A "Small Business Act" for Europe' (Communication) COM (2008) 394.

[131] Commission (EC), 'Proposal for a Council Regulation on the statute for a European private company' COM (2008) 396/3 (hereinafter 'Draft SPE Statute').

[132] Council of the European Union, 'Proposal for a Council Regulation on a European private company – Political agreement' 1061/11 DRS 84 SOC 432 (hereinafter 'Revised Draft SPE Statute').

[133] Draft SPE Statute (n 131) 2.

[134] See R Drury, 'The European Private Company' (2008) *European Business Organization Law Review* 125, 127.

[135] Drury 2008 (n 134) 126–27.

[136] See A Radwan, 'European Private Company and the Regulatory Landscape in the EU – An Introductory Note' (2007) *European Business Law Review* 769, 769.

the proposed Regulation with European and US multinational companies confirmed the view that the possibility of setting up a private company with the EU 'brand' would be well-received by major enterprises that wished to benefit from both the psychological benefits of a supranational brand, as well as a recognisable vehicle for transnational joint ventures which would do away with the cost of expenditure on lawyers' fees which could be prohibitive to smaller enterprises.[137] The proposed SPE Statute therefore offers an alternative to national business vehicles of any dimension, save for the caveat that the SPE's shares 'shall not be offered to the public by the SPE or by its members and shall not be traded on a regulated market or on a multilateral trading facility.'[138] Accordingly, the draft regulation marks a new approach to corporate law and conflicts of corporate law in that it allows promoters of companies to bypass national regulation entirely by setting up a European business vehicle that is far more permissive to shareholders than national alternatives.

A further distinguishing feature is the direct access to an SPE – unlike the SE, it is not intended that shareholders will need to establish a company under national law in order to have access to this supranational company form.[139] However, as noted above, the SPE presents an opportunity for public companies to bypass their obligations by setting up an SPE as the principal motor of their enterprises. Article 5a of the revised draft Regulation empowers both legal and natural persons to set up SPEs, while article 5 provides additional opportunities for the establishment of SPEs through the transformation, merger or division of existing companies.

The private international law provisions of the SPE Statute as originally proposed would have marked the most liberal contractual approach to date in the EU's legislation. The preamble to the draft Regulation, even in its revised formulation, states that 'as many matters as possible should be left to the contractual freedom of shareholders'.[140] This was the first explicit reference to contractual freedom in European corporate law legislation and, if accepted, will constitute a legislative endorsement of a view of corporate choice of law that had hitherto been shunned by several Member States. The preamble of the original draft went on to state that:

> In order to enable businesses to reap the full benefits of the internal market, the SPE should be able to have its registered office and principal place of business in different Member States and to transfer its registered office from one Member State to another, with or without also transferring its central administration or principal place of business.[141]

Thus, in contrast to every other harmonising or unifying legislative measure, the SPE would have allowed shareholders a free rein on the choice of jurisdiction in which to establish the private company, as well as the freedom to revise that choice from time to time by transferring the company's seat.[142] This has since been revised:

[137] Drury 2008 (n 134) 126–27.
[138] Revised Draft SPE Statute (n 132) art 3(2a).
[139] Revised Draft SPE Statute (n 132) arts 5–5a.
[140] Draft SPE Statute (n 131) recital 3.
[141] ibid recital 4.
[142] ibid c VII.

> In order to enable businesses to reap the full benefits of the internal market, the SPE should be able to transfer its registered office from one Member State to another.[143]

The seat of the company is now to be determined 'in accordance with the applicable national law'.[144] The revision of the original draft resulted from lack of agreement in the Council regarding the manner in which the seat of the SPE was to be determined.[145] Indeed, the Council remains undecided on the manner in which Member States may limit evasion of obligations which would arise from incorporation in a more closely connected Member State.[146] Accordingly, it is clear that, notwithstanding the legal developments of the past two decades, there remains significant divergence regarding the extent to which EU law should grant autonomy to incorporators of companies.

What is more, the freedom conferred by the original proposal should not to be mistaken with contractual freedom in the fullest sense. The crux of the SPE proposal is that the business vehicle will be uniform throughout the EU and that the choice of state of incorporation will not substantially affect the rights and obligations of stakeholders in the firm:[147]

> To ensure a high degree of uniformity of the SPE, as many matters pertaining to the company form as possible should be governed by this Regulation, either through substantive rules or by reserving matters to the articles of association of the SPE.[148]

Indeed, the draft SPE Statute is one of the most comprehensive instruments of private law that has yet been introduced in the Union. Among the benefits of detailed regulation is the resulting internal coherence in the body of law governing the SPE. To a great extent the choice of law regime of the draft Regulation was therefore neutral, in that few substantive benefits were to be had from shopping for Member States in which to register an SPE. The wording of the relevant recital has now been revised to shift the emphasis to the contractual freedom of the incorporators.[149] However, this does not appear to have the substantive effect of increasing contractual freedom, particularly in view of further revisions to the SPE Statute which are addressed hereunder.

The amendment that is, perhaps, the most significant from the perspective of the incorporators' contractual freedom concerns employee participation. Unlike the SE Statute, the original draft SPE Statute did not contain any substantive provisions concerning employee participation. Instead it deferred to the employee participation rules of the Member State in which the registered office is situated, if

[143] Revised Draft SPE Statute (n 132) recital 4.
[144] ibid art 7.
[145] ibid 2.
[146] ibid recital 6a.
[147] Draft SPE Statute (n 131) recital 5–6.
[148] ibid recital 6.
[149] Revised Draft SPE Statute (n 132) recital 6.

any such rules exist.[150] Because some states have employee participation rules for private companies, and because of the liberal choice of law regime in the original draft, the rules applicable to the SPE from one Member State to another would have diverged, and a degree of forum shopping would be likely to have ensued. As in previous experiences of the adoption of EU corporate law legislation, agreement among the Member States regarding employee participation remains lacking.[151] Revisions to the draft reflect the fact that the 'end of history' of transnational corporate law has not yet occurred, and nor has convergence on a shareholder oriented model that would confer greater autonomy to shareholders. The original formulation of the Statute was revised to include conditions whereby the employee participation rules of the state in which at least 500 employees of the SPE work habitually would apply in respect of those employees, provided that these rules prescribe a higher standard of participation rights than those of the Member State of the SPE's registered office.[152] What is more, both the original and the revised draft contain provision for the protection of the rights of employees in the event of a transfer of the company's registered office.[153]

Perhaps because of the quasi-partnership nature of the relationship between shareholders in private companies, the statute addresses shareholder protection in a limited way. The only specific provision concerning minority protection in the ordinary course of business is the right to request a general meeting.[154] This is in addition to more general shareholder rights included in the fairly exhaustive list of matters that are to be decided by resolutions of a simple or qualified majority of shareholders, as well as information rights to which shareholders are entitled.[155] What is more, the Statute provides that the protection of minority members who oppose the transfer shall be governed by the law of the state in which the SPE had its registered office prior to the transfer.[156] The fact that similar provision for the withdrawal of shareholders under such circumstances was contemplated in the more liberal original draft vindicates the argument that choice of law remains a matter of significant concern for European lawmakers,[157] notwithstanding the contractual turn following the *Centros* line of judgments.

[150] Draft SPE Statute (n 131) art 34(1). The absence of employee participation rules could, perhaps, have been explained with reference to the perceived dimensions of private companies and the extent of their societal impact. The context of the SPE proposal, that is a package of incentives for the promotion of small and medium enterprises that will lead to an entrepreneurial culture comparable to that of the United States of America (Draft SPE Statute (n 132), 9) would also appear to militate against the introduction of measures that might curtail the freedom of entrepreneurs to conduct business with as little external restraint as possible. Further, only a small minority of Member States find it necessary for shareholders in private companies to share control over the enterprise with employees: Commission (EC), '"Think Small First": A "Small Business Act" for Europe' (Communication) COM (2008) 394, 3.

[151] Revised Draft SPE Statute (n 132) 2.

[152] ibid art 35(1a(a)).

[153] ibid art 35(1a(b)); Draft SPE Statute (n 132) art 38.

[154] Revised Draft SPE Statute (n 132) art 30.

[155] ibid arts 28–29.

[156] Art 37(5).

[157] See Draft SPE Statute (n 131) art 36(6).

4.6 Conclusions

The history of article 50(2)(g) and the directives promulgated under its authority reveals evolving consent of the Member States as to the meaning of the provision. From its origins as a safeguard against the Delawarisation of European corporate law, the article has become an instrument for the furtherance of free movement of companies. Yet throughout this evolution, the Member States have never expressed a preference for unbridled party autonomy in European choice of corporate law. Nevertheless, this conclusion must be qualified. Firstly, although the EU's legislator has never legislated for the unequivocal furtherance of party autonomy, nor has the legislator legislated the unification of corporate law that would deny party autonomy altogether. Indeed, the lack of progress towards further harmonisation intrinsically preserves at least a measure of autonomy, as much as it evidences jealous guarding of corporate traditions in the Member States. Further, the introduction of supranational business vehicles, and the facilitation of cross-border establishment reveal a preference for at least some measure of autonomy.

It is to the cogency and coherence in the interpretation of the law in the *Centros* judgments and to the remaining flaws and open questions that this book will turn next. This is intended to contextualise discussion in Chapter 6 with reference to the challenges posed and the parameters within which legislators may resolve existing dilemmas.

5

The Freedom of Establishment Judgments

5.1 Introduction

As noted in the previous chapter, whereas the Union's legislator has not made a clear choice regarding the place of party autonomy in choice of corporate law, judgments of the Court have had the effect of giving a free rein to party autonomy in most respects.[1] The case law is best viewed in the context of a legislative backdrop which has failed to fulfil its promise. The judgments were preceded by an unsuccessful attempt to harmonise European conflict rules positively through the 1968 EC Convention on the Mutual Recognition of Companies and Bodies Corporate, a convention that was concluded under the authority conferred to the Member States by article 220 of the EEC Treaty (later article 293 EC). This article has now been repealed by the Lisbon Treaty. Authority to legislate remains in articles 50(2)(g) and 81 TFEU (articles 44(2)(g) and 65 EC), but the only legislation of general application is to be found in generic provisions of the Treaty concerning freedom of establishment.[2] Failure to legislate comprehensively has necessitated recourse to a judiciary that has been less restrained or nuanced in its approach to the establishment of the internal market than the legislator. Indeed, there is an undeniable tension between the liberalism of the jurisprudence emanating from Luxembourg and the protectionism that several Member States advocate through the legislation to which they have assented, the legislation they have blocked, as well as through their submissions to the Court.[3]

[1] Case C-212/97 *Centros Ltd v Erhvervs-og Selskabsstyrelsen* [1999] ECR I-01459; Case C-208/00 *Überseering BV v Nordic Construction Company Baumanagement GmbH* (NCC) [2002] ECR I-9919; Case C-167/01 *Kamer van Koophandel en Fabrieken voor Amsterdam v Inspire Art Ltd* [2003] ECR I-10155; Case C-411/03 *Sevic Systems AG* [2005] ECR I-10805; Case C-210/06 *Cartesio Oktató és Szolgáltató bt* [2008] ECR I-9641.

[2] Arts 49 and 54 TFEU.

[3] Case law which does not conform to the expected meaning of the Treaties is commonplace in the history of European integration, which has often been led by an activist, federalist court. See eg T Hartley, 'The European Court, Judicial Objectivity and the Constitution of the European Union' (1996) *Law Quarterly Review* 95, 95–109; H Rasmussen, *On Law and Policy in the European Court of Justice* (Lancaster, Kluwer, 1986) 10–13; KJ Alter, 'Who Are the "Masters of the Treaty"?: European Governments and the European Court of Justice' (1998) *International Organization* 121, 121–47. For a more nuanced view of judicial activism, see JHH Weiler, 'A Quiet Revolution: The European Court of Justice and its Interlocutors' (1994) *Comparative Political Studies* 510, 510–34; J Bengoetxea, N MacCormick and L Moral Soriano, 'Integration and Integrity in the Legal Reasoning of the European Court of Justice' in G de Búrca and JHH Weiler (eds), *The European Court of Justice* (Oxford, Oxford

This chapter charts the development of the case law and identifies the legal reasoning as well as some policy choices that have made the Court the principal motor of harmonisation. More importantly, it identifies flaws in the process of negative harmonisation that have resulted in case law which is internally contradictory, which is dissonant with elements of EU legislation, and which leaves many questions unanswered. In the final analysis, it is argued that the Court of Justice is an inappropriate forum for harmonisation of private international law of companies, both because of the idiosyncrasies of the institution, and because the complexity of the challenges posed cannot be fully resolved in a judicial forum.

The discussion is set out as follows. Section 5.2 outlines the relevant Treaty provisions, the EC Convention on the Mutual Recognition of Companies and Bodies Corporate and the judgment in *Daily Mail*[4] in order to contextualise discussion of the liberalising judgments, which are addressed in section 5.3. Section 5.4 addresses the cautious judgment in the most recent relevant case decided by the ECJ, *Cartesio*.[5] Section 5.5 highlights the effects that the Treaty of Lisbon may have on the case law and appraises the present state of EU law. This is followed by a concluding section which reiterates the argument that negative harmonisation is inadequate and that legislation is needed.

5.2 *Centros* et al in Context: the Treaty Provisions, the 1968 Convention and *Daily Mail*

This section briefly discusses the provisions of the Treaty that are relevant to the private international law of companies, the EC Convention on the Mutual Recognition of Companies and Bodies Corporate which was intended to harmonise European private international law of companies, as well as the judgment of the Court of Justice in *Daily Mail*.[6] The Convention and *Daily Mail* are addressed in the present section principally because they have formed the foundation for the development of the case law. *Daily Mail* represents a conservative, textual reading of the Treaty and is the precedential judgment from which discussion tends to depart, notwithstanding that it is not the first relevant judgment of the ECJ.[7]

The only overt reference in the EC Treaty to the conditions for the harmonisation of rules governing the recognition of companies was to be found in article 293

University Press, 2001) 43–85. For a view which is supportive of the ECJ's approach, see eg A Arnull, 'The European Court and judicial objectivity: a reply to Professor Hartley' (1996) *Law Quarterly Review* 411, 411–23.

[4] Case 81/87 *The Queen v HM Treasury and Commissioners of Inland Revenue, ex p Daily Mail and General Trust plc* [1988] ECR 5483.

[5] *Cartesio* (n 1).

[6] ibid.

[7] See eg Case 79/85 *DHM Segers v Bestuur van de Bedrijfsvereniging voor Bank- en Verzekeringswezen, Groothandel en Vrije Beroepen* [1986] ECR 2375 para 16; Case 270/83 *Commission v France* [1986] ECR 273.

EC which invited, or indeed obliged, Member States to enter into negotiations to determine conditions for the mutual recognition of companies. Notwithstanding the repeal of article 293 EC by the Lisbon Treaty, this provision is addressed in some depth in this chapter because it has helped to shape the case law. Its treatment by the Court of Justice also illustrates some of the contradictions in the evolution of the law. It should be recalled that articles 50 and 81 TFEU (articles 44 and 65 EC) continue to provide a basis for legislation on the private international law of companies. However, article 293 EC was deemed to be particularly important because it provided an explicit basis for legislation regarding the recognition and mobility of companies:

> Member States shall, so far as is necessary, enter into negotiations with each other with a view to securing for the benefit of their nationals:
>
> . . . the mutual recognition of companies or firms within the meaning of the second paragraph of Article 48 [Article 54 TFEU], the retention of legal personality in the event of transfer of their seat from one country to another, and the possibility of mergers between companies or firms governed by the laws of different countries.

The Court of Justice took note of the explicit authority for the adoption of legislation in article 293 EC in *Daily Mail.* This informed the Court's decision to adopt a conservative approach to the direct effect of freedom of corporate establishment in that early judgment.[8] Remnants of caution inspired by article 293 EC remained as recently as the Court's most recent judgment in *Cartesio.*[9] In the absence of further legislation, article 293 EC could not accord any substantive rights to individuals and companies, since it was merely an empowering clause which was further qualified by the phrase 'so far as is necessary'. The same can be said of articles 50 and 81 TFEU, which are also empowering clauses having no substantive content. Notwithstanding the fact that the need for a European choice of corporate law regime was deemed to be worthy of specific mention in the European treaties since the Treaty of Rome,[10] Member States never successfully concluded negotiations to that end.

5.2.1 The 1968 Convention

Yet the absence of legislation governing the transnational recognition of companies should not lead one to the conclusion that it was considered unnecessary to endeavour towards the ends established in article 293 EC. Nor is it tenable to conclude that all matters relating to mobility of companies are addressed by the Treaty.[11] Indeed the Commission recently indicated that it may initiate a legislative

[8] *Daily Mail* (n 4) para 21.

[9] *Cartesio* (n 1) para 114.

[10] The repeal of art 293 should not be understood to be a negation of authority for the adoption of legislation, but is better viewed in the context of a rationalisation of the Treaty whereby authority in arts 50 and 81 TFEU was deemed to be sufficient. See section 5.5 below.

[11] See *Cartesio* (n 1) para 109.

process that will lead to the enactment of legislation on this matter.[12] What is more, the founding Member States did in fact seek to harmonise the private international law of companies and concluded a treaty to that effect. However, the 1968 Convention on the Mutual Recognition of Companies never came into force, for want of ratification by the Netherlands.

The Convention placed the incorporation theory as the point of departure for a mutual recognition regime:

> Companies under civil or commercial law, including co-operative societies, established in accordance with the law of a Contracting State which grants them the capacity of persons having rights and duties, and having their statutory registered office in the territories to which the present Convention applies, shall be recognised as a right.[13]

The apparent liberalism of article 1 was followed by provisions which allowed so much room for exception that the Convention would have given contracting states extensive room to deny recognition or to proscribe the scope of the law of the state of incorporation and supplant this with their own substantive law. Article 3 enabled contracting states to declare that they would not recognise companies whose only connection to the Community was the formal act of incorporation in one of the Member States:

> Notwithstanding the foregoing, any Contracting State may declare that it will not apply the present Convention to any companies or bodies corporate specified in articles 1 and 2 having their real registered office outside the territories to which the present Convention applies, if such companies or bodies corporate have no genuine link with the economy of one of the said territories.[14]

This limitation lacked clear definition of what constituted a 'genuine link with the economy' of a contracting state.

Article 4 surely provided an even more far-reaching and problematic exception to the general rule by allowing the bifurcation of a company's governing law where a company's real seat and place of incorporation were situated in different states:

> Any Contracting State may also declare that it will apply any provisions of its own legislation which it deems essential, to the companies or bodies corporate specified in Articles 1 and 2 having their real registered offices on its territory, even if these have been established in accordance with the law of another Contracting State.
>
> The [supplementary] provisions of the legislation of the state making such a declaration shall apply in only one of the following two cases:
>
> [If the memorandum and articles of association do not derogate from the said law], if necessary by any express general reference to the law in accordance with which the company or body corporate has been established,

12 Commission (EC), 'An area of freedom, security and justice serving the citizen' (Communication) COM (09) 262 final 14.

13 EC Convention on the Mutual Recognition of Companies and Bodies Corporate of 29 February 1968, Bulletin of the European Communities, Supplement 2/69, 7–18 (hereinafter 'EC Convention 1968') art 1.

14 ibid art 3.

> [If, in the absence of any such derogation in the memorandum and articles of association,] the company or body corporate fails to show that it has actually exercised its activity for a reasonable time in the Contracting State in accordance with the law under which it was established.[15]

The Convention did not define which matters could be deemed to be essential, or how any conflicts between essential provisions of the law of the seat and the general provisions of the law of incorporation would be resolved. This would have made two laws incumbent on companies, and would have left stakeholders with the task of guessing how courts would have resolved any conflicts between the two governing laws.[16] Recourse to the European Court of Justice may have resolved some questions,[17] but it is hardly plausible for the Court to have resolved all potential conflicts. Accordingly, the main features of the Convention have been aptly described as a 'half-hearted compromise' in view of the fact that it failed to effect any real bridging between the real seat and incorporation theories.[18]

The 1968 Convention will surely remain dead letter law, but it remains notable that the only legislative initiative concerning the governing law of companies which was brought to some conclusion vested a significant degree of prescriptive jurisdiction in the state which was most closely connected to a company. Nevertheless, it is pertinent to qualify the relevance of the 1968 Convention: the Community was at the time made up of only six states, as opposed to the present 27. Five of the founding Member States applied the real seat theory, and the only state that did not do so, namely the Netherlands, did not ratify the Convention, precisely for fear that it gave effect to the real seat theory.[19] In addition, the 1968

[15] EC Convention 1968, art 4. The text in square brackets replaces the apparently erroneous translation in the Bulletin, which reads as follows: 'If the memorandum and articles so permit, if necessary by any express general reference to the law in accordance with which the company or body corporate has been established; If, the memorandum and articles of association so permitting, the company or body corporate fails to show that it has actually exercised its activity for a reasonable time in the Contracting State in accordance with the law under which it was established'. This is not faithful to the French text: 'si les statuts n'y dérogent pas, le cas échéant par une référence expresse et globale à la loi en conformité de laquelle la société ou personne morale s'est constituée; si, à défaut d´une telle dérogation dans les statuts, la société ou personne morale ne démontre pas qu´elle a exercé effectivement son activité pendant un temps raisonnable dans l´Etat contractant en conformité de la loi duquel elle s´est constituée'. Nor is it faithful to the Italian text : 'Se l'atto costituivo o lo statuto non vi derogano, eventualmente mediante un riferimnento espresso e globale alla legge in conformità della quale la società o persona giuridica si è costituita; Se, in mancanza di tale deroga nell'atto costituivo, o nello statuto, la società o persona giuridica non dimostra di avere effettivamente esercitato la propria attività durante un periodo di tempo adeguato nello Stato contraente secondo la legge del quale essa si è costituita'. The author is grateful to Ms Aude Fiorini for her guidance in making sense of the poorly drafted and poorly translated texts. For criticism of the drafting of the Convention, see A Santa Maria, *European Economic Law* (Netherlands, Kluwer, 2009) 10.

[16] See Santa Maria (n 15) 11; S Rammeloo, *Corporations in Private International Law: A European Perspective* (Oxford, Oxford University Press, 2001) 35.

[17] See Protocol Concerning the Interpretation by the Court of Justice of the Convention of 29 February 1968 on the Mutual Recognition of Companies and Legal Persons (signed at Luxembourg on 3 June 1971), Bulletin of the European Communities, Supplement 4/71, 6–16.

[18] Rammeloo (n 16) 35.

[19] See RR Drury, 'The Regulation and Recognition of Foreign Corporations: Responses to the Delaware Syndrome' (1998) *Cambridge Law Journal* 165, 181–82; T Ballarino, 'Sulla mobilità delle

Convention predates the relevant judgments of the ECJ and the bulk of the harmonising laws. In sum, the Convention was concluded in a context that is far removed from the regulatory environment which subsists presently, both in terms of the substantive regulation and in terms of the participants in that process.

5.2.2 The TFEU

In the absence of secondary legislation, articles 49 and 54 TFEU (arts 43 and 48 EC), concerning freedom of establishment, are the only provisions of the Treaty that could confer substantive rights to companies operating in the Union. Those articles do not elaborate conditions for mutual recognition, seat transfers or cross-border mergers. Rather, the language employed is of a generic nature. Article 49 provides a general prohibition on restrictions to the freedom of establishment of nationals of Member States in the territory of other Member States:

> Within the framework of the provisions set out below, restrictions on the freedom of establishment of nationals of a Member State in the territory of another Member State shall be prohibited. Such prohibition shall also apply to restrictions on the setting-up of agencies, branches or subsidiaries by nationals of any Member State established in the territory of any Member State.
>
> Freedom of establishment shall include the right to take up and pursue activities as self-employed persons and to set up and manage undertakings, in particular companies or firms within the meaning of the second paragraph of Article 54, under the conditions laid down for its own nationals by the law of the country where such establishment is effected, subject to the provisions of the Chapter relating to capital.

Article 54 TFEU then extends the benefits of article 49 TFEU to companies and firms formed in accordance with the law of a Member State and having their registered office, central administration or principal place of business within the Union:

> Companies or firms formed in accordance with the law of a Member State and having their registered office, central administration or principal place of business within the Union shall, for the purposes of this Chapter, be treated in the same way as natural persons who are nationals of Member States.

The natural meaning of article 54 TFEU does appear to embrace the principle of mutual recognition.[20] However, the article poses significant difficulties because it does not elaborate how companies and natural persons are to be treated equally –

società nella Comunità Europea. Da *Daily Mail* a *Überseering*: norme imperative, morme di conflitto e libertà comunitarie' (2003) *Rivista delle società* 669, 670. In addition to the Netherlands' objections to the content of the Convention, there is some evidence to suggest that the Netherlands was in no mood to be accommodating, following General De Gaulle's veto of the accession of the United Kingdom to the Community. See E Stein, 'Conflict-of-Laws Rules by Treaty: Recognition of Companies in a Regional Market' (1970) *Michigan Law Review* 1327, 1337.

[20] FJ Garcimartín Alférez, 'La Sentencia «Centros»: una visión a través de los comentarios' (2001) *Revista Jurídica* 169, 176–77.

'unlike natural persons, companies are creatures of the law and, in the present state of Community law, creatures of national law. They exist only by virtue of the varying national legislation which determines their incorporation and functioning.'[21]

For several decades, the above-quoted provisions of the Treaty were not applied to companies in a manner that affected choice of corporate law directly. It was generally understood that the Treaty itself could not confer directly effective rights in respect of corporate mobility.[22] This may have been a consequence of the rejection of the 1968 Convention, which had the effect of stalling both the positive and negative harmonisation of private international law of companies.[23] Member States therefore retained sovereignty to determine how a company was connected to a jurisdiction. In this construct, freedom of establishment was understood in a limited sense of granting market access to truly foreign companies, rather than a private international law regime which limited the extent to which Member States could prescribe the connecting factors which enabled a company to be recognised. Member States had no European obligation to recognise pseudo-foreign companies incorporated under the laws of other Member States. Nor did Community law limit the connecting factors which Member States could require of companies chartered under their authority. Over the past two decades the extent to which prescriptive jurisdiction is retained by Member States has been rolled back, and articles 43 and 48 EC (articles 49 and 54 TFEU) have been cited as grounds for the striking down of state private international law and practices that limit freedom of incorporation in the EU.

It has been left to the judicial branch to determine whether prescriptive jurisdiction concerning the recognition of companies continued to vest in the Member States, or if it could be resolved with reference to the Treaty. The fact that article 293 EC had not borne fruit rendered the question of its significance, if any, particularly unclear. In view of the ambiguity of the relevant provisions of the Treaty, particularly the absence of phrases which explicitly subjected articles 43 and 48 EC (articles 49 and 54 TFEU) to article 293 EC or vice versa, the Court's judgments were destined to be controversial to some extent. The Court was left with the unenviable task of establishing whether an article of the Treaty that invited Member States to consider whether or not it was necessary to enter into multilateral negotiations to an undefined end have the effect of limiting substantive rights which were purportedly accorded by articles 43 and 48 EC. The ECJ's more recent judgments in *Centros*[24] and the cases that followed were consistent with that

[21] *Daily Mail* (n 4) para 19. This was reiterated in the Court's most recent judgment on the private international law of companies: *Cartesio* (n 1) para 104. To the same effect, see FM Mucciarelli, 'Company "Emigration" and EC Freedom of Establishment: *Daily Mail* Revisited' (2008) *European Business Organization Law Review* 267, 294.

[22] M Goldman, 'La nationalité des sociétés dans la Communauté économique européenne' (1969) *Travaux du Comité français de droit internationale privé* 215, 219–26; Stein (n 19) 1329–31.

[23] Santa Maria (n 16) 11; Rammeloo (n 16) 36–37; Stein (n 19) 1330; T Ballarino, 'From *Centros* to *Überseering*: EC Right of Establishment and the Conflict of Laws' (2002) *Yearbook of Private International Law* 203, 208.

[24] *Centros* (n 1).

Court's historic role as a catalyst and guardian of the liberalisation of the internal market. As has been the case in other fields such as the free movement of goods and persons, the Court has ensured that the process of integration was not stalled by the inaction of Member States. While European company legislation was experiencing an isolated case of Eurosclerosis,[25] the judicial branch compensated for the lack of legislative development by accelerating integration through its judgments with the Commission's express support, or at its instigation, as evidenced in the latter's submissions to the Court. The absence of the express consent of the Member States is therefore not unique in the history of European integration and it could reasonably be argued that party autonomy in choice of corporate law is a natural progression in the evolution of European law.

This notwithstanding, from the perspective of a purposive interpretation of the Treaty, it is perhaps surprising that article 293 EC should have been set aside, and that instead articles 43 and 48 EC should have conferred directly effective rights for choices of corporate law to be recognised. If it were the case that articles 43 and 48 EC were intended to confer freedom of choice of corporate laws, one would have to explain away the Community's founders' rationale for including article 293 EC in the Treaty. The intended purpose of article 293 EC is confirmed by the Member States' endeavours to draft a treaty establishing the conditions for recognition as provided in that article. When viewed together with article 293 EC, it is quite clear that articles 43 and 48 EC were not intended to grant absolute freedom of incorporation within the Community, but that the Member States wished to determine the manner in which corporate mobility would be allowed through specific legislative intervention. What is more, there is no evidence to suggest other than that the repeal of article 293 EC is to be viewed in the context of a spring-cleaning exercise in the Reform Treaty, rather than a recalibration of what are now articles 49 and 54 TFEU (articles 43 and 48 EC).

5.2.3 *Daily Mail*

The ECJ adopted a cautious interpretation of the Treaty in the matter of *Daily Mail*.[26] The Court was asked to consider the legality of a UK tax law which Daily Mail and General Trust plc alleged infringed its freedom of establishment. The law prescribed that a company incorporated in the United Kingdom and having its registered office there was to request permission from the Treasury, which could refuse, prior to transferring its centre of management to another Member State. The Court noted that companies were creatures of national law, and existed only by virtue of the law under which they were established.[27] Further, article 48 EC (article 54 TFEU) does not elevate any connecting factor to a superior standing,

[25] See AJ Gildea, '*Überseering*: A European Company Passport' (2004) *Brooklyn Journal of International Law* 257, 258.
[26] *Daily Mail* (n 4).
[27] ibid para 19.

but instead 'places on the same footing, as connecting factors, the registered office, central administration and principal place of business of a company.'[28] Noting that no agreement had been concluded under the power conferred by article 293 EC, and noting further that none of the company law directives harmonised the manner in which a company's seat may be transferred from one Member State to another, the Court concluded that:

> the Treaty regards the differences in national legislation concerning the required connecting factor and the question whether – and if so how – the registered office or real head office of a company incorporated under national law may be transferred from one Member State to another as problems which are not resolved by the rules concerning the right of establishment but must be dealt with by future legislation or conventions.[29]

Accordingly, it was held that the right to freedom of establishment as then, and indeed presently, articulated in the legislation of the Union could not be interpreted as conferring the unfettered right upon a company to transfer its seat while retaining its juridical personality. The Court was more inclined to take the restrictive view that 'In the case of a company, the right of establishment is generally exercised by the setting-up of agencies, branches or subsidiaries, as is expressly provided for in the second sentence of the first paragraph of Article [54 TFEU]'.[30] Accordingly, it was found that the Treaty said nothing about the factors which connect a company to a jurisdiction or the conditions under which a company could transfer its seat.[31] The Court was satisfied that UK law did not impose any restrictions on transactions of the kind ordinarily used for companies to exercise their freedom of establishment. Further, the ECJ noted that the law at issue did not encumber corporate mobility since the consent of the Treasury was only required where the company intended to transfer its centre of management while retaining its status as a UK company.[32] Accordingly, on that occasion the Court adopted an approach which was cautious and demonstrated an understanding of Member States' concerns regarding the governance of companies as expressed in the strictest possible interpretation of the written laws of the Community.[33] Nevertheless, the judgment was viewed as a blow to the functioning of the internal market. Indeed, one commentator described the judgment hyperbolically as 'a setback to the entire process of European integration'.[34]

[28] ibid para 21.
[29] ibid para 23.
[30] ibid para 17.
[31] ibid para 23.
[32] ibid paras 17–18.
[33] C Timmermans, 'Impact of EU Law on International Company Law' (2010) *European Review of Private Law* 549, 554.
[34] Ballarino 2002 (n 23) 208.

5.3 The ECJ's Liberalising Judgments

5.3.1 *Centros*

The ratio of the judgment in *Daily Mail* was soon revisited in *Centros*,[35] a judgment that gave effect to the principle of mutual recognition and liberalised choice of corporate law in the European Union. The latter judgment marked the birth of freedom of choice in corporate law, a right which some saw as 'inherent in the exercise of the right of establishment within the single market.'[36] Thus *Centros* was to freedom of corporate establishment what *Cassis*[37] was to the free movement of goods.[38] The hypothesis that the development of the Court's jurisprudence evidences a judicial reaction to the Union's legislative process and the Commission's priorities becomes more compelling with reference to the fact that the harmonisation process was progressing at a rapid pace at the time of the Court's cautious judgment in *Daily Mail*. The Commission's submissions in *Daily Mail*, as reported in the Court's judgment, were highly nuanced and do not appear to have advocated liberalisation strongly.[39] In subsequent cases beginning with *Centros*[40] more than a decade after *Daily Mail*, perhaps because the legislative process subsequently lost the momentum that it had garnered in the 1980s, the Commission has consistently argued that the conflict of corporate laws legislation at issue constituted an unjustified restriction to freedom of establishment.

The holding of the ECJ in *Centros* marks the first major departure from the restrained approach which had been adopted in *Daily Mail*. That noted, the facts in *Centros* are certainly distinguishable from those in *Daily Mail*. *Centros* concerned the legality of the refusal by the Danish Trade and Companies Board (hereinafter the 'Board') to register a branch of an English private limited company, which had been set up by shareholders who resided in Denmark and wished to operate the company in Denmark. This case therefore concerned the recognition of a formally foreign company, rather than the connection between a company and its state of incorporation. In *Centros*, it was not contested that the purpose of the establishment of the English company was in fact to circumvent Danish minimum capital requirements, and to operate the business entirely in Denmark by means of a branch of the English company.[41] The Board refused to register the branch, citing the fact that the company in fact intended to set up its principal place of business in Denmark, as opposed to establishing its secondary establishment there through a branch of a company that

[35] *Centros* (n 1).

[36] A Looijestijn-Clearie, 'Centros Ltd – A Complete U-Turn in the Right of Establishment for Companies?' (2000) *International and Comparative Law Quarterly* 621, 634. This echoes the judgment in *Centros* (n 1) para 27.

[37] Case 120/78 *Rewe-Zentral AG v Bundesmonopolverwaltung für Branntwein* [1979] ECR 649.

[38] Garcimartín Alférez (n 20) 169.

[39] *Daily Mail* (n 4) paras 14, 16 and 20.

[40] *Centros* (n 1).

[41] ibid para 17.

truly operated in another Member State. Centros Ltd appealed that decision on the grounds that it felt that its freedom of establishment had been unlawfully restricted.

The Danish government argued that the EC Treaty did not apply to the facts. It was submitted that all relevant factors pointed to a finding that this was a purely Danish matter: the litigation concerned a company the shares in which were held by Danish nationals residing in Denmark who wished to bypass Danish minimum capital requirements.[42] In Denmark's view, there were not sufficient transnational elements to trigger the application of articles 43 and 48 EC (articles 49 and 54 TFEU). Denmark did not contest that article 48 EC bound Member States to register branches of companies established under the laws of another Member State,[43] but the Board was of the view that the registration of Centros Ltd's branch was problematic because the company did not conduct any business whatsoever in the United Kingdom and was therefore unconnected to that jurisdiction.[44] In other words, Denmark did not contest the registration of a branch of a pseudo-foreign corporation that conducted some business in its state of incorporation, but it was of the view that the matter in *Centros* was entirely a case of *fraude à la loi* in a purely Danish context. Recalling its judgment in *Segers*[45] the Court rejected Denmark's argument, noting that 'it is immaterial that the company was formed in the first Member State only for the purpose of establishing itself in the second, where its main, or indeed entire, business is to be conducted'.[46]

In *Centros*, the ECJ did not take into account the scheme of the Treaty which suggested possible limiting effects of article 293 EC on articles 43 and 48 EC (articles 49 and 54 TFEU), as it had done in *Daily Mail*.[47] Accordingly, it did not overtly consider, confirm or override its earlier judgment. The Court's omission could not be readily explained, and this had the inevitable consequence of causing some uncertainty.[48] However, the Court did depart from the interpretation of article 48 EC and its correlation to article 293 EC which it had adopted in *Daily Mail*. In *Daily Mail* the Court was of the view that the phrase 'Companies or firms formed in accordance with the law of a Member State and having their registered office, central administration or principal place of business within the Community' does not give preference to any of the connecting factors mentioned therein. The word 'or' therefore did not render the three connecting factors alternately applicable, but the status of the connecting factors was to be determined by future legislation. In contrast, in *Centros* it was held that 'The location of their registered office, central administration or principal place of business serves as the connecting factor with the legal system of a particular state in the same way as does nationality in the case

[42] ibid.
[43] ibid para 15.
[44] ibid para 16.
[45] *Segers* (n 7) para 16.
[46] *Centros* (n 1) para 17.
[47] See AG Colomer in Case C-208/00 *Überseering BV v Nordic Construction Company Baumanagement GmbH* (NCC) [2002] ECR I-9919 paras 35–40.
[48] WG Ringe, 'No Freedom of Emigration for Companies?' (2005) *European Business Law Review* 621, 628; WH Roth, 'From *Centros* to *Ueberseering*: Free Movement of Companies, Private International Law, and Community Law' (2003) *International and Comparative Law Quarterly* 177, 189.

of a natural person.'[49] Thus the latter judgment departed from the former since the equivalence between the three connecting factors as viewed in *Centros* is such as to make the existence of any of the three trigger the application of article 43 and 48 EC, rather than being such as to empower the Member States to choose one or more of the connecting factors through secondary legislation, as was the view in *Daily Mail*.

Despite any uncertainty which might result from a formal juxtaposition of *Daily Mail* and *Centros*, the latter judgment certainly nudged European law firmly towards the incorporation doctrine. This was not overt, since the Court did not rule that a company's governing law is to be determined with reference to its place of incorporation.[50] However, what is left unsaid and apparently unconsidered is the fact that, when viewed in the context of the doctrinal controversy between the real seat and incorporation theories, it cannot be argued that there is any such thing as strict equivalence between the three connecting factors if they are to coexist. To enforce a company's freedom of establishment if any of the registered office, central administration or principal place of business is present in a Member State has the practical effect of adopting elements of the incorporation theory and granting a free choice of law to the incorporators – the recognition of a company's right to freedom of establishment on the basis of its formation under the laws of a Member State and the presence of its registered office thereat is tantamount to accepting the incorporation doctrine. Indeed, in his Opinion in *Centros*, AG La Pergola endorsed the view that contractual freedom should be given a free rein in European private international law of companies.[51] This was a matter that the Member States originally intended to be resolved by virtue of an agreement under the power conferred by article 293 EC, and that the institutions retain authority to determine through articles 50 and 81 TFEU (articles 44 and 65 EC).

The departure from the prior holding is not readily explicable in terms of a change in the written law that would logically require the Luxembourg Court to change its approach – the relevant treaties, regulations and directives of the Community had not changed in the intervening period.[52] Nor is the Court's reliance on *Segers* rather than *Daily Mail* plain to understand in the context of the affinity of the two precedents to the subject matter in *Centros* – *Daily Mail* and *Centros* both address matters concerning the governing law of companies, whereas *Segers* concerned workers' entitlement to sickness benefits in a context more closely associated with the free movement of persons. Freedom of establishment was ancillary to the principal issue of the said entitlements. Nevertheless the ECJ followed the less relevant precedent and adopted an analysis that was consistent with its jurisprudence on the fundamental freedoms and possible limitations thereto, rather than an approach that also accounted for the provisions of the Treaty that made specific reference to the conflict of corporate laws.

[49] *Centros* (n 1) para 20.

[50] E Micheler, 'Recognition of Companies Incorporated in Other EU Member States' (2003) *International and Comparative Law Quarterly* 521, 521.

[51] AG La Pergola in *Centros* (n 1) para 20.

[52] AG Colomer in *Überseering* (n 1) paras 35–40.

Having satisfied itself that the matter was not purely internal to Denmark, and that article 48 EC was not qualified by article 293 EC, the ECJ went on to consider the extent to which the Board's behaviour impinged upon the company's freedom of establishment. The Court's reasoning freed it to adopt a classic fundamental freedoms approach, as opposed to a more cautious approach that deferred to the positively expressed will of the Member States to pool their sovereignty within limited parameters. The Court recalled the *Gebhard* test[53] which prescribes the four conditions which must be present to justify measures that hinder the exercise of fundamental freedoms or render the exercise thereof less attractive, restrictive as they are when compared to the latitude that the Court had allowed Member States in *Daily Mail*:

> they must be applied in a non-discriminatory manner; they must be justified by imperative requirements in the general interest; they must be suitable for securing the attainment of the objective which they pursue; and they must not go beyond what is necessary in order to attain it.[54]

It was found that the practice in question failed on the third condition because it did not fulfil its purported purpose of protecting the company's creditors – the branch of the company would have been registered had it conducted business in the United Kingdom.[55] The Court also found that the measures in question went beyond what was necessary to attain the objective thereof because 'it is possible to adopt measures which are less restrictive, or which interfere less with fundamental freedoms, by, for example, making it possible in law for public creditors to obtain the necessary guarantees.'[56] The only residual powers that the Court's judgment allowed the Member States concerned the prevention or penalisation of fraud, albeit without allowing them to do so by refusing to register a branch of a company incorporated in another Member State.[57]

It is noteworthy that in order to quash Denmark's protestations against the circumvention of its minimum capital requirements, the Court cited protections to creditors that are provided in the secondary legislation of the Union, including disclosure requirements arising from the Fourth and Eleventh Company Law Directives.[58] Accordingly, the considerations of the Court were not restricted to the primary legislation of the Union, but were informed further by the directives that specify the manner in which the broad constitutional goals of the Treaty are to be attained. This is consistent with the Court's approach to mutual recognition in areas of EU law which have been harmonised. However, the reference to the Community's secondary legislation cannot of itself explain the Court's departure from *Daily Mail*. On one level, the logic that disclosure requirements in secondary

[53] Case C-55/94 *Reinhard Gebhard v Consiglio dell'Ordine degli Avvocati e Procuratori di Milano* [1995] ECR I-4565 para 37.

[54] *Centros* (n 1) para 34.

[55] ibid para 35.

[56] ibid para 37.

[57] ibid para 38.

[58] ibid para 36.

legislation should justify the circumvention of minimum capital requirements is somewhat strained. The secondary legislation was not intended to serve as a basis for allowing incorporations in Member States with which companies had no real connection, but only as a means of protecting creditors in an integrated market. What is more, if the principle of mutual recognition were to rely on the existence of secondary legislation, Member States would have ample room for manoeuvre given that few areas of company law are harmonised. This would have the effect of an easily winnable lottery in which the Member States could rely on unharmonised areas of corporate law in order to deny recognition of companies from other Member States.

Still, the ECJ's ruling marked the genesis of freedom of incorporation within the EU of a fashion not dissimilar to that pertaining in the United States. What followed was a significant exodus of incorporations to Member States whose company laws were more accommodating.[59] However, there was some doubt as to the extent to which *Centros* had rendered the real seat theory incompatible with the prevalent interpretation of the EC Treaty in view of the fact that *Centros* only addressed secondary establishment. In addition, the fact that the states involved in *Centros* were both incorporation states offered some hope to real seat states, in that they could justify their approach on the basis that the practices adopted in their states differed from the repudiated practices of Denmark in *Centros*.[60] Finally, doubts remained as to the apparent divergences between *Daily Mail* and *Centros*, doubts that are compounded by the fact that in the latter judgment the Court did not address its earlier holding. In this respect, one will note that *Centros* set the tone for later judgments also in that each judgment resolves some matters but also adds some uncertainties.

5.3.2 *Überseering*

The absence of clear precedent coupled with the underlying problem of the written law's capacity for multifarious interpretation left room for further questions to be referred to the ECJ. Such was the uncertainty that prevailed following *Centros* that a number of national courts referred the question of the compatibility of the real seat theory with the Treaty in proceedings that were not adversarial. The Court of Justice therefore summarily declined jurisdiction.[61] The prevalent lack of certainty is highlighted with reference to the fact that eminent scholars proposed five significantly different explanations for the differences between the *Daily Mail*

[59] Following the judgment in *Centros* there was a more than fourfold increase in incorporations from other EU Member States in the United Kingdom alone, with Germany experiencing the highest loss of incorporations to the UK: M Becht, C Mayer and HF Wagner, 'Where do Firms Incorporate?' (2008) *Journal of Corporate Finance* 241, 242.

[60] See Garcimartín Alférez (n 20) 179–82; M Gestri, 'Mutuo Riconoscimento delle Società Comunitarie, Norme di Conflitto Nazionali e Frode alla Legge: il caso *Centros*' (2000) *Rivista di Diritto Internazionale* 71, 78–79; Roth 2003 (n 48) 188–90.

[61] Case C-86/00 *HSB-Wohnbau Ltd* [2001] ECR I-5353; Case C-447/00 *(Reference for a preliminary ruling from the Landesgericht Salzburg): Holto Ltd* [2002] ECR I-735. See Micheler (n 50) 523.

and *Centros*:[62] (i) *Daily Mail* addressed a question of private international law, whereas *Centros* addressed a question of substantive law;[63] (ii) *Centros* only addressed a company's right to secondary establishment, whereas *Daily Mail* addressed a company's right to primary establishment;[64] (iii) *Daily Mail* dealt with corporate emigration whereas *Centros* concerned immigration;[65] (iv) *Centros* overturned *Daily Mail*;[66] (v) *Centros* only bound Member States that applied the incorporation theory to recognise foreign companies, and left untouched Member States that applied the real seat theory.[67]

In *Überseering*[68] a German court requested clarification regarding the compatibility with the Treaty of the refusal to recognise the legal personality of a company that had its seat in Germany but that was incorporated under Netherlands law. The question referred could have elicited a response that would dispel all doubts as to the extent of liberalisation of incorporations in the Union occasioned by the judgment in *Centros*:

> The Bundesgerichtshof wonders whether, in view of *Centros*, the Treaty provisions on freedom of establishment preclude, in a situation such as that in point in the main proceedings, application of the rules on conflict of laws in force in the Member State in which the actual centre of administration of a company validly incorporated in another Member State is situated when the consequence of those rules is the refusal to recognise the company's legal capacity and, therefore, its capacity to bring legal proceedings in the first Member State to enforce rights under a contract.[69]

The Court found that the company must be recognised and that the real seat theory could not be applied to the facts. Still, notwithstanding the clarity of the question referred, the Court appears to have been at pains to consolidate the apparent contradictions in the two precedents. The consolidation of the two judgments is, of course, impossible to achieve without mitigating the logical consequences of one holding or the other. The attempt to consolidate precedents through strained logic has been of disservice to legal certainty.

The defendant in the main proceedings, supported by the governments of Germany, Spain and Italy, argued that article 293 provided evidence of the Member States' intention that a company should not automatically retain its legal personal-

[62] For an overview of the different approaches, see Ringe (n 48) 628; Roth 2003 (n 48) 189.

[63] WH Roth 'Case note on *Centros*' (2000) 37 *Common Market Law Review* 147, 154; Micheler (n 50) 522.

[64] The German Supreme Court adopted this view as a consequence of the prevailing scholarly consensus in Germany: see WF Ebke, 'The European Conflict-of-Corporate-Laws Revolution: *Überseering, Inspire Art* and Beyond' (2004) *International Lawyer* 813, 820–21. See also Looijestijn-Clearie (n 36) 637.

[65] M Andenas 'Free Movement of Companies' (2003) *Law Quarterly Review* 221, 222.

[66] JC Dammann 'The future of codetermination after *Centros*: Will German corporate law move closer to the U.S. model?' (2003) *Fordham Journal of Corporate and Financial Law* 607, 616–17; K Heine and W Kerber, 'European Corporate Laws, Regulatory Competition and Path Dependence' (2002) *European Journal of Law and Economics* 47, 50.

[67] See Garcimartín Alférez (n 20) 179–82; Gestri (n 60) 78–79; Roth 2003 (n 48) 188–90.

[68] *Überseering* (n 1).

[69] ibid para 20.

ity in the event of a transfer of its seat.[70] The Court rejected the notion that article 293 constituted a reserve of legislative competence in the Member States. Following the Advocate General's reasoning,[71] it took the view that article 293 enabled the Member States to enter into negotiations to the extent that it is necessary to do so where the Treaty provisions did not achieve the goals established therein.[72] Noting that the adoption of directives is not a *sine qua non* for the direct effect of the Treaty provisions concerning the fundamental freedoms, it was held that by analogy nor could the adoption of a convention pursuant to article 293 EC be necessary for the effectiveness of the freedom of establishment of companies.[73]

This is a curious interpretation of the powers conferred by article 293 EC. While the Court's view is broadly consistent with the body of EU law concerning direct effect,[74] it is difficult to justify the statement that article 293 EC is empowering only 'so far as is necessary, that is to say if the provisions of the Treaty do not enable its objectives to be attained.' Indeed, if the Member States were to conclude a Treaty which exceeded the powers that the Court deemed article 293 EC to confer, it is unlikely that there could be any grounds to curtail the purportedly ultra vires effects of the hypothetical treaty. The extent of the limitation of the meaning of article 293 EC is therefore baffling, since a hypothetical convention would have the same standing at international law as the EC Treaty itself, and indeed it could explicitly render applicable or inapplicable any manner of things that the ECJ deems to have direct effect under the Treaty. Further, notwithstanding the *sui generis* nature of EU law, the power conferred by article 293 EC need not have been so conferred in order that the Member States would be empowered to conclude a convention among themselves. The limits to State power are not such as to deny the right to conclude agreements of a constitutional nature that limit or elaborate the fundamental freedoms. Accordingly, while one can understand that the general body of EC law would allow the Court to follow its previous reasoning in extending the applicability of the rights conferred by the fundamental freedoms despite the provisions of article 293 EC, the statement that article 293 EC conferred only limited powers appears to have no legal basis.

While the Court was eager to address, and overturn, the interpretation of article 293 EC which was handed down in *Daily Mail*, it did not go so far as to set that judgment aside entirely. Instead, in its reasoning in *Überseering* the Court drew distinctions between the facts in that case and those in *Daily Mail*:

> It must be stressed that, unlike *Daily Mail and General Trust*, which concerned relations between a company and the Member State under whose laws it had been incorporated in a situation where the company wished to transfer its actual centre of administration to another Member State whilst retaining its legal personality in the State of incorporation, the present case concerns the recognition by one Member State of a company

[70] ibid paras 23–28.
[71] AG Colomer in *Überseering* (n 1) para 42.
[72] *Überseering* (n 1) para 54.
[73] ibid para 55.
[74] ibid para 60.

> incorporated under the law of another Member State, such a company being denied all legal capacity in the host Member State where it takes the view that the company has moved its actual centre of administration to its territory, irrespective of whether in that regard the company actually intended to transfer its seat.[75]

The distinction is therefore twofold. First, *Daily Mail* concerned the relationship between the state of incorporation and the company, whereas *Überseering* addressed the relationship between a Member State and a company incorporated elsewhere in the EU; hence, a distinction between emigration and immigration. This first innovation in *Überseering* is problematic because it suggests that the Court is willing to read its case law in a quite different light to that which a literal reading might suggest. *Daily Mail* did not rely on a distinction between emigration and immigration, but was a fairly straightforward denial of mobility on the basis that the Treaty and secondary legislation did not provide a single connecting factor to determine conditions for the recognition of companies.[76]

Secondly, and perhaps more importantly from a theoretical perspective, is the question of the extent to which the company intended to transfer its seat. The concluding phrase in the above-quoted extract of the judgment in *Überseering*, namely the words 'irrespective of whether in that regard the company actually intended to transfer its seat', lends credence to the view advocated by proponents of the incorporation doctrine that the decision-makers in companies are competent to establish the conditions under which a company is connected to the law of a jurisdiction. The Court is therefore, perhaps inadvertently, taking a view about corporate legal theory and its relationship to the private international law of companies. The result curtails the powers of states to determine the manner in which a company is governed, and vests authority instead in the hands of corporate decision-makers. This is at odds with the Member States' concessionary approach to the corporate form and its transnational recognition, as illustrated through the inclusion of articles 44 EC (article 50 TFEU) and 293 EC. The effect of *Überseering* is therefore not only to confirm the holding in *Centros*, but also to introduce a normative foundation based on the principle of party autonomy in European conflict of corporate laws.

5.3.3 *Inspire Art*

In *Inspire Art*[77] the ECJ continued to develop the law on the basis of the reasoning that it had adopted in *Centros* and *Überseering*. Once more, the Court reiterated the restricted scope of application of the judgment in *Daily Mail* without overtly overturning the said judgment. On this occasion the Court was invited to consider the validity of outreach statutes governing pseudo-foreign corporations.[78] In view

[75] ibid para 62.

[76] *Daily Mail* (n 4) paras 21–23.

[77] *Inspire Art* (n 1).

[78] See M Andenas and F Wooldridge, *European Comparative Company Law* (Cambridge, Cambridge University Press, 2009) 97; Rammeloo (n 16) 114, and the references therein.

of earlier dicta regarding legitimate restrictions to the fundamental freedoms,[79] it was unclear whether Member States could subject recognition of pseudo-foreign corporations to compliance with mandatory rules. The litigation in *Inspire Art* concerned a UK private company that conducted business exclusively in the Netherlands by virtue of a branch in Amsterdam. The sole director of the company resided in The Hague. The dispute concerned a Dutch outreach statute that required that the company should be registered as a formally foreign company, the consequences of which would be the imposition of further legal requirements upon the company. In default of registration as such, Dutch law provided that the director of the company would be jointly and severally liable with the company.[80] The law at issue did not deny recognition to the pseudo-foreign corporation, but pierced the corporate veil in default of registration as such. Thus freedom of establishment was not denied; the controversy concerned the extent to which the said freedom was made less attractive.

The convoluted development of the relevant case law allowed the parties to refer to conflicting precedent in support of their opposite arguments. The Netherlands argued that article 293 had the effect of limiting the competence of the Community in matters relating to private international law. Its arguments were supported by the governments of Germany, Austria and Italy, all real seat states. The German and Austrian governments made representations to the effect that the freedom of establishment contemplated in the Treaty was not intended as a conflict of laws principle that enabled 'brass-plate companies' to operate in other Member States. Rather, 'as a matter of principle the purpose of Articles 43 and 48 EC [articles 49 TFEU and 54 TFEU], as regards freedom to set up branches, is to enable undertakings carrying on activities in one Member State to achieve growth in another Member State, which is not so in the case of brass-plate companies.'[81] Had this argument been accepted, the Court would have effectively reverted to the position articulated in *Daily Mail* whereby the private international law of companies would remain within the reserved competence of the Member States. However, the Court persisted in distinguishing between the conflicting precedents by drawing attention to the differing substance of the cases. The Court recalled in particular that *Daily Mail* addressed the relations between a company and the Member State under the laws of which it had been established, whereas in *Inspire Art* 'the national court has asked the Court of Justice whether the legislation of the State where a company actually carries on its activities applies to that company when it was formed under the law of another Member State.'[82]

The parties and the interveners in the case did not overtly request that the Court overturn the ruling in *Centros*. Rather, it was submitted that the said judgment enabled Member States to prevent the fraudulent evasion of national rules through the superimposition of obligations over and above the law of incorporation, albeit

[79] *Centros* (n 1) para 38.
[80] *Inspire Art* (n 1) para 25.
[81] ibid para 84.
[82] ibid para 103.

without denying the company recognition.[83] Accordingly, the crux of the argument against further liberalisation was that outreach statutes are not incompatible with the Treaty as interpreted in *Centros*, so long as a pseudo-foreign corporation is recognised and enabled to carry on business. In this construct, freedom of establishment is not an unlimited right, but one that is subject to imperative requirements of the host state in respect of corporations that are foreign only insofar as the legal fiction of their act of incorporation is concerned. Further, it was emphasised that the outreach statute at issue was not discriminatory because it merely rendered stakeholder-protection laws that were applicable to Dutch companies equally applicable to pseudo-foreign corporations.[84] As against this position, the defendant in the main proceedings, the government of the United Kingdom and the Commission, submitted that the relevant legislation rendered the exercise of freedom of establishment less attractive.[85] The Court found in favour of the arguments submitted in support of Inspire Art Ltd and pronounced that the law at issue impeded the exercise of freedom of establishment.[86] The only room that the Court left for Member States to control fraud was on a case-by-case basis,[87] a somewhat opaque position that leaves little, if any, room for Member States to protect the interests of the stakeholders recognised in their company laws against abuse of EU law by brass-plate companies – it is hard to fathom a system whereby a public authority could prevent fraud on a case-by-case basis without a legislative basis which applies across the board.

Following the judgments in *Centros*, *Überseering* and *Inspire Art*, the question of the status of the connecting factors in article 48 EC (article 54 TFEU) appeared to have been laid to rest. What is more, *Inspire Art* served to entrench the distinction between corporate immigration and emigration by restating the revised ratio for the judgment in *Daily Mail*. The Court had consistently ruled that legislative authority was merely facultative. It added that the powers conferred by the EC Treaty were limited to the necessity for agreement where articles 43 and 48 EC (articles 49 and 54 TFEU) did not resolve the difficulties of divergent conflict of corporate laws legislation. It also held that limitations to freedom of establishment may only be adopted for the prevention of fraud on a case-by-case basis. The net effect is the importation of the American internal affairs doctrine which requires that the only state which is entitled to regulate the organisation of companies is the state under whose laws the company is incorporated.[88] This can be limited only under extremely stringent conditions.

[83] ibid paras 86–88; see *Centros* (n 1) para 38.
[84] *Inspire Art* (n 1) para 82.
[85] ibid paras 92–93.
[86] ibid para 101.
[87] ibid para 105.
[88] See Restatement (Second) of Conflict of Laws § 302; C Kersting, 'Corporate Choice of Law – A Comparison of The United States and European Systems and a Proposal for a European Directive' (2002) *Brooklyn Journal of International Law* 1, 3–6; RM Buxbaum, 'The Origins of the American "Internal Affairs" Doctrine Rule in the Corporate Conflict of Laws' in HJ Musielak and K Schurig (eds), *Festschrift für Gerhard Kegel* (Berlin, Kohlhammer, 1987) 75–76; NP Beveridge, 'The Internal Affairs Doctrine: The Proper Law of a Corporation' (1989) *The Business Lawyer* 693, 693–94.

5.3.4 *de Lasteyrie du Saillant*, *Marks and Spencer*, and *Cadbury Schweppes*

The 'second wave' of liberalising judgments of the Court of Justice were hailed by some as the wave of judgments that 'would break firms out of their prisons'.[89] The judgments in *de Lasteyrie du Saillant*,[90] *Marks and Spencer*,[91] and *Cadbury Schweppes*[92] concern fiscal policies that acted as barriers to the enjoyment of freedom of establishment. The judgments provided indications of the Court's thinking with regard to companies' freedom to emigrate from one Member State to another. However, the argument that these judgments struck down the final barriers to corporate mobility was rash, since none of the judgments address *Daily Mail* or the question of a company's relationship to its state of incorporation explicitly. Indeed, the later judgment in *Cartesio* reiterated the view expressed in *Daily Mail* that companies are creatures of national law and that it is for national law to determine the factors which connect a company to a jurisdiction.[93] Accordingly, the judgments which are considered in this section are best viewed as further evidence of case law that sends mixed signals to stakeholders.

The case of *de Lasteyrie du Saillant* concerned a French law that required shareholders who were resident in France to pay taxes on capital gains that had not yet been realised, in the event that they wished to transfer their residence to another Member State. AG Mischo took the view that the laws at issue were discriminatory and impinged upon the capacity of shareholders to transfer their residence, particularly in view of the fact that they were expected to make payments on profits that had not been realised, and for which they therefore did not necessarily have the available funds as they would if the relevant profits were not prospective.[94] The Court concurred with the Advocate General's approach and concluded that the taxation of latent profits could not be a justifiable restriction on freedom of establishment. Of particular note is the Court's statement that Member States may not hinder the establishment of their nationals in another Member State:

> Even if, like the other provisions concerning freedom of establishment, Article 43 EC [article 49 TFEU] is, according to its terms, aimed particularly at ensuring that foreign nationals are treated in the host Member State in the same way as nationals of that State,

[89] B Angelette, 'The Revolution that Never Came and the Revolution Coming – *De Lasteyrie du Salliant, Marks & Spencer, Sevic Systems* and the Changing Corporate Law in Europe' (2006) *Virginia Law Review* 1189, 1205–6.

[90] Case C-9/02 *Hughes de Lasteyrie du Saillant v Ministère de l'Économie, des Finances et de l'Industrie* [2004] ECR I-2409.

[91] Case C-446/03 *Marks & Spencer plc v David Halsey (Her Majesty's Inspector of Taxes)* [2005] ECR I-10837.

[92] Case C-196/04 *Cadbury Schweppes plc, Cadbury Schweppes Overseas Ltd v Commissioners of Inland Revenue* [2006] I-7995.

[93] *Cartesio* (n 1) paras 108–10.

[94] AG Mischo in *de Lasteyrie du Saillant* (n 90) paras 32–40.

> it also prohibits the Member State of origin from hindering the establishment in another Member State of one of its own nationals.[95]

When applied to legal persons, the logical consequence of the judgment in *de Lasteyrie du Saillant* is that Member States may not impose fiscal barriers to the emigration of companies. However, this reasoning assumes the existence of a right to emigration for companies. The Court's most recent judgment in *Cartesio* rejected the notion on the grounds that corporations are presently creatures of national law.[96] The Commission has suggested that legislation should be adopted to allow companies to transfer their seat without the need of being wound up.[97] Later judgments that refer to *Daily Mail* have all confirmed the passages of the judgment concerning the relationship between a company and the state in which it is incorporated. Nevertheless, *de Lasteyrie du Saillant* may be contrasted with *Daily Mail* in that the later judgment emphatically affirms that Member States may not erect barriers to the right of establishment on the basis of prospective taxation, albeit with reference to natural persons rather than legal persons.[98] If *Daily Mail* is viewed as a tax-law case, this may be viewed as a considerable departure from previous doctrine. However, the better view is that *de Lasteyrie du Saillant* does not address the crucial question of the relationship of legal persons to their state of incorporation.[99] *Daily Mail* therefore remains good law, although it does appear that *de Lasteyrie du Saillant* could offer a possible basis for the Court of Justice to revisit the validity of the dicta in *Daily Mail*.[100]

Marks & Spencer concerned United Kingdom legislation which allowed a company incorporated in the United Kingdom to deduct losses made by its local subsidiaries from its taxable profits, but did not accord the same benefit to losses made by non-resident subsidiaries.[101] Profits made by non-resident subsidiaries were only taxable if they were generated from economic activity in the United Kingdom. The Court found that the discrimination as between losses incurred by local and foreign subsidiaries discouraged companies from exercising their freedom of establishment and was therefore in breach of the Treaty. The judgment is particularly noteworthy in that it strikes down practices that indirectly hinder companies' enjoyment of freedom of establishment, as opposed to the earlier judgments which addressed practices that were found to constitute a more direct restriction of freedom of establishment. Thus *Marks & Spencer* could have been to corporate law what *Dassonville*[102] is to the free movement of goods.[103]

[95] *de Lasteyrie du Saillant* (n 90) para 42.

[96] *Cartesio* (n 1) paras 108–10.

[97] Commission (EC), 'An area of freedom, security and justice serving the citizen' (Communication) COM (09) 262 final, 14.

[98] Angelette (n 89) 1208.

[99] Ringe (n 48) 640.

[100] See AG Maduro in *Cartesio Oktató és Szolgáltató bt* (n 1) para 25.

[101] *Marks & Spencer* (n 91).

[102] Case 8-74 *Procureur du Roi v Benoît and Gustave Dassonville* [1974] ECR 837.

[103] Angelette (n 89) 1217–18.

The litigation in *Cadbury Schweppes* also addressed the United Kingdom's treatment of the taxation of groups of companies and discrimination as between resident and non-resident subsidiaries.[104] Whereas profits of resident subsidiaries were not included in the parent company's taxable income, profits of non-resident controlled companies were taxable in the United Kingdom if they were subject to a lower level of taxation in the state in which the subsidiaries were established. The government of the United Kingdom argued that this distinction was intended to prevent resident parent companies from avoiding taxation by offloading profits generated in the United Kingdom to its foreign subsidiaries in order to avoid the higher rates of corporate taxation which were applicable in the UK. Thus the net result was that profits generated by resident and non-resident subsidiaries were taxable on an equal pegging. The Court emphasised that 'a national measure restricting freedom of establishment may be justified where it specifically relates to wholly artificial arrangements aimed at circumventing the application of the legislation of the Member State concerned'.[105] This was in keeping with earlier dicta in *de Lasteyrie du Saillant* and *Marks and Spencer*.[106] However, it differed to some extent in that the earlier judgments referred to fiscal legislation, whereas *Cadbury Schweppes* provided a blanket statement which Advocate General Maduro would later refer to in support of the prohibition of non-fiscal restrictions to freedom of establishment.[107]

5.3.5 *Sevic Systems*

Sevic Systems[108] introduced the first, and presently the only, proviso to the notion that the relationship between a company and the Member State in which it is established is not subject to articles 43 and 48 EC (articles 49 and 54 TFEU). The litigation concerned the legality of the refusal by the court of a Member State to register a cross-border merger. German law provided that mergers could only be registered as between companies formed under German law. However, the merger at issue concerned the merger by acquisition by a German company of a Luxembourgish company. Accordingly, the judgment did not concern the governing law of companies directly, but addressed one of the principal motivations of European regulation of the conflict of corporate laws, namely corporate mobility.

At the time of the merger there was no European law governing cross-border mergers, as the Cross-Border Merger Directive[109] was still to be finally approved by the Community's institutions. Advocate General Tizzano opined that 'it should be recalled that the Commission has, for several years, been making efforts to

[104] *Cadbury Schweppes* (n 92).
[105] Angelette (n 89) 1217–18.
[106] *de Lasteyrie* (n 90) para 50; *Marks & Spencer* (n 91) para 57.
[107] *Cartesio* (n 1) para 29 (AG Maduro).
[108] *Sevic Systems* (n 1).
[109] Directive (EC) 2005/56 of the European Parliament and of the Council of 26 October 2005 on cross-border mergers of limited liability companies [2005] OJ L310/1.

introduce in relation to cross-border mergers a Community legal instrument that meets the needs for cooperation and consolidation between companies from different Member States.'[110] The Opinion goes on to explain that the Cross-Border Merger Directive was at an advanced stage at the time of the proceedings in *Sevic Systems*.[111] These statements are not elaborated further in the AG's opinion. One is therefore left with a curious pair of paragraphs that beg the question as to why 'it should be recalled' that legislation was in the pipeline at the time. Draft legislation has absolutely no standing before a court of law. Had the AG's Opinion cited extracts of the preamble to the draft directive in order to highlight the internal market imperative for allowing cross-border mergers,[112] it would perhaps have lent support to his argument. However, this is not the case, and it therefore appears that it was the Advocate General's view that the fact of the Commission's efforts to introduce legislation should have a bearing on the analysis of law that was actually in force. This is not to say that there is any evidence that the reasoning in the Opinion and the subsequent judgment would have reached a different conclusion had it not been for the Commission's legislative efforts – the Court's analysis is not wanting in terms of a consistent analysis of the fundamental freedoms. However, the reference to irrelevant considerations in preliminary remarks is indicative of an approach that defers to the legislative goals of the Commission, as opposed to a strict analysis of the law.

Notwithstanding the absence of any instrument governing cross-border mergers, the AG was of the view that the refusal to register such a merger constituted an unjustified restriction on a company's freedom of establishment. He argued that by taking over a Luxembourgish company, the German company would be establishing a secondary economic presence in Luxembourg, and the refusal to register the merger constituted a restriction of the German company's freedom to establish itself in another Member State.[113] By the same measure, he was of the view that the preclusion of cross-border measures constituted a barrier to access to the German market because it barred companies from other Member States from merging with established German companies as a means to establishing themselves in that territory.[114] The Advocate General explained, and the Court concurred,[115] that:

> The instrument of merger is a particularly effective means of transforming a company in so far as it makes it possible, within the framework of a single operation, to pursue a particular activity in new forms and without interruption, thereby reducing considerably the complications, times and costs associated with other forms of company consolidation such as those which entail, for example, the dissolution of a company with liquidation of assets and the subsequent formation of a new company, the transfer of individual assets, and the exchange of title deeds, etc.[116]

[110] *Sevic* (n 1) para 7 (AG Tizzano).
[111] ibid para 8.
[112] See recital 1.
[113] ibid para 35.
[114] ibid para 50.
[115] *Sevic Systems* (n 1) para 21.
[116] *Sevic Systems* (n 1) para 47 (AG Tizzano).

Having found that mergers are an effective means of company consolidation, particularly when compared to the option of liquidation and reincorporation,[117] the Court found that discrimination between domestic and international mergers constituted a restriction of freedom of establishment.[118] Thus through an emphasis on discrimination, the judgment restricted the scope of the *Daily Mail* proviso that the relationship between a company and the Member State in which it is established is outwith the scope of the Treaty. Given that the rationale for the judgment in *Sevic Systems* was in part based on discrimination, one may have expected that in due course the *Daily Mail* proviso would be done away with altogether.

The judgment in *Sevic Systems* highlights the difficulties associated with negative harmonisation perhaps more than any of the other liberalising judgments of the Court of Justice. The Court's judgment simply stated that cross-border mergers were to be permitted by the Member States, but left unsaid the manner in which those mergers were to be conducted and how the conflict of laws as between the governing laws of the companies was to be resolved.[119] In the event, the judgment has since been superseded by the Cross-Border Merger Directive, discussed in section 4.4.1 above. However, in the interim period there was no clarity as to how, if at all, the requirements of the directive on domestic mergers were to be applied,[120] or which law should govern the rights of minority shareholders, creditors and employees.[121] Thus the Court's apparent eagerness to support the Commission's legislative agenda actually opens up a host of questions that the Court itself cannot resolve, both because those questions were not asked and because the Court cannot make good for lacunae of such fine detail, even if it were so inclined to do. This is quite clearly the case in the matter of *Sevic Systems*, and it is also the case in respect of other liberalising judgments where the Court struck down protective laws and left nothing in their place but unworkable formulae for the prevention of fraud.

5.4 *Cartesio*

5.4.1 AG Maduro's Opinion

It is quite clear that the reasoning of the Court in *Daily Mail* was at odds with the rest of the ECJ's jurisprudence, notwithstanding the Court's repeated partial confirmation of the judgment in *Daily Mail* on the basis of the peculiar facts of the said

[117] *Sevic Systems* (n 1) para 21.

[118] ibid paras 22–23.

[119] MM Siems, '*Sevic*: Beyond Cross-Border Mergers' (2007) *European Business Organization Law Review* 307, 309.

[120] Council Directive (EEC) 1978/855 of 9 October 1978 based on Article 54(3)(g) of the Treaty concerning mergers of public limited liability companies [1978] OJ L295/36.

[121] Siems (n 119) 309.

case. The reasoning in *Daily Mail* was based upon the pre-eminence of article 293 EC, and on the absence of a single connecting factor in article 48 EC (article 54 TFEU). In *Centros* and consistently thereafter, it was found that articles 43 and 48 EC (articles 49 and 54 TFEU) had direct effects and were not subject to future legislation promulgated under the authority of article 293 EC. Further, the *Daily Mail* caveat to the *Centros* doctrine also appeared to have been overturned in *Sevic Systems* where the Court appeared to overturn the adage that the relationship between a company and its state of incorporation is outwith the scope of the Treaty. However, the fact that the Court had avoided explicitly overturning *Daily Mail* left room for uncertainty, at least insofar as the restated *Daily Mail* reasoning is concerned.

The reference for a preliminary ruling in *Cartesio*[122] concerned similar facts to those at issue in *Daily Mail*, and therefore provided the Court with an opportunity to confirm or reject the earlier judgment and to truly settle its case law. In *Cartesio*, a Hungarian Court of appeal requested a ruling on the legality of a court's refusal to allow a Hungarian limited partnership to transfer its seat to Italy while remaining incorporated under Hungarian law. In accordance with the real seat theory, Hungarian law provided[123] that a company must have its operational headquarters in its state of incorporation. The similarity of the facts to those in *Daily Mail* provided the Court with an opportunity to either uphold its distinction between the legal consequences of the facts in *Daily Mail* and those in *Überseering* and *Inspire Art*, or to depart from that reasoning and adopt a more coherent approach to articles 43 and 48 EC (articles 49 and 54 TFEU).

If the *Daily Mail* approach, as revised in subsequent judgments, had been adopted, the fact that the litigation concerned the relationship between a company and its state of incorporation would render inapplicable articles 43 and 48 EC. However, Advocate General Maduro took the view that *Daily Mail* is no longer good law. He noted that efforts by the Court and others to consolidate the conflicting precedents 'were never entirely convincing'.[124] He found that, in view of the later judgments of the Court, EU law had developed since *Daily Mail*, and the thrust of subsequent judgments runs counter to the earlier ruling.[125]

Thus freed of the logical constraints that the Court has imposed upon itself in refusing to explicitly override the judgment in *Daily Mail*, the Advocate General took the view that the refusal to allow a Hungarian body corporate to transfer its operational headquarters to another Member State was incompatible with the Treaty. Relying on the more recent judgments of the Court, and in particular on their emphasis on discrimination between national and cross-border situations,

[122] *Cartesio* (n 1).

[123] Hungarian law has since been amended and the ruling will therefore have no impact on companies incorporated in Hungary. See KPMG International, 'Euro Tax Flash: Issue 90' (2008) www.kpmg.be/dbfetch/52616e646f6d495613e0c3885001ac474ddc7501a1f057e0258c22de5277b322/euro_tax_flash_2008_06_11.pdf 1.

[124] *Cartesio* (n 1) para 28 (AG Maduro).

[125] ibid para 27.

Maduro concluded that one cannot consider a company's emigration to be outwith the scope of the Treaty:

> The view that the present case falls outside the scope of the Treaty rules on the right of establishment is, in my opinion, incorrect. National rules that allow a company to transfer its operational headquarters only within the national territory clearly treat cross-border situations less favourably than purely national situations. In effect, such rules amount to discrimination against the exercise of freedom of movement.[126]

The reliance on discrimination constituted a departure from earlier distinctions of a more formal nature – namely distinctions that were premised on the fact that a company can only be born of national law and that the relationship between a company and its governing law is *sui generis*. AG Maduro's Opinion was based on reasoning that is consistent with jurisprudence concerning the maximisation of freedom of establishment. Having found authority for an effects-based approach in AG Tizzano's Opinion in *Sevic Systems*, the Opinion in *Cartesio* explores the practical effects of restrictions on corporate mobility:[127] 'an intra-Community transfer of operational headquarters may be a simple and effective form of taking up genuine economic activities in another Member State without having to face the costs and the administrative burdens inherent in first having to wind up the company in its country of origin and then having to resurrect it completely in the Member State of destination.'[128] The Advocate General argued that, in the context of the current state of EU law, that is in the state of the law as developed by the Court of Justice, it is not tenable to argue that Member States retain absolute control over the life and death of companies constituted under their laws. The alternative would be to allow Member States to deny the benefits of freedom of establishment to companies incorporated in their territories, and to impose a 'death sentence' on companies that had decided to exercise that freedom.[129] Thus in the Advocate General's view, EU law drastically limits the effects of the concessionary principle that dictates that companies are creatures of the law of the state under whose laws they are established; freedom of establishment severs the umbilical chord that binds a company to the state that gave birth to the company and renders its continuing existence dependent upon the said state.

The AG's Opinion also suggested a new approach to the limits within which Member States may act to prevent abuse of a company's right to freedom of establishment. Citing *Cadbury Schweppes*, the AG suggested that Member States were in fact entitled to be 'wary of "letter box" or "front" companies'. He noted that the Court 'also emphasised that Member States may take measures to prevent "wholly artificial arrangements, which do not reflect economic reality" and which are aimed at circumventing national legislation.'[130] Maduro observed, correctly it is submitted, that 'this represents a significant qualification of the rulings in *Centros*

[126] ibid para 25.
[127] ibid para 28.
[128] ibid para 31.
[129] ibid.
[130] ibid para 29.

and *Inspire Art*.'[131] Had the Court of Justice accepted this restriction, qualified though it was by subsequent references to the Court's limited acceptance of pleas based on abuse of Community rights,[132] this would have merely added a further dimension to the lack of certainty that emanates from the Court's judgments.

Moreover, the Opinion proposed a potential safeguard for Member States, which, had it been endorsed by the Court, would have been costly in terms of its diminution of legal certainty:

> it may be acceptable for a Member State to set certain conditions before a company constituted under its own national company law can transfer its operational headquarters abroad. It might, for instance, be possible for the Member State to consider that it will no longer be able to exercise any effective control over the company and, therefore, to require that the company amends its constitution and ceases to be governed by the full measure of the company law under which it was constituted.[133]

The qualification is worrisome on two levels. First, as is often the norm in the dicta of the ECJ, a reference to 'certain conditions' simply invites Member States to test the limits of what those conditions might be, deferring precise definition to future litigation which would, no doubt, result from such an unclear condition, and which would be costly. In support of this contention, Maduro cited article 8 of the SE Statute which stipulates the procedural requirements for the transfer of an SE's seat and a change in its governing law.[134] The Commission supported this view in its submissions to the Court.[135] The suggestion that legislation governing a supranational business vehicle should be applicable mutatis mutandis to national business vehicles is, however, manifestly flawed. The SE may provide a template for legislative intervention, but it is not of itself applicable to cross-border transfers of the seat of national companies.[136] What is more, the SE statute refers to seat transfers which are accompanied by changes in the governing law of companies, a situation unlike that in *Cartesio* where the Hungarian entity wished to retain its Hungarian nationality.[137] Accordingly, the Advocate General's suggestion would in fact operate in the absence of legislation of direct relevance.

The second difficulty, which is closely associated with the first, relates to the suggestion that the governing law of a company may be subjected to bifurcation. This is not an intrinsically unreasonable approach by any measure, if that is in fact what the Advocate General meant by 'to require that the company amends its constitution and ceases to be governed by the full measure of the company law under which it was constituted'.[138] Maduro's suggestion is somewhat fanciful

[131] ibid.

[132] ibid.

[133] ibid para 33.

[134] Council Regulation (EC) 2157/2001 on the statute for a European company (SE) [2001] OJ L294/1.

[135] *Cartesio* (n 1) paras 115–16.

[136] ibid paras 117–20.

[137] ibid.

[138] Extra-curial writings by the Judge-Rapporteur in *Cartesio* suggest that he understood Maduro's recommendation to refer to a change in the company's governing law: Timmermans (n 33) 555–56.

because it operates in a legislative vacuum. It emanates from an institution with no legislative initiative, whereas it would require legislative action at a supranational level. Implementation would require Member States other than the state of incorporation to assent to the company being governed in part by their own laws. In addition, it is not immediately apparent how requiring a company to be governed in part by foreign law would make the relationship between that company and its state of incorporation any less tenuous, in the absence of a system of cooperation between Member States. Quite the contrary might be true in that, in the absence of formal mechanisms for cooperation between incorporating authorities, the incorporating authority would be less equipped to ensure compliance with norms with which it is unfamiliar. In sum, the novel suggestion put forward by the AG may be valid in a legislative forum where Member States devise an instrument of cooperation between authorities, but if it were to become law by virtue of a judgment, this would add a further dimension to a prevalent lack of certainty and would therefore be costly.

The Advocate General's Opinion is also open to criticism because it is devoid of any sustained analysis of the primary source of EU law, namely the Treaty. In the analysis of the limitation of State powers the Opinion takes the Court's case law as its point of departure, never once referring directly to the underlying controversy concerning the interpretation of the relationship between article 293 EC and the fundamental freedoms.[139] It is submitted that from a formal perspective, the Opinion was therefore severely flawed in that it treated judgments of the Court as though they were the only primary sources of law, and disregards the Treaty, which ought to form the basis of the Opinion.

However, aside from the qualifications that Maduro adds to his main findings, the effort to replace the internal contradictions in the case law with a clear direction is commendable. If the Court had followed the reasoning of the Advocate General, it would have marked a welcome break from the convoluted precedents that have led to a somewhat incoherent body of law that is difficult to understand from a systemic perspective.

5.4.2 The Court's Judgment[140]

Despite the seemingly inexorable momentum of the *Centros* doctrine,[141] the ECJ chose to re-examine its case law in quite a different manner to what one might

However, this does not sit comfortably with the Court's dismissal of Maduro's suggestion on the basis of the fact that *Cartesio* concerned a seat transfer without a change in the governing law at paras 115–20 of the judgment.

[139] See AG Maduro in *Cartesio* (n 1) paras 29–30.

[140] This section is based on parts of a published article by the author: J Borg-Barthet, 'European Private International Law of Companies after *Cartesio*' (2009) *International and Comparative Law Quarterly* 1020, 1024–27. The author gratefully acknowledges the editorial remarks of Prof Peter McEleavy.

[141] See FJ Garcimartín Alférez, 'Cross-Border Listed Companies' (2007) 328 *Recueil des Cours de l'Académie de Droit International* 13, 67–68.

have expected.[142] The Court concluded that a Member State may indeed require that a company incorporated under its laws must retain its operational headquarters within its territory. The judgment relies heavily on the dicta in *Daily Mail*, which, notwithstanding the similarity of the facts in the two cases, is somewhat surprising, given the judgment in *Sevic Systems*. The judgment in *Cartesio* is also surprising because it engages in reasoning that contradicts much of the case law that appeared to be settled.

5.4.2.1 The Status of the Connecting Factors in article 54 TFEU

When considering the equivalence of the connecting factors in article 48 EC (article 54 TFEU), the Court relied on its reasoning in *Daily Mail*, rather than contradictory reasoning in the later *Centros* judgment. In *Centros* the Court had concluded that 'The location of [a company's] registered office, central administration or principal place of business serves as the connecting factor with the legal system of a particular state in the same way as does nationality in the case of a natural person.'[143] Consequently, the Court was of the view that the existence of any of the connecting factors would suffice to trigger the application of freedom of establishment. In *Cartesio* the equivalence of the connecting factors was seen in a very different light.[144] In relying on dicta in *Daily Mail*,[145] the Court concluded that the equivalence of the connecting factors indicated that there was no preference for any of the connecting factors, and the applicable connecting factor was to be determined by future legislation.[146] The implication of equivalence is therefore viewed in diametrically opposed fashions. *Centros* viewed that equivalence as permissive of the fundamental freedoms in the event of the existence of any of the connecting factors; *Daily Mail* and *Cartesio* deemed the equivalence to be a denial of direct effects.[147]

The Court observed that the right to transfer a company's seat was subject to the adoption of future legislation under articles 44(2)(g) EC (article 50(2)(g) TFEU) and 293 EC, as stated in *Daily Mail*, rather than a directly effective right emanating from the Treaty. The qualifying effects of articles 44 and 293 EC had been omitted from the considerations in *Centros*[148] and explicitly contradicted in *Überseering*, where the Court had held that article 293 EC did not constitute a reserve of legislative competence in the Member States, but only empowered them to adopt legislation to facilitate the attainment of the ends of the Treaty.[149] Further, such legislation could only be adopted so far as might be necessary to resolve discrepancies in national laws that had not been resolved directly by the Treaty.[150] *Cartesio* returned

[142] AW Wisniewski and A Opalski, 'Companies' Freedom of Establishment after the ECJ *Cartesio* Judgment' (2009) *European Business Organization Law Review* 595, 602.
[143] *Centros* (n 1) para 20.
[144] *Cartesio* (n 1) paras 106–9.
[145] *Daily Mail* (n 4) para 21.
[146] *Cartesio* (n 1) para 106.
[147] *Daily Mail* (n 4) paras 21–23; *Cartesio* (n 1) para 109.
[148] See AG Colomer in *Überseering* (n 1) paras 35–40.
[149] *Überseering* (n 1) para 54.
[150] ibid.

to the earlier position enunciated in *Daily Mail.* Having found that the existence of freedom of establishment could not be inferred directly from the Treaty in the event of the existence of any one of the three connecting factors, the Court concluded that Member States retained the power to decide the connecting factor that was required for a company to be established and to continue to exist under their laws. However, the judgment failed to refer to the relevant tracts of the contradictory judgments – there was no explicit overturning of *Centros* and *Überseering* that could lead one to the incontrovertible conclusion that a new precedent had been set. One is therefore left at a loss as to the circumstances in which articles 49 and 54 TFEU are directly applicable.

5.4.2.2 A Distinction between Emigration and Immigration: the Internal Affairs Doctrine by Another Name

The limitation of the direct effects of article 48 EC (article 54 TFEU) in relation to emigration begs the question as to why the *Centros* doctrine remains valid at all. If articles 44(2)(g) EC (article 50(2)(g) TFEU) and 293 EC qualified the effects of articles 43 and 48 EC (articles 49 and 54 TFEU) in relation to emigration, why then does a Member State not also retain the power to determine the extent to which companies incorporated abroad should be recognised?

The Court's answer is, of course, to be found in the *Daily Mail* ratio, as revised in *Überseering* – companies incorporated in a Member State must be recognised throughout the Union, but the relationship between a company and its state of incorporation is outwith the scope of the Treaty.[151] Thus the emphasis of the Court has moved towards the power of Member States to grant legal personality to companies and to regulate them thereafter. The Member States' powers are enforced through the concomitant obligation to recognise companies incorporated under, and governed by, foreign law. Freedom of corporate establishment therefore becomes a matter of comity among Member States, rather than one of rights of legal persons. This is redolent of the internal affairs doctrine that permeates American choice of law, a doctrine that has no clear authority in the Treaty.

The focus on the rights and obligations of states renders the net effect of the Court's judgments all the more questionable. Freedom of establishment is intended to benefit individuals and legal persons. Nowhere in the relevant articles of the Treaty is there any mention of administrative comity among states. It is therefore surprising that comity should become the only pervasive principle in the Court's jurisprudence. Mutual recognition was only mentioned in article 293 EC as a matter which was subject to future legislation. In addition, given the declared equivalence of the connecting factors in article 48 EC (article 54 TFEU), if states rather than persons are at the core of the Court's reasoning, it would perhaps be more logical to regulate immigration of pseudo-foreign companies than emigration, since the state interest in the former is far stronger than in the latter.

[151] See *Cartesio* (n 1) paras 121–23.

The insistence on emphasising an internal affairs doctrine that finds no authority in the Treaty compelled the Court to flawed reasoning. In order to maintain the internal affairs doctrine without reversing any earlier judgments, the Court had to distinguish *Cartesio* from *Sevic Systems*. It found that *Sevic Systems* related to the relationship between a Member State and a company connected to another jurisdiction. This is true to the extent that the question referred by the German court related to the right of a Luxembourgish company to be absorbed by a German company.[152] However, it was the acquiring German company which had applied for the registration of the merger,[153] and which objected to its refusal.[154] In *Cartesio* the Court returned to reliance on the facts of a case, arguably skewing them in the process, rather than relying on the reasoning itself:

> *SEVIC Systems* concerned the recognition, in the Member State of incorporation of a company, of an establishment operation carried out by that company in another Member State by means of a cross-border merger, which is a situation fundamentally different from the circumstances at issue in the case which gave rise to *Daily Mail and General Trust*, but similar to the situations considered in [*Centros*, *Überseering* and *Inspire Art*].[155]

Had the court relied on the reasoning in *Sevic Systems*, its point of departure would have been a question of discrimination.[156] *Sevic Systems* adopted a classic fundamental freedoms analysis that explores whether there is a restriction to the fundamental freedoms and, if so, whether that restriction is justified.[157] The existence of a restriction to freedom of establishment by the Court was partly founded on the fact of discrimination between domestic and cross-border mergers.[158] By the same measure, discrimination as between the transfer of a company's seat within a jurisdiction and cross-border seat-transfers is prima facie an unjustified restriction of freedom of establishment.[159] However, in *Cartesio*, reliance on the facts of *Sevic Systems* allowed an approach that essentially distinguishes between immigration and emigration. This is reminiscent of the revisionist approach to the judgment in *Daily Mail*, a worrying approach to judicial law-making that does little for legal certainty.

This approach is flawed not only because the legal principle espoused therein discriminates between like situations and as such continues to be at odds with the general body of jurisprudence dealing with the fundamental freedoms.[160] It is also flawed because, notwithstanding the manner in which the question was framed by the referring court, the facts in *Sevic Systems* deal with the relationship between the German court and the German acquiring company, rather than the German court and the Luxembourgish company which was absorbed through the merger. It is

[152] *Sevic Systems* (n 1) para 10.
[153] ibid para 2.
[154] ibid para 8.
[155] ibid para 122.
[156] See AG Maduro in *Cartesio* (n 1) para 25.
[157] *Sevic Systems* (n 1) paras 20–31.
[158] ibid paras 20–23.
[159] See AG Maduro in *Cartesio* (n 1) para 25.
[160] ibid.

likely that this minor inconsistency will be noted by practitioners seeking to instigate further revision of the case law on the basis of the discrimination test.

5.4.2.3 *Reincorporation: Cartesio's Unprompted Innovation*

Cartesio introduces one major innovation that may appease proponents of liberalisation who might have been disappointed by the general thrust of the judgment. The Court contrasts the facts of the case with a situation where the company wishes to change its governing law in the process of transferring its headquarters. In the latter case, the Court found that a Member State may not restrict a company's emigration from its territory by requiring the winding-up of the company.[161] However, Member States may restrict relocation if the restriction is justified on the basis of 'overriding requirements in the public interest', subject to the stringent proportionality test.[162] The logic of this distinction lies in the fact that, by electing to change its governing law in the process of emigrating, the company frees itself of its dependence on its governing law and the connecting factors prescribed therein.[163] In a perhaps vain attempt to settle all potential future questions, the Court here answered a question that was not asked of it, namely that of reincorporation under a different national law without the need for winding up. However, it left unanswered the academic question of whether a company could change its governing law without relocating its headquarters, although the Court's reasoning suggests that this should be possible given that the company would equally be breaking the connecting factor between itself and its governing law.

5.5 The Present State of EU Law

Where legislators have failed, the ECJ has shown only fleeting reluctance in harmonising conflicts of corporate laws.[164] In essence, the plethora of questions

[161] *Cartesio* (n 1) paras 111–12.

[162] ibid para 113. In support of potential justifications based on overriding requirements in the public interest, the Court cited paras 7 and 11 of Case C-442/02 *CaixaBank France v Ministére de l'Économie* [2004] ECR I-8961. It should be noted, however, that in that judgment, the repudiated measure failed the proportionality test: paras 17–24. Similarly, in the *Viking* case, in which a trade union attempted to take industrial action to prevent the reflagging of a Finnish vessel to Estonia, 'overriding justifications in the public interest' failed the proportionality test. The conflict between the fundamental freedoms and the fundamental right to collective action highlights the limited scope for justifications to the fundamental freedoms: Case C-438/05 *International Transport Workers' Federation v Viking Line ABP* [2007] ECR I-10779. See J Malmberg and T Sigeman, 'Industrial Actions and EU Economic Freedoms: the Autonomous Collective Bargaining Model Curtailed by the European Court of Justice' (2008) *Common Market Law Review* 1115, 1115–46; P Syrpis and T Novitz, 'Political and Social Rights in Conflict: Political and Judicial Approaches to their Reconciliation' (2008) *European Law Review* 411, 411–26; A Hinarejos, '*Laval* and *Viking*: the right to collective action versus fundamental freedoms' (2008) *Human Rights Law Review* 714, 714–29. For further academic commentary on the proportionality test, see C Barnard, *The Substantive Law of the EU: The Four Freedoms,* 3rd edn (Oxford, Oxford University Press, 2010) 516, 516–18 and the references therein.

[163] *Cartesio* (n 1) para 112.

[164] *Daily Mail* (n 4).

that have been referred to the ECJ can be boiled down to just one issue: do articles 49 and 54 TFEU (articles 43 and 48 EC) confer directly effective rights upon legal persons, or is the enjoyment of freedom of establishment dependent upon the adoption of future legislation? Unfortunately, the answers provided by the Court are far too nuanced, and contradictory, for a single sentence to suffice in response. The difficulty is compounded by the fact that article 293 EC has been repealed by the Treaty of Lisbon. In a recently published article, former Judge Timmermans, the Judge-Rapporteur in *Cartesio*, reaffirmed the historical importance of article 293 EC to the Court's analysis of the connecting factors in article 54 TFEU.[165] It is unclear whether the Court's dicta concerning the equivalence of the connecting factors in article 54 TFEU must now be read in a different light.

Judgments of the ECJ, most notably the seminal judgment in *Centros*,[166] have limited the extent to which protective laws may be applied in Europe, principally because non-recognition of pseudo-foreign companies incorporated in another Member State is deemed to unjustifiably limit freedom of establishment.[167] In its present state, EU law guarantees that a company incorporated in a Member State must be recognised throughout the Union, provided that it has any of its registered office, central administration or principal place of business in a Member State,[168] subject only to the nebulous notion of the prevention of fraud on a case-by-case basis.[169] Besides formal recognition of companies as legal persons, Member States must recognise the law of the state of incorporation as the governing law of the company, and they may not impose further obligations on pseudo-foreign corporations or their officers.[170] Member States must also allow companies governed by their laws to merge with companies governed by the laws of other Member States.[171] Further, they may not prevent a seat transfer accompanied by a change of a company's governing law, provided that this is possible under the law of the Member State whose laws the company wishes to adopt, and subject also to the limited public interest exception.[172] Hence, the emergence of a market-driven conflicts regime.

Notwithstanding the ECJ's judgments, and indeed sometimes because of them, the tensions between liberalism and protectionism remain unresolved to this day. First, Member States retain the right to dictate the situation of the operational headquarters of companies governed by their laws.[173] This has been framed in unfortunate terms that place the relationship between a company and the Member State in which it is incorporated beyond the scope of freedom of establishment.[174]

[165] Timmermans 2010 (n 33) 554.
[166] *Centros* (n 1).
[167] *Centros* (n 1); *Überseering* (n 1); *Inspire Art Ltd* (n 1).
[168] *Centros* (n 1); *Überseering* (n 1).
[169] *Inspire Art* (n 1) para 105.
[170] ibid para 101.
[171] *Sevic Systems* (n 1).
[172] *Cartesio* (n 1) paras 111–113.
[173] *Daily Mail* (n 4); *Cartesio* (n 1).
[174] *Überseering* (n 1) para 62.

Moreover, there exist a number of conflicting precedents regarding the role of legislation,[175] while a reluctance to overturn earlier judgments leaves the law in a constant state of flux.[176] Indeed, the relatively simple schema set out in the immediately foregoing paragraph masks the truth of the convolution that permeates the ECJ's case law. Some aspects of the Court's reasoning are internally incoherent, to such an extent that it has become impossible to discern a cogent line of thought.[177] The Court has stated that article 293 EC vested legislative competence in the Member States,[178] that the article was relevant only insofar as the Treaty does not confer rights directly,[179] while on other occasions the Court has ignored article 293 EC altogether.[180] The Court has considered corporate mobility from the perspective of a classic analysis of the fundamental freedoms in some judgments,[181] from the perspective of discrimination in others,[182] and on other occasions from the perspective of administrative comity.[183] The equivalence of the connecting factors in article 48 EC (article 54 TFEU) has been deemed to trigger freedom of establishment in the event of the presence of any of them,[184] whereas the Treaty's employment of three connecting factors has been deemed to leave the choice to secondary legislation in other judgments.[185] The Court did not adopt these divergent approaches in a manner suggesting an implicit overturning of precedent, but swayed between the various positions. The reasoning is so inconsistent that there can be little doubt that further references will ensue.

Moreover, if one attaches importance to the historical development of the law,[186] the Court's reference to article 293 EC in the most recent judgment in *Cartesio* may call aspects of the case law into question, now that the Treaty of Lisbon has come into force and the said article is repealed. Given that authority to legislate remains in article 50(2)(g) and article 81 TFEU (articles 44(2)(g) and 65 EC), albeit indirectly, the conflicting signals may still be relevant in the absence of article 293 EC. It is arguable that article 54 TFEU (article 48 EC) should now be read without qualification. However, the better view is that dicta to the effect that a company is a creature of State law and dependent on the state under whose law it is constituted for its continued existence,[187] and consequently cannot benefit from absolute freedom without further legislation, remain relevant even in the absence of article 293 EC. Still, the removal of article 293 does not resolve the

[175] Contrast *Daily Mail* (n 4) paras 23–25 with *Centros* (n 1).

[176] By way of example, the Court relies on restating and revising the rationale of earlier judgments, rather than actually overturning precedent. Contrast *Überseering* (n 1) para 62 with *Daily Mail* (n 4); and *Cartesio* (n 1) para 122 with *Sevic Systems* (n 1).

[177] Borg-Barthet (n 140) 1024–27.

[178] *Daily Mail* (n 4).

[179] *Überseering* (n 1).

[180] *Centros* (n 1).

[181] ibid.

[182] *Sevic Systems* (n 1) para 22.

[183] *Cartesio* (n 1) paras 121–23.

[184] *Centros* (n 1) para 20.

[185] *Daily Mail* (n 4) para 21; *Cartesio* (n 1) paras 106–9.

[186] See Timmermans (n 33) 554.

[187] *Cartesio* (n 1) paras 109–10.

conflicting precedents concerning the equivalence of the connecting factors in article 54 TFEU.

5.6 Conclusions

The law as developed by the Court achieves two perceived goods, namely the maximisation of party autonomy, and the mobility of companies within the Union. Yet the Court's judgments have redefined state sovereignty and replaced shared sovereignty with horizontal transfers of sovereignty[188] which may lead to the hegemony of those states that are most willing to facilitate the incorporation of companies without encumbering incorporators with obligations that are deemed to be onerous. This is not to say that regulatory competition does not have the potential to stimulate economic growth – the lowering of costs to incorporators does, at least in theory, afford better allocation of resources in the market. Yet it most certainly is not within the competence of the Union to coerce Member States to amend their laws for the purposes of the maximisation of regulatory competition, and indeed the ECJ has on no occasion purported to address the matter of regulatory competition.

Negative harmonisation in the form of the ECJ's rulings could affect social policy concerns that do not appear to be fully appreciated in the Court's jurisprudence.[189] To some extent it is inevitable that the judiciary will not be able to attach conditions as the legislator would where it is called upon to resolve a limited matter to compensate for a legislative lacuna.[190] The conflict of corporate laws revolution disregards the principled policy motivations upon which the protective conflicts rules are premised. The said rules constitute a negation of party autonomy, inter alia on the grounds that the corporate form is a concession which is granted by states under specified conditions. A free market in corporate charters cannot be equated with the other major contributions that the ECJ has made to the harmonisation of laws and the establishment of the internal market. Here we do not have the liberalisation of a market in products or services, but the liberalisation of systems of social and economic governance. The court's judgments do not merely allow a bottle of cassis de Dijon to be displayed on the shelves of a German supermarket and to be sold as an alcoholic beverage.[191] Nor do they simply allow natural persons to enjoy equal rights as citizens of the Union. Rather, they allow incorporators to become consumers of corporate forms and, through the creation of a market for incorporations, to exploit their demand for laws that accommo-

[188] See MP Maduro, 'So Close and Yet So Far: the Paradoxes of Mutual Recognition' (2007) *Journal of European Public Policy* 814, 819.

[189] See D Komo and C Villiers, 'Are Trends in European Company Law Threatening Industrial Democracy?' (2009) *European Law Review* 175, 189–201.

[190] Wisniewski and Opalski (n 142) 621–22.

[191] See Case 120/78 *Rewe-Zentral AG v Bundesmonopolverwaltung für Branntwein* [1979] ECR 649.

date the shareholders' needs in preference to the socio-economic systems that social history and political fiat had previously preferred. Indeed, to return to the analogy with *Cassis*,[192] the *Centros* and *Inspire Art* decisions are far more akin to a hypothetical scenario where the ECJ might determine that a French supermarket chain should be allowed to sell alcoholic beverages outside France at the same times and to persons of the same ages as it would be allowed to do in France.

Notwithstanding a debatable Treaty basis and the possible extent of social repercussions occasioned by its judgments, the ECJ has charted a route that maximises party autonomy in European choice of corporate law. This is subject only to limited exceptions, principally relating to the Member States' continued ability to restrict seat transfers which are not accompanied by a change in the governing law.[193] Statistical indicators confirm the attraction of jurisdictions that liberally allow companies to be incorporated under their laws with minimal financial cost to incorporators.[194] If a state is liberal in its chartering policy and its substantive law is also accommodating of the needs of incorporators, competition theory dictates that this jurisdiction will attract incorporations in preference to jurisdictions that are less accommodating; the attraction to incorporators lies in the fact of lower costs and the attendant increase in market-access for start-up businesses that are denied the benefits of the corporate form in jurisdictions that impose onerous start-up capital and capital maintenance requirements.[195] By way of example, Switzerland has been explicit in touting business expediency as the motivation for its recent statutory adoption of the incorporation model.[196] The alternative argument, namely that jurisdictions such as Delaware which attract incorporations coincide with expert administrative and judicial services,[197] fails to account for the coincidence of those services with lower standards of protection for non-controlling stakeholders in the company. The emergence of expert human resources is not likely to be a phenomenon that is wholly unrelated to the availability of corporate clientele. What is more, it appears that the status of Delaware as the jurisdiction of choice in corporate litigation is becoming progressively weaker.[198] Whichever the better view may be, the fact remains that a free market for incorporations allows incorporators to contract in favour of the particular corporate model that best allows them to fulfil their own aspirations.

The ECJ could equally have adopted an approach that deferred to the Member States' judgment of how best to regulate socio-economic affairs in their territories, much like it has done recently in allowing states to restrict freedom to provide

[192] ibid.

[193] *Cartesio* (n 1).

[194] Becht, Mayer and Wagner (n 59) 248–55.

[195] ibid.

[196] See G Broggini, 'Regole societarie del nuovo diritto internazionale privato svizzero' in E Brem et al (eds) *Festchrift zum 65. Geburstag von Mario m. Pedrazzini* (Berne, Verlag Stämpfli, 1990) 267.

[197] R Daines, 'Does Delaware Law Improve Firm Value?' (2001) *Journal of Financial Economics* 525, 540.

[198] J Armour, B Black and C Cheffins, 'Is Delaware Losing its Cases?' ECGI Working Paper xx/2010 http:ssrn.com/abstract=1578404, 6–17.

services in the online gaming market in order to protect societal norms.[199] The prevention of vice in the regulation of gambling is no different in principle to the protection of societal goods in corporate laws. Indeed, it is arguable that the restrictions on freedom of incorporation do not create barriers to the markets of the Member States, whereas the Court's jurisprudence concerning gambling does so. Further, the ECJ had no clear Treaty basis to support restrictions in the gambling market, but could have persisted in the *Daily Mail* approach to the need for secondary legislation to clarify the standing of the connecting factors in article 48 EC (article 54 TFEU). All things considered, one might hypothesise that the ECJ may have found in its private deliberations that the diversity in Member States' substantive corporate law norms does not warrant vigorous protection, as does gambling. The Court did allow Member States to retain the connecting factors which they required of companies incorporated under their own laws,[200] but this has no bearing on corporate law itself when promoters of companies are free to select any law within the Union. The Court may have considered that the conflict of corporate laws is too important an area to allow for a reproduction of the convoluted regulatory environment that obtains in the gambling market, where the residual power of Member States to limit the freedom to provide services gives rise to great uncertainty in ascertaining which state enjoys prescriptive jurisdiction.[201]

The result of the piecemeal harmonisation of the conflict of corporate laws is a legislative landscape that is internally incoherent, a reflection of the different forces at play in the making of EU law as it stands today, as well as the realignment of policy priorities over time. Judicial development has not been accompanied, much less led, by concomitant political will. Indeed, the general scheme of the Treaty of Rome suggests that the *Centros* line of judgments is not in keeping with the intentions of several Member States, and is instead deferent to federalist ambitions.[202] The Union's legislation is often at odds with the judgments of the Court, arguably because the judgments of the Court have no roots in the collective will of the Member States as expressed in the primary and secondary legislation of the Union to which the latter have assented. By way of example, the SE statute and the revised Draft SPE Statute are far more restrictive of corporate establishment and emigration than the judgments of the Court.[203] Indeed, the full import of the judgments of the ECJ is not completely clear, particularly as regards its effects on European legislation.[204] Despite overtures by the legislature to the

[199] Case C-258/08 *Ladbrokes Betting & Gaming Ltd, Ladbrokes International Ltd v Stichting de Nationale Sporttotalisator* [2010] ECR I-0000 (nyp).

[200] *Cartesio* (n 1) paras 109–10.

[201] See A Littler, 'Regulatory Perspectives on the Future of Interactive Gambling in the Internal Market' (2008) *European Law Review* 211, 211–29; J Borg Barthet, 'Online Gambling and the Further Displacement of State Regulation: *A Note on PMU v Zeturf*' (2008) *International and Comparative Law Quarterly* 417, 417–26.

[202] On the federalist goals of the Court of Justice, see Hartley (n 3) 566.

[203] See section 4.5 above.

[204] Timmermans argues that, given that the Member States are free to choose the connecting factors required of companies incorporated under their laws, it follows that so must the Union be able to choose connecting factors: Timmermans (n 33) 557. However, this is to be contrasted with the fact that

judicial branch,[205] it appears that the two branches continue to pull in different directions. The policy considerations underpinning legislative efforts are, at times, in direct contradiction to the liberalisation for which the Court's judgments have set the course. The state of development of EU law therefore does not afford market actors with the certainty of a coherent system the import of which is clear without the necessity of recourse to the interpretative authority of the ECJ.

The tools that have been employed to date are unsatisfactory. Following the failure of the 1968 EC Convention on the Mutual Recognition of Companies and Bodies Corporate, a piecemeal approach to harmonisation has been adopted. This has allowed for the harmonisation of those areas upon which agreement can be reached, without undue distraction and gridlock in areas where fundamental disagreement would have stalled progress. Yet the lack of a grand design opens up the process of harmonisation to the accusation that it 'lacked clear objectives and a clear programme, and was therefore mainly a matter of "muddling through"'.[206] It is conceded that the present state of development is not amenable to evaluation as a final product since the relevant norms remain in flux and are but a snapshot of a particular phase in the evolution of norms that will eventually lead to a more coherent and complete regulatory environment. Nevertheless, it is submitted that the slow development that has been experienced to date provides little comfort or confidence in the continued use of a piecemeal approach that by its very nature leads to internal incoherence. Moreover, due to the peculiar nature of the EU, the development of the relevant norms has occurred in poorly integrated fora, negotiated by experts in different fields or litigated before judges who could not be asked to be mindful of norms and negotiations that are unrelated to the matters which they have been asked to resolve.

the Member States are not enabled to restrict the conditions under which they will recognise companies incorporated in other Member States on the basis of the fact that they are not incorporated in the state in which their seat is situated: WG Ringe, 'The European Company Statute in the Context of Freedom of Establishment' (2007) *Journal of Corporate Law Studies* 185, 191–98. See section 4.5.2 of this book.

[205] Directive 2005/56/EC of the European Parliament and of the Council of 26 October 2005 on cross-border mergers of limited liability companies [2005] OJ L310/1 recital 3.

[206] CWA Timmermans 'Company Law as Ius Commune?' (2002) Walter van Gerven Lecture, Leuven Centre for a Common Law of Europe www.law.kuleuven.ac.be/ccle/pdf/wvg1.pdf 2.

6

Options for Future Development

6.1 Introduction

This chapter explores a number of possible avenues for the development of the conflict of corporate laws in the European Union. As noted above, the Commission has recently invited the European Parliament and the Council to consider whether legislation concerning the governing law of companies should be introduced.[1] The Stockholm Programme includes a somewhat tentative endorsement of this suggestion: 'There is a need to explore whether common rules determining the law applicable to matters of company law . . . could be devised.'[2] It is argued in this chapter that it is possible to devise a regulation which would serve the goal of an integrated market, without denying Member States the opportunity to retain some protection of the norms which they consider most important.

The analysis in this chapter is divided into four sections. In Section 6.2 the present trajectory of the law is addressed. It is concluded inter alia that the development of the law does not properly account for genuine State interests in the protection of their corporate law doctrines. Having found that the present direction of legal development is unsatisfactory, section 6.3 briefly considers a return to the state of affairs antecedent to *Centros*. This too is found to be unsatisfactory, both in practice and in principle. Section 6.4 briefly addresses the possibility of unifying corporate law, whether by increments or through a single measure. It is found that this is an unlikely project that would stagnate the development of corporate law if ever it were taken on. Finally, section 6.5 elaborates a proposal for a new regulatory framework which would build upon elements of the liberalisation of corporate law, but which also rolls back some elements of the liberalisation by limitedly catering for the inclusion of interests that Member States may wish to protect. It is concluded that imaginative compromises, coupled with the use of information technology, may allow for the adoption of a new conflicts regime that is acceptable to all Member States, without being too burdensome from an administrative perspective or harmful to legal certainty.

[1] Commission (EC), 'An area of freedom, security and justice serving the citizen' (Communication) COM (09) 262 final, 14.

[2] Council of the European Union, 'The Stockholm Programme – An open and secure Europe serving and protecting the citizens' Document 17024/09, 33.

6.2 Option 1: the Status Quo

In order to justify any significant changes in the law, it is necessary to demonstrate that the law which is presently in force is not fit for purpose, or that the chosen vehicles for the development of the law are inadequate.

To date, the market has been the main driving force for legal reform. Entrepreneurs who wished to benefit from freedom of establishment have, generally, found a sympathetic Court of Justice which has maximised market freedoms in preference to the concerns of some Member States. From the perspective of the establishment of the internal market, this has certainly been positive. What is more, the judicial development of the law does away with the need to strike compromises, which led to poor legislative solutions in the Hague and EC Conventions, both of which are now dead letters. The regulations and directives of the EU also include a number of poor compromises which have led to the adoption of ineffective instruments. By way of example, the SE Regulation produced a business vehicle which few market actors wished to use, and this after 40 years of negotiation. Indeed, one might speculate that the Commission's decision to abandon the proposed Fourteenth Company Law Directive may have been motivated by the fact that law-making in the EU is a difficult process, which is often unrewarding.[3]

However, negative harmonisation has not been flawless. As was shown in Chapter 5, some of the ECJ's judgments contradict one another, while others are revisionist and misrepresent the ratio of earlier judgments. The unclear signals which the Court is broadcasting are harmful to legal certainty and may be costly to the market. In fact, despite a palpable movement towards liberalising the conflict of corporate laws to allow corporate decision-makers to freely select a company's governing law, there are also some instances where the Court has been cautious.[4] This has surprised the market, which had expected the ECJ to continue to develop the case law with a view to allowing the greatest enjoyment of the fundamental freedoms.[5] On the other hand, the Court's efforts to elaborate the fundamental freedoms in *Cartesio*[6] and *Sevic Systems*[7] shows that the Court will occasionally strike down the laws of the Member States and leave a legislative vacuum in their place.[8] Indeed, it is quite clear that negative harmonisation alone is insufficient when coordination of the laws is needed, as is the case in respect of cross-border mergers and changes in a company's governing law.

Still, if the narrative remains unchanged, it seems likely that the internal affairs doctrine will become entrenched in a manner that does not account for the

[3] See section 4.4.3.

[4] *Cartesio Oktató és Szolgáltató bt* [2008] ECR I-9641 paras 110–13.

[5] See KPMG International, 'Euro Tax Flash: Issue 90' (2008) www.kpmg.be/dbfetch/52616e646f6d495613e0c3885001ac474ddc7501a1f057e0258c22de5277b322/euro_tax_flash_2008_06_11.pdf.

[6] *Cartesio* (n 4).

[7] Case C-411/03 *Sevic Systems AG* [2005] ECR I-10805.

[8] See sections 5.3.5 and 5.4.

legitimate policy concerns of real seat states. Freedom to incorporate and subsequently reincorporate a company in any jurisdiction is not fully justifiable in terms of corporate legal theory, or the general scheme of the Treaty. What is more, even if one accepts that the ultimate goal should be a European internal affairs doctrine, it is unlikely that this will be achieved in full. There are a number of directives in force which provide for some involvement of states other than the state of incorporation, and it is highly unlikely that those laws will be repealed.[9] The net result of the judgments and the legislation is also contradictory. By way of example, the sum effect of the Works Council Directive[10] and the liberalising judgments is that companies that conduct transnational activities will have to consult employees in the decision-making process, whereas companies that have their seat in a state which requires employee participation of its companies may evade that requirement simply by incorporating elsewhere. Similarly, the Cross-Border Merger Directive[11] creates a singular class of companies that are bound by foreign law in respect of employee participation. Since no conditions are currently attached to a company's right to reincorporate under *Cartesio*, it might be possible to avoid the requirements of the directive by reincorporating the company to be absorbed in the state of the acquiring company. There will remain a number of exceptions to an otherwise liberal regime, and a number of significant loopholes that encumber legal certainty and create an internally incoherent body of law.

The encroachment of the incorporation theory will continue to occur against the backdrop of resistance by those states that hold the protection offered by the real seat doctrine most dear. For as long as this state of affairs persists, the Commission's approach of virtually delegating the task of harmonisation to the Court of Justice will continue to be more pragmatic than attempting to introduce laws in the face of lack of consensus in the Council of Ministers. Yet this approach is not without its shortcomings. The judgment in *Cartesio* demonstrates that the Court of Justice might not always be willing to follow the Commission's recommendations, in part because the Court appears to have realised that some of those suggestions are in fact unworkable.

However, legislative resistance seems likely to be gradually replaced by an acceptance of European law as articulated by the Court of Justice, as has been the case historically in respect of formerly controversial judicial developments in EU law such as the supremacy of EU law.[12] Indeed, courts in Germany and Austria have declared that the real seat theory is no longer applicable in their jurisdictions, since it is incompatible with the Treaty.[13] Thus, although the executive branch in

[9] See sections 4.4 and 4.5.

[10] Council Directive (EC) 1994/45 on the establishment of a European Works Council or a procedure in Community-scale undertakings and Community-scale groups of undertakings for the purposes of informing and consulting employees [1994] OJ L254.

[11] Directive (EC) 2005/56 of the European Parliament and of the Council of 26 October 2005 on cross-border mergers of limited liability companies [2005] OJ L310/1.

[12] JHH Weiler, 'A Quiet Revolution: The European Court of Justice and Its Interlocutors' (1994) *Comparative Political Studies* 510, 510–34.

[13] FJ Garcimartín Alférez, 'La Sentencia «Centros»: una visión a través de los comerntarios' (2001) *Revista Jurídica* 169, 180.

those states demonstrates resistance to the ECJ's line of thought through their submissions to the Court, the judiciaries are bound to apply the interpretation of the Treaty that is handed down by the Luxembourg Court since they are de facto subsidiary courts of the Union. Further evidence of acceptance of irreversible liberalisation is to be found both in the preamble to the Tenth Company Law Directive, which refers to the judgments of the Court.[14] However, the more recent draft Regulation on a European Private Company, as revised, adopts a neutral approach to the determination of a supranational company's governing law and leaves the matter to the applicable national law.[15] This is relatively liberal when compared to earlier comparable legislation such as the SE Statute.[16] However, it is noteworthy that the Council continues to oppose the more liberal contractual approach which was proposed in the Commission's original proposal.[17] Elsewhere the lack of progress in the adoption of positive harmonisation measures affecting companies created by state law has allowed the Court to continue to take the lead.[18] Accordingly, the Member States are not in a particularly strong position to stem the flow of liberalisation, even where some of their number are inclined to do so.

Notwithstanding the likelihood of eventual acceptance of a European internal affairs doctrine, cultural attachment to the social and political construct of the firm, coupled with the prima facie rights of states to govern socio-economic affairs within their territories, militate against judicially imposed liberalisation. That liberalisation and deference to party autonomy will most likely be accepted in the long-term as though it had always existed as a matter of right does nothing to alter the fact that the present social, economic and political construct is not in harmony with the direction that negative harmonisation has signalled. The power of states to exercise exclusive prescriptive jurisdiction over corporate law within their territories has long been lost. Yet the result of a fully functioning market for incorporations will be that rather than a Union where Member States pool sovereignty, the prescriptive jurisdiction of states with more accommodating laws will encroach on the territory of states whose corporate laws are more protective of non-shareholder constituencies. Thus, in the absence of further Union legislation, the legislation of some Member States will be of extraterritorial relevance as much as it is of relevance within their own territories.[19] By way of example, if the legislation of Member State X is particularly attractive to the promoters of companies, the legal persons prescribed by the law of that state will be taken up by promoters of companies in other Member States. The resulting legal persons that are the

[14] Directive (EC) 2005/56 of the European Parliament and of the Council of 26 October 2005 on cross-border mergers of limited liability companies [2005] OJ L310/1 recital 3.

[15] Council of the European Union, 'Proposal for a Council Regulation on a European private company – Political agreement' 1061/11 DRS 84 SOC 432 (hereinafter 'Revised Draft SPE Statute') art 7.

[16] Council Regulation (EC) 2157/2001 on the statute for a European company (SE) [2001] OJ L294/1 art 7.

[17] Draft Council Regulation on the statute for a European private company COM (2008) 396/3 recital 4.

[18] *Cartesio* (n 4) paras 110–13.

[19] See MP Maduro, 'So Close and Yet So Far: the Paradoxes of Mutual Recognition' (2007) *Journal of European Public Policy* 814, 819.

product of the prescriptive and administrative acts of Member State X will have a widespread presence within the territories of other Member States that would otherwise prescribe a different legal form. With the harmonisation of company laws stalled as it is, it is unlikely that other Member States will be able to use the legislative avenues of the Union to modify the nature of the corporate forms entering their jurisdiction by way of the laws of state X to a greater extent than positive harmonisation has allowed to date. Prescriptive jurisdiction over corporate law will thus be haphazardly situated throughout the Member States, a phenomenon that may be described as displaced sovereignty as opposed to shared sovereignty.[20]

The approach to the establishment of the internal market based on negative harmonisation may change following the cautious judgment in *Cartesio*. This has led both the Commission and the Council to re-engage with legislation, joining the European Parliament, which is the only institution to have consistently advocated the adoption of legislation. Re-engagement with a regulatory approach is positive. However, legislating for the sake of legislating is not adequate. The Union requires a principled approach to the private international law of companies.

6.3 Option 2: the Status Quo Ante

Given that the *Centros* line of judgments is open to criticism on account of more than a hint of judicial activism, there is a principled argument in favour of judicial or legislative reversal of those judgments. The result would be a closer reflection of the intended meaning of the Treaty. However, such a step is both impractical and implausible. Despite the ECJ's recent cautious approach to further liberalisation in *Cartesio*, there is no indication that the Court of Justice is inclined to roll back the liberalisation that has been achieved to date. Quite the contrary is true in fact as each relevant judgment confirms the wide application of the principles enshrined in *Centros*. Nor is there a legislative appetite to return to the pre-*Centros* state of affairs. Save for the judgment in *Cartesio*, the Court's judgments are actually in conformity with the submissions of the Commission, while the Member States have not brought pressure to bear to induce the Commission to introduce protective legislation.

Moreover, returning to the status quo ante *Centros* would call into question the legal status of all companies that have legitimately taken advantage of liberalisation. Even if transitional measures were adopted to cater for such companies, reversing *Centros* would be a cumbersome process that would be open to abuse – unless complicated safeguards were introduced, there would almost certainly be a market for off-the-shelf *Centros* companies that would severely limit the benefits of the U-turn. Indeed, there can be little doubt that forward-thinking opportunistic

[20] See J Borg Barthet, 'Online Gambling and the Further Displacement of State Regulation: A Note on *PMU v Zeturf* (2008) *International and Comparative Law Quarterly* 417, 417–26.

entrepreneurs would avail themselves of their right to establish several shell companies in the interim period prior to the legislation coming into force, for the purposes of resale at a mark-up at a later date.

Even if the complete reversal of *Centros* were attainable, with or without negative side effects, it is submitted that the position that obtained prior to liberalisation was far from desirable. Prior to *Centros* there existed irreducible conflicts of conflicts norms as between incorporation states and real seat states. The uncertainty that obtained previously would re-emerge and would be compounded further by lack of clarity as regards the compatibility of the real seat doctrine and the fundamental freedoms.

A return to the pre-*Centros* environment would simply be a return to the co-existence, and opposition, of two flawed theories that connect companies to a jurisdiction. The incorporation theory is only valid if one disregards the role of the state in the establishment of companies, and contorts reality to accommodate an entirely private view of companies; the real seat theory is only valid if one contorts reality to disregard the private aspects of companies and further distorts reality by adding the fiction of the seat as the closest connection between the company and a given jurisdiction. The real seat theory also does little to provide legal certainty in a transnational context, while the application of exceptions to the incorporation doctrine reduces the benefits that the said doctrine otherwise provides.

In view of the foregoing, the option of returning to the situation that obtained prior to the ECJ's liberalising judgments is a non-option and can safely be set aside.

6.4 Option 3: Unification or Supranationalisation of Corporate Law

The legislative agenda of the Union has consistently included projects whose goals surpass mere harmonisation and extend to the creation of supranational business vehicles.[21] What is more, the academic European Model Company Law Project sets out to provide a template for voluntary convergence on an ideal law.[22] These initiatives have the potential to further the industrial policy goals of freedom of establishment, and of minimising the effects of conflicts of laws. The supranational business vehicles created by EU law do not unify corporate law, since they do not replace national laws with a European code.[23] However, the introduction of supranational legal persons must be viewed as part of a process towards making

[21] See section 4.5.

[22] T Baums and P Krüger Andersen, 'The European Model Company Law Project: ECGI Law Working Paper No 097/2008' (2008) http:// ssrn.com/abstract=1115737, 7–8.

[23] Besides the SE and the proposed SPE that are discussed in the immediately foregoing chapter, Community law has created the European Economic Interest Grouping (EEIG), the European Cooperative, and European Mutual Societies.

supranational business vehicles more attractive than those available under national law and thus becoming the vehicles of choice for entrepreneurs in the Union. As such, the net result of supranationalisation would be to render the conflict of corporate laws less relevant in the long run, while unification could do away with conflict of corporate laws altogether. The recent Communication on a Small Business Act signals the Commission's intention to persist in an approach which sets out to bypass the difficulties posed by a plurality of national laws.

Still, there does not appear to be any prospect for unification of corporate laws, whether throughout the Union or only among some Member States through the enhanced cooperation procedure. To date there has not even been any movement in that direction in Member States that have similar legal systems, let alone across legal families. Rather any similarity in changes to national laws has been occasioned by traditional imitation and transposition rather than concerted action, save of course where harmonisation measures were adopted. Further, if one looks to monetary union for analogous enlightenment in the context of a two-speed Europe, one will note that one of the motivations for monetary union was the expectation that the euro would become a reserve currency in global markets. By analogy, unification of corporate law would be attractive to Member States only if there were a quid pro quo, such as increased revenue from incorporations. While the European corporate brand would no doubt be attractive to incorporators from third countries,[24] a European company would likely have to offer lower standards of stakeholder protection if it is to attract widespread use. Further, the law would have to allow the seat of the company to be situated in third countries.

In addition, the unification of corporate laws would encumber the development of the entire Union's corporate law with the burden of a European legislative process that is not capable of responding to challenges as expediently as the Member States are individually.[25] In a global economy that requires responsive legislators, it is inadvisable to strip Member States of the capacity to respond to challenges efficiently, as would be the case if amendments to the law were subject to negotiation within and among the Union's institutions. Moreover, unification would deny European corporate law of the benefit of legislative competition that has on occasion served the Member States so well by allowing them to borrow innovative solutions adopted elsewhere. Unification is therefore both unlikely in political terms, and undesirable in practical terms. Accordingly, the unification of corporate law would be a fanciful project in Europeanisation that would be more costly than it would be beneficial. Even if this were not the case, the experience of 40 years of negotiation which led to the adoption of an SE which few wanted to use suggests that interim measures would be required while legislation establishing a European corporate code is devised and negotiated.

[24] R Drury, 'The European Private Company' (2008) *European Business Organization Law Review* 125, 126–27.

[25] See Baums and Krüger Andersen (n 22) 3.

6.5 Option 4: a New Regulatory Framework

Given the proven imperfection of negative harmonisation, piecemeal positive harmonisation or the absence of any harmonisation of conflict of corporate law norms, it is submitted that European legislators should introduce an instrument that will provide a comprehensive and coherent regime to replace the present laws and the foreseeable development of the law. The case-by-case approach that has been adopted to date has been successful in some measure, but a lack of a coherent legislative vision compounded by the sometimes insensitive intervention of the judiciary has failed to provide stakeholders with a clear legal landscape.

Nevertheless, the progress that has been made in unifying conflicts of corporate laws through legislation and through the Court's judgments should not be set aside completely. Indeed, the German Council on Private international Law has recommended that legislation be adopted to clarify the scope of mutual recognition of companies and to remove the internal contradictions.[26] Several authors have suggested that, in the interests of legal certainty, the Union should re-engage with the legislative process.[27] This would be preferable to the present state of affairs, in that there would be an unmistakeable point of reference. Codification of case law would provide certainty, particularly to Member States of a civilian tradition who are less accustomed to dealing in judicial subtleties. However, it would fall short of what is ideal within the limits of possibility. Rather, the 'present state of Union law' should provide the political impetus, as well as the legislative groundwork, to move Member States towards adopting legislation that will unify the conflict of corporate laws in a manner that underwrites the principle of freedom of establishment and the free movement of companies, but that also accounts for genuine state interests in the governance of corporations which have their operational headquarters within their territory. Thus, without discarding greater freedom of choice, it is preferable to adopt legislation that does not disregard the symbolic and real importance of corporations in the governance of socio-economic affairs within each Member State.

This is made more urgent by the fact that the harmonisation programme is not likely to progress much further in substantive terms, and that Member States will be free to adopt diverse laws only within the limits of the harmonisation that has been achieved to date. This presents an opportunity for Member States, particularly smaller states with an offshore tradition, to prescribe corporate laws whose

[26] Conseil allemand pour le droit international privé, 'Proposition du Deustcher Rat für Internationales Privatrecht en vue de l'adoption d'une réglementation du droit international des sociétés au niveau européen/national' (2006) *Révue Critique* 712, 712–34; EM Kieninger, 'The Law Applicable to Corporations in the EC' (2009) *RabelsZ* 607.

[27] See eg Kieninger (n 26) 619–20; C Timmermans, 'Impact of EU Law on International Company Law' (2010) *European Review of Private Law* 549, 566; E Wymeersch, 'Is a Directive on Corporate Mobility Needed?' (2007) *European Business Organization Law Review* 161, 166; AW Wiśniewski and A Opalski, 'Companies' Freedom of Establishment after the ECJ *Cartesio* Judgment' (2009) *European Business Organization Law Review* 595, 621–23.

real target is corporations that have their headquarters in other Member States that have more stringent corporate law policies. Accordingly, if core features of the corporate law of some Member States are to be safeguarded against encroachment of foreign laws, the solution must be a private international law regime which accounts for those core features that might otherwise be at risk. Legislation would also add legitimacy in that the unquestionable assent of the Member States would be granted. If properly constructed, it might also add clarity and legal certainty.[28]

In formulating new legislation concerning the governing law of companies, it is submitted that one must first acknowledge that past efforts at harmonisation of conflicts norms form an inadequate basis for future development. The adoption of one or the other is neither attainable nor sufficient. However, both the Hague and EC Conventions show that compromises between the real seat and incorporation theories are necessary. The abortive conventions also show that the schism between the incorporation and the real seat theories may be bridged without completely disregarding the reasoning that underpins the two theories.[29] From the incorporation theory one must accept that corporations are in great measure an instrument for the generation of profit, principally for the benefit of the initiators of an enterprise and those who invest funds for the furtherance of that enterprise. Thus, pragmatism dictates that one must defer to party autonomy in great measure. From the real seat theory one must accept that every state has a political history and a socio-economic reality that has led to the acceptance of a particular corporate form. In most states that particular form includes elements of social solidarity that should be respected transnationally, if it is practical to do so.

The regulatory framework that is proposed below therefore provides that companies incorporated in the EU should be recognised in each Member State and subject to the law of their state of incorporation, provided that companies incorporated in a Member State other than that of their real seat will be subject to a limited number of norms prescribed by the law of the state of the real seat. Accordingly, rather than applying the full spectrum of the law to which a company is most intimately connected, as the real seat theory would require, only such elements of corporate law as are most vigorously protected by the state of the real seat should be mandatorily applied to companies whose seat and state of incorporation do not coincide.

6.5.1 Legal Basis

The legal basis for the unification of the conflict of corporate laws was to be found explicitly in article 293 of the EC Treaty. The Treaty of Lisbon has repealed article 293.[30] The remaining legal bases are to be found in less direct language in articles

[28] Kieninger (n 26) 619–20.

[29] See section 1.4.

[30] Treaty of Lisbon amending the Treaty on European Union and the Treaty establishing the European Community, signed at Lisbon, 13 December 2007 [2007] OJ C306/1 art 2(280).

50 and 81 TFEU (articles 44 and 65 EC). Article 50 refers to the coordination of safeguards in corporate law with a view to making them equivalent throughout the Union. Reference to the equivalence of safeguards was originally intended as an instrument for the substantive harmonisation of laws, but this article has served as a basis for the adoption of the Cross-Border Merger Directive, which is principally an instrument of transnational law.[31] Article 81(2)(c) refers to the adoption of legislation to ensure 'the compatibility of the rules in the Member States concerning conflict of laws and of jurisdiction'. Legislation under either article would be adopted through the ordinary legislative procedure. However, article 50 provides for the approximation of laws through directives, whereas article 81 allows for the adoption of regulations. A regulation would be preferable because this allows for the unification of conflicts legislation. Unification would better serve legal certainty, since it would eliminate differences which would lead to a costly and unpredictable system.

6.5.2 Aims and Principles

The recent development of European law has been characterised in great measure by the notion that the absence of substantive harmonisation implies that 'competition among rules must be allowed free play'[32] – promoters of companies should be free to choose the company law that they deem most apt to accommodate their goals. AG La Pergola observed that 'the purpose of [freedom of establishment] is to guarantee to all Community citizens alike the freedom to engage in business activities through the instruments provided by national law'.[33] As noted in Chapters 4 and 5, this is a somewhat surprising reading of the aims of the Treaty. Article 50(2)(g) TFEU, which provides for the harmonisation of corporate law, was included in the Treaty of Rome specifically to prevent unrestrained freedom of choice.[34] This provided an additional safeguard against Delawarisation at a time when the application of the real seat theory in all but one Member State limited, or indeed excluded, party autonomy.[35] Both a textual and a teleological reading of

[31] Directive (EC) 2005/56 of the European Parliament and of the Council of 26 October 2005 on cross-border mergers of limited liability companies [2005] OJ L310/1 recital 1.

[32] Case C-212/97 *Centros Ltd v Erhvervs-og Selskabsstyrelsen* [1999] ECR I-01459 para 20 (AG La Pergola).

[33] ibid.

[34] Further evidence of this intention is to be found in art 50(2)(g), which deals with substantive harmonisation of corporate law rather than private international law. This article provides that in order to attain freedom of establishment, directives shall be adopted to coordinate safeguards for the protection of corporate stakeholders 'with a view to making such safeguards equivalent throughout the Union'. This suggests that it was never intended that the harmonisation of corporate law should be market-driven. See S Grundmann, 'The Structure of European Company Law: From Crisis to Boom' (2004) *European Business Organisation Law Review* 601, 605; CWA Timmermans, 'Company Law as Ius Commune?' (2002) Walter van Gerven Lecture, Leuven Centre for a Common Law of Europe www.law.kuleuven.ac.be/ccle/pdf/wvgl.pdf, 5; J Wouters, 'European Company Law: *Quo Vadis*?' (2000) *Common Market Law Review* 257, 269–70.

[35] Timmermans (n 34) 5; Wouters (n 34) 283–84.

the Treaty would more likely have led one to the conclusion that freedom of choice of national business vehicles was only to be allowed subject to legislation under article 293 EC which was then still in force.

Between the proposition that freedom of establishment grants absolute freedom of choice and the requirement of extensive substantive harmonisation lies the possibility of granting free choice of law, but recognising that the absence of harmonisation is symptomatic of diverse corporate cultures.[36] The logic of a conflicts model which allows almost absolute autonomy in choice of law in the absence of substantive convergence is certainly questionable.[37] A plurilegal system need not be entirely market-driven, but nor is the only other option the exclusion of legal competition. In the absence of a clear legal basis for legal competition, however, free movement of companies in Europe is built on poor foundations. As noted in Chapters 4 and 5, a clear legal basis is indeed lacking. It is the purpose of this section to provide a possible framework for free movement that will account for both efficiency and the proper locus of prescriptive power.[38] Further, in the interests of legal certainty and internal coherence, it is pertinent to introduce a system that governs the private international law of both national and supranational companies. The proposed regulation would function on the basis of slight modification to the incorporation theory whereby Member States that incorporate companies having their seat in another state may be bound to enforce elements of foreign law by requiring their inclusion in corporate statutes. While it may also be opportune for legislators to turn their minds to recognition of companies incorporated in third countries, the present proposal is limited to the governing law of companies formed in accordance with the laws of a Member State or those of the Union.

6.5.2.1 Case Law as a Constitutional Foundation

Central to the present proposal is the codification of the principle enunciated in *Centros*[39] and *Überseering*,[40] which requires that companies incorporated in a Member State be recognised throughout the EU and accorded the full extent of the

[36] See CM Schmitthoff, 'Company Structure and Employee Participation in the EEC – the British Attitude' (1976) *International and Comparative Law Quarterly* 611, 611–20; B Pasa, GA Benacchio and L Orme (tr), *The Harmonization of Civil and Commercial Law in Europe* (Budapest, Central European University Press, 2005) 365.

[37] See H Hansmann and R Kraakman, 'The End of History for Corporate Law' (2001) *Georgetown Law Journal* 439, 454.

[38] While the discussion in this section sets out the possible content of legislation, it is paramount that the Union's legislators adopt a cautious and studied approach. To date, a lack of holistic vision has caused internal incoherence that should be avoided going forward. Further, codification should neither perpetuate existing shortcomings, nor introduce new incoherence. The suggestions made here are therefore intended as part of a larger debate leading to European legislation that, unlike its present incarnation, is internally coherent, philosophically sound, and the drafting of which is of a quality that provides certainty to market actors and that is not reliant on clarification by the Court of Justice. See generally A Fiorini, 'The Codification of Private International Law: The Belgian Experience' (2005) *International and Comparative Law Quarterly* 499, 499–519.

[39] *Centros* (n 32).

[40] Case C-208/00 *Überseering BV v Nordic Construction Company Baumanagement GmbH (NCC)* [2002] ECR I-9919.

fundamental freedoms. This is to be complemented by the principle that Member States must remove fiscal barriers to the mobility of companies.[41]

However, given that provisos to the general rule on recognition are recommended, it is also incumbent to address whether the Treaty, as interpreted by the Court, delimits the manner in which legislators may act. The first challenge is posed by the statement in *Überseering* to the effect that article 293 EC (and by implication articles 50 and 81 TFEU) does not constitute a reserve of legislative competence in the Member States but enables them to enter into negotiations only to the extent that it is necessary to do so where the Treaty provisions do not achieve the goals established therein.[42] In addition, the judgment in *Inspire Art*[43] declared the application of local law to pseudo-foreign corporations incompatible with the Treaty.[44] However, legislators may take comfort in the plurality of contradictory statements on the effects of article 293,[45] the fact that the judgments addressed national legislation imposed unilaterally on foreign companies rather than Union legislation enacted under the authority of article 50 or article 81, as well as the potential justifications for restrictions to freedom of establishment cited by the Court itself.[46] Accordingly, it is submitted that the requirements of the judgments of the Court should pose no barrier to the enactment of legislation that guarantees freedom of establishment, subject to the requirement that pseudo-foreign corporations account for local norms in their corporate statutes.

6.5.2.2 Theoretical Basis

The *Centros* doctrine requires that companies incorporated in one Member State be recognised in other Member States, regardless of the situation of their seat. Indeed, European law has been shaped by AG La Pergola's view that party autonomy is central to the attainment of the goals of the internal market:

> The right of establishment is essential to the achievement of the objectives set in the Treaty . . . it is the opportunity to exercise business activities that is protected, and with it the contractual freedom to make use of the instruments provided for that purpose in the legal systems of the Member States.[47]

[41] Case C-9/02 *Hughes de Lasteyrie du Saillant v Ministère de l'Économie, des Finances et de l'Industrie* [2004] ECR I-2409; Case C-446/03 *Marks & Spencer plc v David Halsey (Her Majesty's Inspector of Taxes)* [2005] ECR I-10837; Case C-196/04 *Cadbury Schweppes plc, Cadbury Schweppes Overseas Ltd v Commissioners of Inland Revenue* [2006] ECR I-7995. For the sake of clarity, and to avoid unnecessary litigation, the law should empower Member States to recuperate reasonable administrative costs incurred in processing an application for a company to transfer its seat to another jurisdiction; these shall not be deemed to be fiscal barriers.

[42] ibid para 54.

[43] *Inspire Art* (n 1).

[44] ibid paras 99–101.

[45] Case 81/87 *The Queen v HM Treasury and Commissioners of Inland Revenue, ex p Daily Mail and General Trust plc* [1988] ECR 5483 paras 20–23; *Cartesio* (n 4) para 109.

[46] *Überseering* (n 40) para 92; *Inspire Art* (n 1) para 132; *Sevic Systems* (n 5) para 28.

[47] *Centros* (n 32) para 20 (AG La Pergola).

For the sake of coherence, party autonomy in choice of law should also be extended to the SE and the nascent SPE without the need of coincidence of the place of incorporation and the seat of the company. Similarly, the ability to change a company's governing law, available for the SE and SPE, should be extended to national companies as a matter of EU law, and not only where it is permitted by the national law of the destination state. Moreover, internal coherence and the protection of identifiable stakeholders would require that seat transfers and reincorporation be allowed, subject to the requirements of the Cross-Border Merger Directive, rather than in the legislative vacuum of negative harmonisation.[48] To the extent that the present proposal is founded on the dual requirements of internal coherence and party autonomy, it is unlikely to be controversial.

Still, there is a principled argument for the limitation of private ordering as a general rule. Indeed, notwithstanding the adoption of the incorporation theory in the revised Draft SPE Statute, the Draft Regulation includes generic provision for the limitation of a company's right to circumvent the law with which it is most closely connected, albeit without any substantive provision to achieve this at the time of writing.[49] This is so notwithstanding that it has become commonplace for authors to suggest that the economic nature of the company is such that party autonomy should be given a free rein in transnational corporate law,[50] and also notwithstanding the Court of Justice's somewhat dogmatic allusion to party autonomy in one of its judgments.[51] The economic claim in support of absolute autonomy falls to be qualified. First, despite a plurality of potential approaches, this claim is premised on a single economic theory of the firm, namely that of Ronald Coase, which emphasises the primacy of entrepreneurs in the governance of firms.[52] Coase's seminal work on the theory of the firm is most certainly indispensable in any discussion of corporate legal theory, but it has been developed and, arguably, superseded by a plethora of authors who benefited from Coase's insights.[53] Secondly, as was shown in Chapter 2 of this book, '[economic] theories

[48] See *Cartesio* (n 4) paras 111–12.

[49] Council of the European Union, 'Proposal for a Council Regulation on a European private company – Political agreement' 1061/11 DRS 84 SOC 432 recital 6a.

[50] See eg S Lombardo, 'Conflict of Law Rules in Company Law after *Überseering*: An Economic and Comparative Analysis of the Allocation of Policy Competence in the European Union' (2003) *European Business Organization Law Review* 301, 320–22; MJ Whincop, 'Conflicts in the Cathedral: Towards a Theory of Property Rights in Private International Law' (2000) *University of Toronto Law Journal* 41, 52–54; EM Iacobucci, 'Toward a Signaling Explanation of the Private Choice of Corporate Law' (2004) *American Law and Economics Review* 319, 319–20.

[51] *Überseering* (n 40) para 62. Overt reference to party autonomy was also made in the Opinion of AG La Pergola in *Centros* (n 32) para 20; this was not reflected in the judgment of the Court: see A Johnston and P Syrpis, 'Regulatory Competition in European Company Law after *Cartesio*' (2009) *European Law Review* 378, 395–96; M Gestri, 'Mutuo Riconoscimento delle Società Comunitarie, Norme di Conflitto Nazionali e Frode alla Legge: il caso *Centros*' (2000) *Rivista di Diritto Internazionale* 71, 90.

[52] RH Coase, 'The Nature of the Firm' (1937) *Economica*, 386, 386–405.

[53] See eg MC Jensen and WH Meckling, 'Theory of the Firm: Managerial Behaviour, Agency Costs and Ownership Structure' (1976) *Journal of Financial* Economics 305, 305–60; AA Alchian and H Demsetz, 'Production, Information Costs and Economic Information' (1977) *The American Economic Review* 777, 777–95; MA Eisenberg, 'The Structure of Corporation Law' (1989) *Columbia Law Review*,

are – naturally – reductionist in their view of the firm, and some would suggest that what they leave out renders their ready acceptance in practice problematical.'[54] Hence, there are theories of the firm that are not purely economic, or that also account for the investment of human capital which is to be considered in the determination of systems of governance.[55]

Indeed, even if one were to accept the primacy of the private profit-making purpose of companies, it is equally true that private law is also 'public, in the sense that it is a social function and that all individuals are, whatever their varying titles, functionaries of society.'[56] This explains the extensive regulation of corporate law in every Member State and the reflection of diversity in national conflicts rules. The schism between the protective real seat theory and liberal incorporation theory masks a truth that virtually all states adopt some protective conflict of laws mechanisms, whether as a matter of course or from time to time.[57] Targeted exceptions to the incorporation theory provide compelling evidence that states attach importance to the connection of companies to their territories. This is reflected in the Union's secondary legislation and in the wording of article 50(2)(g) TFEU. It is therefore submitted that, in a Europe of diverse legal cultures and plural sources of law, legislation should account for genuine policy concerns that are not intended to pose a barrier to trade or the genuine enjoyment of the internal market.

6.5.2.3 *A Modified Incorporation Theory*

In 1955 ER Latty proposed a formula within the limits of which pseudo-foreign corporations should be regulated by local law in the United States. He proposed a

1461, 1461–1525; EF Fama, 'Agency Problems and the Theory of the Firm' (1980) *Journal of Political Economy* 288, 288–307; ML Weitzman, 'Increasing Returns and the Foundations of Unemployment Theory' (1982) *The Economic Journal* 787, 787–804; OE Williamson, *The Economic Institutions of Capitalism* (Free Press, New York 1985); OE Williamson, 'The Theory of the Firm as Governance Structure: From Choice to Contract' (2002) *Journal of Economic Perspectives* 171, 171–95. For an account of the spectrum of theories of the firm and their potential deployment in company law, see eg J Paterson, 'The Company Law Review in the UK and the Question of Scope: Theoretical Concerns, Practical Constraints and Possible New Directions' in R Cobbaut and J Lenoble (eds), *Corporate Governance. An Institutional Approach* (Netherlands, Kluwer Law International, 2003) 141, 141–79; J Dine, *The Governance of Corporate Groups* (Cambridge, Cambridge University Press, 2000) 1–36; A Belcher, 'The Boundaries of the Firm: The Theories of Coase, Knight and Weitzman' (1997) *Legal Studies* 22, 22–39.

[54] Paterson (n 53) 150.

[55] See eg MM Blair, 'Firm-Specific Human Capital and Theories of the Firm' in M Blair and M Roe (eds), *Employees and Corporate Governance* (Washington DC, Brookings Institution Press, 1999) 58, 58–91; LA Stout, 'Bad and Not-So-Bad Arguments for Shareholder Primacy' (2002) 75 *Southern California Law Review* 1189, 1189–1210.

[56] E Durkheim and G Simpson (tr), *The Division of Labor in Society* (Glencoe IL, The Free Press, 1964) 68.

[57] By way of example, *Daily Mail* (n 45) concerned the United Kingdom's obstruction of a transfer of a company's headquarters for tax purposes notwithstanding the UK's application of the incorporation theory; *Centros* (n 32) concerned the refusal to register a subsidiary of a pseudo-foreign corporation in Denmark, also an incorporation state, because the primary establishment in the UK was intended to avoid Danish capital requirements; Case C-167/01 *Kamer van Koophandel en Fabrieken voor Amsterdam v Inspire Art Ltd* [2003] ECR I-10155 concerned the legality of outreach clauses applied by the Netherlands, another incorporation state, to companies having their seat in the Netherlands but formally constituted under foreign law. For further discussion, see Chapter 3.

test based on (i) the identification of those areas of corporate law that demonstrate a 'vigorous legislative intention', that is those areas of law that are not merely enabling but that seek to protect local interests such as the rights of minority shareholders;[58] (ii) the definition of a pseudo-foreign corporation based on ad hoc tests, the result of which would depend on the extent of local or foreign interests in the particular matter at hand;[59] and (iii) the identification of the manner in which local law should be applied by accumulating obligations under the local and the foreign law provided that it is ensured that (a) no stakeholder is exposed to greater liability than he would be under the law of either relevant state; and (b) the local law is applied only if it is more stringent/protective than the foreign law.[60] In a similar vein, proponents of the *Überlagerung* principle suggest that a company need not have a single governing law;[61] companies should be organised under the law of the state of incorporation, but the mandatory laws of the real seat may replace the law of the state of incorporation in certain circumstances.[62] This allows stakeholders to rely on the mandatory rules of the state where the company is factually situated,[63] which presumably reflect a 'vigorous legislative intention'.

Notwithstanding the merits of the argument that states should be able to protect important corporate policy, Latty's system is cumbersome. In the absence of clear and predictable legislative framework, outreach statutes are likely to expose the corporation and its officers to conflicting obligations.[64] The most difficult situations arise where conflicts of mandatory obligations are irreducible. Buxbaum describes this as a 'paradigmatic conflict'.[65] One such example is where the mandatory rules of the state in which a company is factually situated require cumulative voting in the election of directors, whereas the law of the state under which the company is organised requires straight voting. [66] It is impossible for the company to comply with both laws.[67] The matter is exacerbated where conflicts between the laws of the relevant states require technical analysis.[68] The example of dividend payments under the laws of California and Delaware highlights this problem. California requires its cash-flow test to be applied by local and pseudo-foreign corporations alike.[69] In contrast, the law of Delaware, which is the most popular

[58] ER Latty, 'Pseudo-Foreign Corporations' (1955) *Yale Law Journal* 137, 159–60.

[59] ibid 160–61.

[60] ibid 161–62.

[61] S Rammeloo, *Corporations in Private International Law: A European Perspective* (Oxford, Oxford University Press, 2001) 22–23.

[62] ibid.

[63] ibid.

[64] DA DeMott, 'Perspectives on Choice of Law for Corporate Internal Affairs' (1985) *Law and Contemporary Problems* 161, 172–79. See also AE Anton and PR Beaumont, *Private International Law: A treatise from the standpoint of Scots law*, 2nd edn (Edinburgh, W Green, 1990) 703.

[65] RM Buxbaum, 'The Threatened Constitutionalization of the Internal Affairs Doctrine in Corporation Law' (1987) *California Law Review* 29, 40.

[66] ibid.

[67] ibid. For a discussion of conflicts of obligations in corporate law, see DeMott (n 64) 172–79; Anton and Beaumont (n 64) 703.

[68] DeMott (n 64) 174–75.

[69] ibid.

corporate law in the United States, adopts a balance sheet test to evaluate the legality of dividend payments.[70] However, paradigmatic conflicts are not the only problematic situations. Where provisions of one or more of the relevant laws are merely facilitative and apply only in case of express provision to the contrary in the corporation's statute, it is necessary for the incorporators to be aware of the default provisions of each law in order to avoid lack of certainty as to the outcome of a conflict of laws. This is undesirable, given that providing for such a conflict in advance requires an understanding of the laws of both states as well as 'competent counselling, planning and drafting'.[71] Hence the well-founded view that making two laws incumbent on a company constitutes an insuperable burden since it imposes further opportunity costs by necessitating the employment of lawyers and accountants to ensure compatibility with both laws.[72]

Although the theses cited in the two immediately foregoing paragraphs are indeed mutually exclusive in great measure, a balanced principle may be derived from the synthesis of the two. Both approaches have merit, as well as flaws. In view of the wider effects of corporations on societies, it is reasonable to suggest that laws that demonstrate a vigorous legislative intention should not be displaced by a foreign legislator that has no interest in the social construct of a territory. However, there is no merit in applying laws to pseudo-foreign corporations if this is done through cumbersome ad hoc tests, as the result would be unworkable from a practical perspective. The application of mandatory laws of the real seat in accordance with the *Überlagerung* principle would be equally cumbersome in the event that this is done in a legislative vacuum, as irreducible conflicts of obligations would be inevitable.

That noted, it is not necessarily the case that applying principles of local law to pseudo-foreign corporations will result in an unwieldy regime. An appropriate balance may be struck between party autonomy and certainty on the one hand, and safeguarding a 'vigorous legislative intention' of the state of the company's seat on the other. To attain that balance, a 'vigorous legislative intention' must be interpreted narrowly – the parameters within which private ordering is restricted should be limited to matters that truly reflect distinct socio-political choices of different Member States. Further, in order to avoid the uncertainty of ad hoc tests or undefined mandatory rules, Member States should be able to prescribe the extent of the application of local norms in advance through an annex to a European regulation. Finally, the formal bifurcation of the governing law may be avoided by requiring pseudo-foreign corporations to include norms that reflect the law of the real seat in company statutes.

A single governing law, subject only to European law, would situate responsibility for compliance in the Member State in which the company is incorporated. Vesting jurisdiction over substantive matters in the authorities and courts of the state of incorporation would maintain a unitary national law and incur none of the

[70] ibid.
[71] ibid 173.
[72] ibid.

expenses of plural counsel cited by opponents of bifurcation. Moreover, in view of the jurisdictional scheme of the Brussels I Regulation,[73] specifically article 22 which provides for the exclusive jurisdiction of the courts of a single Member State over the internal affairs of a company, it is preferable for the laws of only one state to apply to a company and to thereby ensure certainty in adjudicatory jurisdiction. This will also have the effect of ensuring that the case law concerning the company laws of each Member State remains coherent and administered by courts that are proficient in the relevant laws. In addition, by retaining a single governing law, albeit modified, bifurcation of the governing law of merged companies in respect of employee participation will not be complicated further and may also be applied with relative ease to seat transfers.

6.5.3 An Electronic Solution

Information technology may provide a relatively seamless solution for the incorporation of foreign norms into corporate statutes. A mechanism that adopts aspects of the iSupport system employed in the new Hague Maintenance Convention[74] could allow incorporating authorities and other stakeholders instant access to the norms to be included in the statutes of pseudo-foreign corporations. iSupport is an electronic case-management and communication system that allows authorities in different states to share information concerning the laws, procedures and services available in their jurisdictions in a manner that is instantly available online in a plurality of languages.[75] Information will be available through a system of country profiles that are submitted in one language and automatically and instantly available in multiple languages.[76] The European Commission has already taken steps towards interconnecting corporate registers through a 2009 Green Paper.[77] This would provide cross-border business actors with information regarding 'a company's legal form, its seat, capital and legal representatives'.[78] The proposal to connect registers has been received enthusiastically by business actors who foresee savings of up to €161 million to the European economy.[79] The e-Justice initiative then provides citizens with access to judicial and legal

[73] Council Regulation (EC) 44/2001 on jurisdiction and the recognition and enforcement of judgments in civil and commercial matters [2001] OJ L12/1.

[74] Hague Convention of 23 November 2007 on the International Recovery of Child Support and Other Forms of Family Maintenance.

[75] See Permanent Bureau of the Hague Conference on Private International Law, 'Preliminary Document No 5 – Draft Business Plan for the Development of iSupport' (2009) www.hcch.net/upload/wop/maint_pd05e2009.pdf 10–12.

[76] ibid; see also P Lortie, 'The Development of Medium and Technology Neutral International Treaties in Support of Post-Convention Information Technology Systems' (2008) *Yearbook of Private International Law* 359, 364.

[77] Commission (EC), 'Green Paper: The interconnection of business registers' (Communication) COM (09) 614 final.

[78] ibid 2.

[79] ibid 3.

information.[80] It is foreseen that e-Justice and the business registers could be partially integrated.[81] This could provide a basis for a private international law solution which would build on other investments which are in the offing.

A future regulation could provide that Member States were to submit information by electronic means regarding the norms that they would require to be included in the statutes of pseudo-foreign corporations. Thus, the database would be employed not only as a source of information about laws, but also as an actual source of law. However, the limitations of such a system must also be acknowledged. As in the case of iSupport, information-sharing will be dependent on the development of prescribed forms that elicit limited information.[82] If information-sharing is to be as efficient as suggested, the norms to be applied to pseudo-foreign corporations may only include an agreed list of matters that are capable of a numerical response, a yes/no answer, or a choice of limited responses. If more elaborate answers were to be provided, the possibility for instant availability would be lost, as translation services would be required as in the ordinary course of the Union's business. Moreover, an extensive list of matters to be included in corporate statutes would be so burdensome on incorporating authorities as to encumber efficiency, effective implementation and monitoring. While this would not be fatal to the present proposal, it would certainly detract from its potential attractiveness.

6.5.4 Substantive Matters to be Included in Future Legislation

This section considers a sample of aspects of corporate law that may be capable of inclusion in the proposed scheme. In particular, it considers which matters of public interest should be accounted for by way of exception to a general rule which endorses the principle of party autonomy. Of particular concern are matters which reflect specific choices about the public purpose of companies, such as the co-determination model of corporate governance.

Prior to addressing in which instances it may be necessary to derogate from the incorporation theory, it is pertinent to determine which matters will in fact be included in the governing law of companies as a matter of course. The German Council for Private International Law recommended the inclusion of the following matters:

1. legal nature, legal capacity and capacity to act;
2. foundation, reorganisation and dissolution;
3. name or company name;
4. organisational and financial constitution;
5. powers of representation of the company bodies;

[80] ibid 8.
[81] ibid.
[82] See Permanent Bureau of the Hague Conference on Private International Law (n 75) 11–13.

6. acquisition and loss of membership and associated rights and obligations;
7. liability of the company, its officers and its members for company obligations;
8. liability arising from the breach of duties imposed by company law;
9. the duty to draw up accounts in accordance with standards imposed under commercial law, in particular annual financial statements and its form, disclosure and the legal consequences of non-compliance, including liability.[83]

The above list provides a sound basis, subject to the qualifications that are set out below.

Most of these matters are fairly uncontroversial, but as is shown below, the law of the state of incorporation should not apply without restriction. In order to determine whether substantive requirements of the law of the real seat should be enforced in the state of incorporation, the following matters should be considered: (i) whether the state of the real seat demonstrates a vigorous legislative intention, (ii) whether the implementation of the requirements of the law of the real seat would be capable of seamless introduction in a company's statute, and (iii) whether the norm in question has the potential to act as a legal irritant that will have unpredictable effects in the legal system of the state of incorporation.[84] As will become more apparent, the combined effect of these requirements is such as to allow only limited room for deviation from the principle of party autonomy. One might also consider whether the state in which the company is incorporated demonstrates a vigorous legislative intention. In this case, the state of incorporation might be allowed to refuse to register companies from certain Member States. However, it is submitted that the interests of the state of incorporation are unlikely to be so clear as to justify further complications, or the denial of a level playing field.

6.5.4.1 Structure and Composition of the Board of Directors

It is arguable that there is little in the size, structure and manner of appointment of a board of directors that could reflect a state's vigorous legislative intention. However, it remains true that states have developed diverse systems of governance over time on the basis of divergent understandings of best practice.[85] By way of example, the continental system of two-tiered boards reflects a policy based on monitoring and separation of powers.[86] In contrast the unitary board of the Anglo-American tradition prefers centralised decision-making.[87] However, one would be hard pressed to argue that the structure itself is a matter of such importance as to require application to pseudo-foreign corporations. In fact, research into targeted exceptions to the incorporation doctrine does not reveal any measures that require

[83] Kieninger (n 26) 624–25.

[84] *cf* E Örücü, 'Law as Transposition' (2002) *International and Comparative Law Quarterly* 205, 209.

[85] L Enriques, H Hansmann and R Kraakman, 'The Basic Governance Structure: The Interests of Shareholders as a Class' in R Kraakman and others (eds), *The Anatomy of Corporate Law*, 2nd edn (Oxford, Oxford University Press, 2009) 56–72.

[86] ibid 56; GF Maasen, *An International Comparison of Corporate Governance Models* (Amsterdam, Spencer Stuart, 1999) 15–16.

[87] Enriques, Hansmann and Kraakman (n 85) 56.

the application of local board structures to unlisted companies.[88] Nor does it appear that concerns about freedom of choice in corporate law resulted from the potential avoidance of board structures. The case for including board architecture in future legislation is therefore not particularly compelling.

In contrast, the threat to worker co-determination laws is arguably the principal reason why the liberalisation of corporate law in Europe has attracted so much academic attention.[89] Harmonisation measures in the field of employee participation add emphasis to its importance, but they do not suffice to compensate for the major differences as between the laws of the Member States.[90] Rather, they create a questionable distinction between (i) community-scale undertakings and certain companies resulting from a cross-border merger, and (ii) companies that are entirely situated within a Member State but which have availed themselves of the opportunity to avoid company laws that include employee participation. Given the continued importance attached to employee participation in a plurality of Member States, future legislation may empower Member States to require the application of their own standards to pseudo-foreign corporations having their headquarters in their territory. A future regulation may remedy the present situation by requiring companies to include employees in corporate decision-making processes to the same extent as they would be bound to do so under the laws of the real seat. In a similar fashion, nascent gender equality regulation could be protected through the proposed regulation,[91] as could any other quota of membership of boards of directors.

6.5.4.2 *Duties and Liability of Officers*

In some jurisdictions the duties of officers are articulated in such a way as to define the relationship of a company to its social and physical environment.[92] By way of example, the UK Companies Act 2006 requires that directors' decisions should account for the impact of corporate activity on suppliers, local communities, and the physical environment.[93] This is, clearly, an expression of a local interest in the governance of companies. There is therefore a prima facie case for allowing the Member State of a pseudo-foreign corporation's seat to define the duties owed. Yet interfering with the duties of officers may have the effect of widening discretion to such an extent as to make obligations unenforceable.[94] In a transnational

[88] See Ch 3.

[89] See WF Ebke, '*Centros* – Some Realities and Some Mysteries' (2000) *The American Journal of International Law* 623, 623–25; WH Roth, 'From *Centros* to *Ueberseering*: Free Movement of Companies, Private International Law, and Community Law' (2003) *International and Comparative Law Quarterly* 177, 177–80.

[90] See section 4.4.2.

[91] S Terjesen and V Singh, 'Female Presence on Corporate Boards: A Multi-Country Study of Environmental Context' (2008) *Journal of Business Ethics* 55, 62.

[92] See Enriques, Hansmann and Kraakman (n 85) 104–5.

[93] Companies Act 2006 s 172.

[94] See MJ Roe, 'The Shareholder Wealth Maximization Norm and Industrial Organization' (2001) *University of Pennsylvania Law Review* 2063, 2065.

context the danger is accentuated by the potential for the foreign norm to act as an irritant that has unexpected effects in the recipient legal system.[95] Moreover, it is perhaps more true that, generally, the duty of care owed by officers to anyone other than the company itself has the character of a mere legal platitude that is not capable of enforcement.[96] In the absence of a common notion of the duty owed, it is submitted that the alteration of officers' duties should be treated with caution and limited to clearly defined obligations.

The liability of officers for breaches of substantive obligations is also a matter of such importance as to justify departure from the incorporation theory in at least one EEA jurisdiction. Article 159 of the Swiss Private International Law Code of 1987 provides that, by way of derogation from the incorporation doctrine, 'when the operations of a company created under a foreign law are carried out in or from Switzerland, the liability of the persons acting in the name of such company is governed by Swiss law.'[97] This is intended to afford third parties with the pertinent level of protection where the relevant foreign legal system is lax in this respect.[98] However, it is not clear that similar provision can be made in a law that depends on incorporation of foreign norms in corporate statutes. Although joint and several civil liability of officers in situations where the law of the real seat would make them liable may be stipulated, this might not be capable of enforcement by third parties. Civil wrongs are not easily accommodated, save to the extent that the contractual obligations of officers towards the company and as surety for the company's obligations towards third parties are covenanted directly to third parties.

6.5.4.3 The Relationship between Parents and Subsidiaries

The incidence of multinational groups of companies is a matter that has consistently been of concern to legislators and academics in Europe.[99] This is symptomatic of the fact that limited liability was not originally intended to allow for multiple insulation of shareholders, but was intended to function in a market environment where the corporation deals with all third parties at arm's length.[100] It would be tempting to address this concern in the present system, but this is yet another matter that does not lend itself to easy resolution. Accordingly, it would be better addressed through the harmonisation or unification of substantive national laws, a process that is occurring organically in some measure,[101] rather than by attempting to introduce potentially unenforceable obligations in corporate statutes.

[95] See Örücü (n 84).

[96] Enriques, Hansmann and Kraakman (n 85).

[97] trans per B Dutoit, *Commentaire de la loi fédérale du 18 décembre 1987* (Frankfurt-sur-le-Main, Helbing und Lichtenhahn, 1996) 429.

[98] ibid.

[99] Pasa, Benacchio and Orme (n 36) 368–71.

[100] K Hofstetter, 'Parent Responsibility for Subsidiary Corporations: Evaluating European Trends' (1990) *International and Comparative Law Quarterly* 576, 576; P Muchlinski, 'Corporations in International Litigation: Problems of Jurisdiction and the United Kingdom Asbestos Cases' (2001) *International and Comparative Law Quarterly* 1, 16.

[101] Pasa, Benacchio and Orme (n 36) 368–71.

6.5.4.4 *Creditor Protection*

Creditor protection has been deemed to be sufficiently important for freedom of establishment to be harmonised through the introduction of minimum capital requirements for public companies, as well as accounting standards and publicity requirements.[102] However, as illustrated with reference to the litigation in *Centros*, harmonisation has not been sufficient to assuage the concerns of some Member States.[103] The Danish government's refusal to register Centros Ltd was motivated by the company's intention to circumvent higher Danish capital requirements by incorporating the company in the UK. As a direct result of *Centros*, several European jurisdictions have relaxed their rules on minimum capital for private companies.[104] Italy is the one remaining major jurisdiction to have kept its rules intact.[105] Competitive pressures might make this untenable, and might erode differences in capital requirements for public companies. If it were felt that this should be averted, minimum requirements regarding start-up capital and capital maintenance could also be included in corporate statutes without doing violence to the integrity of the underlying corporate law of the state of incorporation. Given the numerical expression of capital, this is also a matter that should not prove excessively burdensome to include in an electronic annex to a regulation.

6.5.4.5 *Shareholder Rights*

In view of the pre-eminence of the shareholder model of corporate governance,[106] and given the emergence of a 'shareholder class' which is no longer confined to the more affluent,[107] Member States are likely to wish to safeguard some aspects of shareholder protection by requiring higher standards than those provided in the state of incorporation. However, to accord the full extent of shareholder rights of

[102] Directive of the European Parliament and of the Council (EC) 101/2009 on coordination of safeguards which, for the protection of the interests of members and third parties, are required by Member States of companies within the meaning of the second paragraph of Article 48 of the Treaty, with a view to making such safeguards equivalent [2009] OJ L258/11; Council Directive (EEC) 77/91 of 13 December 1976 on coordination of safeguards which, for the protection of the interests of members and others, are required by Member States of companies within the meaning of the second paragraph of Article 58 of the Treaty, in respect of the formation of public limited liability companies and the maintenance and alteration of their capital, with a view to making such safeguards equivalent [1977] OJ L26/1; Council Directive (EEC) 1978/660 based on Article 54(3)(g) of the Treaty on the annual accounts of certain types of companies [1978] OJ L222/11; Council Directive (EEC) 1983/349 based on the Article 54(3)(g) of the Treaty on consolidated accounts [1983] 193/1; Council Directive (EEC) 1984/253 based on Article 54(3)(g) of the Treaty on the approval of persons responsible for carrying out the statutory audits of accounting documents [1984] OJ L126/20; Council Directive (EEC) 1989/666 concerning disclosure requirements in respect of branches opened in a Member State by certain types of company governed by the law of another State [1989] OJ L395/36.

[103] *Centros* (n 32).

[104] J Armour, 'Legal Capital: An Outdated Concept?' (2006) *European Business Organization Law Review* 5, 26.

[105] J Armour, G Hertig and H Kanda, 'Transactions with Creditors' in Kraakman and others (n 85) 130–31.

[106] Hansmann and Kraakman (n 37) 439–41.

[107] ibid 451–53.

the law of the real seat would be to fundamentally redefine the company law of the state of incorporation. In addition, there is a principled argument that shareholders, whose participation in a company is an expression of contractual liberty,[108] should not be able to rely on laws other than those which they have chosen. Still, European law expresses a preference for the protection of minority shareholders from exposure to foreign law.[109] This bias for shareholder protection may be reflected in the present scheme in respect of such matters as voting thresholds and rights to information which can be accommodated in a corporate statute. This could include matters such as supermajority voting on amendments to corporate statutes. In this case, a company incorporated in Italy but having its seat in the United Kingdom would have to adopt the UK's 75 per cent threshold for amendments to corporate statutes,[110] rather than Italy's two-thirds threshold.[111] In the reverse situation, a company incorporated in the UK and having its seat in Italy would have to adopt Italy's mandatory representation of minority shareholders on corporate boards.[112]

6.5.4.6 Seat Transfers

In this section the meaning of seat transfers is understood in two senses. First, there is the matter of the transfer of a company's operational headquarters, and secondly the matter of a change of the state of incorporation without the winding up and reincorporation of a company. The economic rationale for legislation concerning seat transfers was repudiated by the Commission through its withdrawal of the Fourteenth Company Law Directive. However, the Commission's submissions in *Cartesio* indicate that there is indeed an economic imperative for the facilitation of seat transfers. When one considers that seat transfers may be effected through a two-step process via cross-border mergers, there can be little doubt of the imperative for the facilitation of transfers through a rational and simple mechanism that minimises costs.

That noted, the Court of Justice may revisit its judgments in *Daily Mail* and *Cartesio*. In the event of a reversal of those judgments, cross-border seat transfers would be allowed as a directly effective right emanating from the Treaty with no need for further legislation. Member States could then unilaterally prescribe the formalities for a seat transfer to be effected, so long as such formalities do not act as a disproportionate barrier to freedom of establishment. Within the context of the present proposal, in the absence of further regulation, where a company intends to transfer its operational headquarters the state of incorporation would

[108] See Case C-214/89 *Powell Duffryn plc v Petereit* [1992] ECR I-01745 para 10.

[109] Directive (EC) 2005/56 of the European Parliament and of the Council of 26 October 2005 on cross-border mergers of limited liability companies [2005] OJ L310/1 art 4(2).

[110] Companies Act 2006 s 21(1).

[111] Codice Civile, art 2369. See L Enriques, H Hansmann and R Kraakman, 'The Basic Governance Structure: Minority Shareholders and Non-Shareholder Constituencies' in Kraakman and others (n 85) 92–93.

[112] Testo Unico della Finanza art 147-*ter* (3). See Enriques, Hansmann and Kraakman (n 111) 90–91.

need to ensure that the requirements in respect of the state of the new seat are respected as of the date of the transfer. Similarly, where a company intends to reincorporate under the laws of another Member State, the new state of incorporation would inherit the rights and obligations of the former state of incorporation. Any further formalities would be determined by the law or laws of the relevant state or states of incorporation.

However, such an approach would be overly simplistic. In the event of a change in the state of incorporation, the mechanics of a transfer would be liable to irreducible conflicts of laws, since two laws would apply to the transfer.

In the case of any change in the governing law, stakeholders, including shareholders, creditors and employees, must at least have some advance notice that a company's governing law is going to change, whether entirely or only partially, or indeed only potentially. Accordingly, future legislation should include some mechanism that accords rights to the said stakeholders over and above the default rights that are accorded by virtue of the governing law. It is submitted that the procedure to be adopted for a seat transfer should be the same as that applicable in advance of a cross-border merger, mutatis mutandis. This would benefit legislative coherence, as well as making it easier for stakeholders to understand and foresee their rights and obligations.

6.5.5 Legal Certainty

Advocates of the real seat theory propose that legal certainty is achieved by reassuring stakeholders that all corporations that have their management centre in a given jurisdiction are subject to the same rules.[113] Insofar as the present proposal would in fact subject companies having their seat in a jurisdiction to the same rules, certainty will be furthered.

On the other hand, the present proposal might compound concerns, since varying the law of incorporation would actually multiply the laws applicable to companies operating in a given European jurisdiction. It is therefore paramount that a European regulation contains provision for information and disclosure. The former is resolved through the accessibility of the electronic database supporting the proposed regulation in which requirements for the inclusion of norms of the real seat are listed. The latter requires further legislation whereby stakeholders may be made aware of the fact that a company is governed by the provisions of the regulation. This could be resolved by highlighting the fact of the incumbency of the regulation in the acronym following the company name in a stipulated format. By way of example, a company incorporated in the United Kingdom and having its real seat in Italy would be called X Company plc (It), while in the reverse scenario the company would be called X SpA (UK). Further, companies that fall within the scope of the regulation could be made to include information to that

[113] WF Ebke, 'The "Real Seat" Doctrine in the Conflict of Laws' (2002) *The International Lawyer* 1015, 1027–28.

effect and an indication of electronic sources of information in all forms of company communications.

However, information that the governing law is modified does not reveal the content of the law of the state of incorporation. Stakeholders in the Member State of the real seat might not be aware of the provisions of the foreign law that otherwise governs the company, and this leaves unresolved the concern of real seat theorists.[114] Although a private international law instrument is not a traditional locus for the resolution of information-sharing, the electronic database supporting the proposed regulation could equally be employed in support of compilation and promulgation of the provisions of national company law in much the same manner as iSupport will do in respect of laws and procedures concerning maintenance obligations.[115] To this end, it is certainly desirable to integrate the present proposal with the e-Justice initiative.[116] Indeed, the creation of appropriate forms that could elicit extensive information in a linguistically transferrable format will serve to assuage existing concerns of opponents of corporate mobility.

6.5.6 An Obligation to Incorporate 'Foreign' Companies

It is pertinent for future legislation to resolve the matter of whether Member States should be obliged to incorporate companies that have their seat elsewhere, and to thereby pre-empt the necessity of costly recourse to the Court of Justice by way of the preliminary reference procedure. Given that Member States will be bound to allow companies incorporated under their laws to transfer their seat to another jurisdiction, it would be incoherent to allow incorporating authorities to refuse to incorporate a company on the grounds that its centre of management is to be situated in another jurisdiction. Indeed, such a prohibition would be easily bypassed by initially setting up a company having fictional operational headquarters in the Member State in question, and subsequently transferring the said headquarters elsewhere. Alternatively, off-the-shelf companies could be acquired with the same purpose in mind. On the other hand, it is arguable that Member States should be allowed to limit the extent to which companies are set up under their laws by not granting the right to have the operational headquarters elsewhere ab initio. Whichever the preferred solution, in the interests of certainty, future legislation should determine whether or not Member States may refuse to incorporate a company on the grounds that its operational headquarters are situated in another Member State.

114 ibid.

115 Permanent Bureau of the Hague Conference on Private International Law (n 75) 10.

116 See section 6.5.3.

6.5.7 Determining the State of the Real Seat, and Applying its Laws

6.5.7.1 Declaration of the Company's Seat

Given that the proposed regulation operates on the basis of a European notion of the real seat of a company, it is pertinent to establish a common system for the determination of where the seat is in fact situated. An appropriate definition is that adopted by German courts, namely 'the place where the management office and the organs representing the company are engaged in business is the place where fundamental decisions of the management and control office are taken and effectively carried out'.[117] However, in a growing minority of cases, mobility of persons and communication technologies may render inoperable a definition on the basis of a single office or locus of decision-making.[118] In such cases, reference may be made to the habitual residence of the person with primary responsibility for the decisions of the company. Alternatively, if a real seat does not in fact exist, there is a compelling argument for acknowledging this at law and thereby rendering the regulation inapplicable to companies whose management transcends a single territory.

In any event, it is submitted that primary responsibility for declaring the situation of a company's seat should lie with promoters of companies and the directors of companies from time to time. Incorporating authorities may require an annual declaration of the situation of a company's centre of management, as well as a report of any subsequent changes in the company's seat in advance. Jurisdiction to decide whether companies have in fact made correct and truthful declarations of their seat would in turn be accorded to the incorporating state. The alternative would be far less workable as it could lead to a plurality of states that purport to exercise jurisdiction over this essential determination. This would undermine legal certainty and possibly render the proposed solution more cumbersome than the status quo, as it would add a legislative basis to the jurisdictional quandary that persists today. Future legislation would therefore be founded on a system of mutual trust and confidence in the administrative decisions of other Member States. Mutual trust and confidence may be enhanced by cooperation between authorities whereby concerns may be raised and dialogue conducted in order to ensure that non-compliance is addressed appropriately.

6.5.7.2 Formulae for the Application of the Law of the Real Seat

A further question concerns how to ensure that the requirements of foreign law have been satisfied. One would have to determine whether choice of form should be left to the parties or whether this should be prescribed in European legislation. A formulaic approach would require states to prescribe the precise wording to be

[117] *Liechtenstein AG* BGH 21 March 1986, BGHZ 97, 269 trans per Rammeloo (n 61) 179.
[118] Rammeloo (n 61) 14.

adopted in company statutes. In addition, it would be necessary to decide whether the state of incorporation or that of the company's seat should prescribe the necessary wording. It is submitted that if a formulaic approach were adopted potentially insurmountable problems might arise including the necessity of making the precise wording available in a plurality of languages and in a manner that is compatible with a plurality of legal systems. This task might be overwhelming. Alternatively, the incorporating state could prescribe the precise formulae to be adopted. However, this too would be cumbersome, as incorporating states would thereby be bound to legislate in accordance with the legislative agenda of every other Member State. This would be so burdensome as to be unrealistic. Accordingly, it is submitted that the better approach would be to shift the burden to the incorporators. This would have the added benefit of allowing incorporators a degree of flexibility, and indeed the opportunity to exceed the requirements of foreign law should they be so inclined.

In order to facilitate the most expeditious processing of applications, jurisdiction to decide whether the requirements of foreign law have been satisfied would best be accorded to the incorporating state. The chartering states would simply ensure that the statute of the company satisfied the requirements listed in the country profile of the state in which the company will have its centre of management.

6.5.7.3 Amendments to the Laws of the Real Seat

Such matters as are permitted to be applied extraterritorially should be capable of inclusion in the country profiles at the discretion of the state of the real seat. The onus for updating the country profiles would, of course, be incumbent on the state whose laws have been amended. This obligation should apply whether national laws have been made more restrictive or less so. However, a future regulation must account for the fact that changes to the law of the real seat which are to be applied to pseudo-foreign corporations will require amendments to corporate statutes. Accordingly, amendments cannot be expected to apply to pseudo-foreign corporations contemporaneously with their coming into force in respect of companies established under the relevant law. Minimum periods of time that account for annual corporate activity must be allowed in order to allow for the necessary changes to be effected, and these periods should be stipulated in European legislation.

Communication of changes and deadlines for their accommodation in corporate statutes can be facilitated by an electronic system. Direct notification of amendments to the relevant laws, or rather relevant requirements under the regulation, could automatically be sent to the officers of every affected company that is incorporated in a jurisdiction other than that of its real seat. This would not resolve the problem of stakeholders, who are also affected by a realignment of the rights and obligations incumbent upon the company and its officers. However, stakeholders presently are not directly advised of amendments to the law, as indeed they cannot be, because they are often impossible to identify with certainty. That said, an electronic system could allow interested third parties to access information at will or indeed to subscribe to electronic feeds which advise them of amendments to the requirements of European law.

6.5.8 Enforcement Mechanisms: the Challenge of the Privity of Contract

The present proposal could afford parties who are extraneous to the corporate contract with rights under the same. However, the maxim that *res inter alios acta*, may render non-shareholder constituencies powerless to enforce their rights. A future regulation may have to account for this apparent loophole by affording redress to third parties who are prejudiced by shareholders' unwillingness to enforce the provisions of the statutes by which they are bound to one another.

A possible solution is for the regulation to harmonise substantive norms in order to render third parties beneficiaries of the statutory contract in a similar fashion to the beneficiaries of a trust. Alternatively, or additionally, the incorporating authority may be empowered, and indeed bound, to ensure that the company abides by the obligations that are required by the state of the real seat. As a matter of European Union law, the penalty for persistent non-compliance with the instructions of the incorporating authority should be dissolution. However, it is unrealistic to expect an incorporating authority to police the minutiae of the behaviour of all companies that it has chartered with the pertinent degree of vigour. Indeed it would be excessively burdensome and potentially ineffective to rely for compliance entirely on enforcement measures initiated by public authorities. Thus, although ex officio control by the incorporating authority need not be excluded, it would be pertinent to add further safeguards. Here too the electronic system proposed above may prove useful. It may allow third party monitoring by stakeholders and other Member States, as well as an appropriate system of communication of complaints concerning non-compliance.

If a company does not comply with its obligations under the regulation, the incorporating Member State could then be bound to dissolve the company and strike it from the register of companies, following appropriate notice and an opportunity to correct its behaviour. By addressing the obligation to Member States, enforcement actions could be brought against those states that might otherwise be lax in their enforcement of the regulation, whether due to administrative shortcomings or through strategic choices to turn a blind eye.

6.6 Conclusions

While there can be little doubt that no legislative proposal may satisfy all of the conflicting concerns of proponents of regulation and deregulation, the strengths of both arguments have led to some bridging of the ideological divide in Europe's present legal system. However, a lack of holistic vision has caused internal incoherence and some legal uncertainty. Accordingly, the Commission's proposal to introduce legislation should be embraced and the opportunity taken to clarify the law by introducing coherence, while still accounting for the genuine concerns of both schools of thought. By founding the law in a clear theoretical setting that restricts private ordering only under limited conditions, the law may retain the benefits of progress achieved to date without entrenching a singular vision of the firm. Information technology, coupled with the preservation of a unitary governing law, provides opportunities to reach compromises that previously appeared impossible. The iSupport system adopted by the Hague Conference provides the impetus for new developments in EU law that could bridge the divide between the two schools of thought. Moreover, it can provide new opportunities for communication, information sharing and publicity to address matters that previously were considered to be outwith the remit of private international law.

7

Concluding Remarks

This book set out to explore the theoretical and legal foundations for choice of corporate law in the European Union. In particular, it set out to evaluate the cogency of party autonomy, which is the dominant paradigm in the development of the law, and in the work of theorists. The discussion was situated in the context of the divergence between the normative bases for the real seat theory and the incorporation theory. The real seat theory is based on a territorial approach to the governing law of companies which requires that companies be governed by the state with which they are most closely connected. The incorporation theory adopts a liberal contractual approach.

To date, the narrative regarding the governing law of companies has been dominated by the conflict between these two schools of thought. Commentators have sought to evaluate which of two mutually exclusive theories is better suited to connect a corporation to a jurisdiction. They have sometimes employed tenuous logic to justify the application of one theory or another, or indeed to discredit one theory or the other. Likewise, legislators and judges acted within the confines of opposing theories, as is reflected in laws, treaties and judgments of national and regional courts. Throughout, there has been no successful broad-based attempt at a meeting of minds and every international attempt at multilateral reconciliation has failed.

Party autonomy is based on the principle of contractual freedom. Accordingly, this book set out to evaluate the extent to which contractual freedom is applicable to choices of corporate law. It was first shown that the contractual principle should be viewed in its fullest form, that is in a manner which includes the limitations to contractual freedom in contractual choice of law. It was found that corporate choice of law bears some resemblance to those areas of contract law where freedom is limited. This suggests that it is possible to limit the dogmatic approach to the contractual elements of choice of corporate law. Contract law itself includes limits to party autonomy, and these limitations are potentially applicable to corporate choice of law.

Contractual principle in corporate choice of law is often closely aligned with economic analyses of the firm. The economic analysis which is cited most often in conflicts literature, namely Coase's theory of the firm, tends to suggest that corporate law should be designed to maximise efficient private ordering. However, corporate legal theory is far from uncontroversial. An approach such as that of

Coase, which focuses on shareholder wealth, might suggest that corporate choice of law should maximise free choice. Nevertheless, even this basic suggestion is capable of limitation, given that the rational apathy of shareholders vests significant control in directors. What is more, corporate legal theory is unsettled on the matter of who should benefit from corporate governance. Several theorists now recognise that companies are made up of several investments, including those of the community, the environment and workers. This leads to a further set of controversies regarding how best to safeguard these investments. Some theorists suggest that stakeholders should protect their interests through contracts, others suggest that directors should account for these interests in decision-making, and a further group recommend that stakeholders should participate in the governance of companies. It follows that a hierarchical design of the company is controversial in itself. It is therefore far from self-evident that corporate legal theory can justify party autonomy in choice of corporate law.

Different views about the economic nature of companies are accounted for in state practice. The general design of corporate law, as well as the finer details, varies from one state to another. What is more, these differences are protected through the private international law of many states. This is so much the case that states that adopt a contractarian view of companies often limit contractual freedom in their private international law of companies, because contractarianism is never unlimited. States are keen to use private international law as a means to limit the extent to which important areas of corporate law may be bypassed through the choice of a foreign law. This suggests that the dogma of party autonomy should be replaced by recognition that the private international law of companies should be aligned with legislative choices, rather than remaining reliant upon controversial principles.

Having established that the private international law of companies is not a matter of dogma, this book then explored whether the European Union had made a clear choice about the treatment of companies in its foundational law. It was found that the Treaties contain contradictory signals. The principle of mutual recognition, which is central to the European economic constitution, requires that states recognise the legal products of other Member States. Party autonomy is a necessary corollary of mutual recognition. However, the Treaty also makes provision for the protection of stakeholders in companies. This suggests that European law does not adopt a contractarian view of the company. This is borne out in secondary legislation which is invariably protective, and supplants contractual covenants by superimposing rights and obligations. What is more, article 293 EC suggests that the founders of the EU had always expected that the private international law of companies should operate on the basis of a legal instrument which was to be agreed by the Member States. The repeal of article 293 does not appear to have been the product of a conscious choice to redefine the basis for mutual recognition because alternative legal bases exist in articles 50 and 81 TFEU.

Still, the lack of clarity in the Treaties has allowed, and perhaps necessitated, recourse to the European Court of Justice. The Court has, generally, adopted an interpretation of the Treaty which furthered economic integration. In view of the foregoing, it appears that the judgments of the ECJ are displacing the proper locus of prescriptive competence. Every Member State may now exercise prescriptive jurisdiction over the corporate policy that is practised in another Member State simply by allowing a 'foreign' entity to be incorporated under its laws. Effectively, the ECJ has banned measures that are genuinely designed to protect societal norms, as opposed to illegitimate restrictions that seek to protect a geographic market from competition. However, liberalisation has not been unqualified and this causes uncertainty. What is more, the judgments reveal numerous inconsistencies in reasoning and results, and the law is in a constant state of flux. Added to the fact that the EU's legislation is less permissive than the Court's judgments, the law lacks clarity.

In view of the fact that the law is unclear, and because negative harmonisation is an inappropriate instrument for the unification of European private international law of companies, this book has shown that legislation is needed. The proposed form of future legislation should account for the fact that states differ on the goals of companies, and that they should be able to protect those areas of corporate law that demonstrate a 'vigorous legislative intention'. However, this does not necessarily lead to a reversion to the real seat theory. It is possible to adopt the incorporation theory, subject to the application of mandatory rules of the state in which a company's seat is factually located. The novel suggestion in this book is that the law of the state of incorporation should govern all matters relating to the company's internal law, but that European law should bind the Member State in which a company is set up to impose 'foreign' norms on that company. This will allow beneficial legal competition as well as ensuring a great degree of individual autonomy, without denying states the opportunity to define aspects of their corporate laws, and indeed to experiment with the development of laws which are not market-oriented. It is submitted that this approach will suffice to ensure legal certainty, while doing justice to the legitimate claims of proponents of both contractual and concessionary choice of law theories.

BIBLIOGRAPHY

Books

AF Alkhafaji, *A Stakeholder Approach to Corporate Governance* (New York, Quorum Books, 1989).

M Andenas and F Wooldridge, *European Comparative Company Law* (Cambridge, Cambridge University Press, 2009).

AE Anton and PR Beaumont, *Private International Law: A treatise from the standpoint of Scots law,* 2nd edn (Edinburgh, W Green, 1990).

J Armour and JA McCahery (eds) *After Enron: Improving Corporate Law and Moderninisng Securities Regulation in Europe and the US* (Oxford, Hart, 2006).

PS Atiyah, *The Rise and Fall of Freedom of Contract* (Oxford, Clarendon Press, 1979)

T Ballarino, *Diritto Internazionale Privato,* 3rd edn (Napoli, Simone, 2006).

C Barnard, *The Substantive Law of the EU: The Four Freedoms,* 3rd edn (Oxford, Oxford University Press, 2010).

SM Bartman (ed) *European Company Law in Accelerated Progress* (The Hague, Kluwer, 2006).

NE Bowie, *Business Ethics: A Kantian Perspective* (Oxford, Blackwell, 1999).

M Blair, *Wealth Creation and Wealth Sharing: A Colloquium on Corporate Governance and Investments in Human Capital* (Washington DC, Brookings Institute, 1996).

M Blair and M Roe (eds) *Employees and Corporate Governance* (Washington DC, Brookings Institution Press 1999).

WW Bratton, 'Corporate Law's Race to Nowhere in Particular' (1994) *Toronto Law Journal* 401.

E Brem et al (eds), *Festchrift zum 65. Geburstag von Mario m. Pedrazzini* (Bern, Verlag Stämpfli, 1990).

P Cartwright (ed), *Consumer Protection in Financial Services* (London, Kluwer, 1999).

A Conard, 'Fundamental Changes in Marketable Share Companies' in *International Encyclopedia of Comparative Law,* vol XIII: Business and Private Organizations, ch 6 (1972).

R Cobbaut and J Lenoble (eds), *Corporate Governance. An Institutional Approach* (Netherlands, Kluwer Law International, 2003).

PL Davies, *Gower and Davies' Principles of Modern Company Law,* 8th edn (Oxford, Oxford University Press, 2008).

G de Búrca and JHH Weiler (eds), *The European Court of Justice* (Oxford, Oxford University Press, 2001).

F Dessemontet (ed), *Le nouveau droit international privé suisse. Travaux des journées d'études organiseés par le Centre de droit de l'entreprise les 9 et 10 octobre 1987, à l'Université de Lausanne* (Lausanne, Cedidic, 1988).

J Dine, *The Governance of Corporate Groups* (Cambridge, Cambridge University Press, 2000).

E Durkheim and G Simpson (tr), *The Division of Labor in Society* (Glencoe IL, The Free Press, 1964).

B Dutoit, *Commentaire de la loi fédérale du 18 décembre 1987* (Frankfurt-sur-le-Main, Helbing und Lichtenhahn, 1996).

J Fawcett and JM Carruthers, *Cheshire, North and Fawcett Private International Law,* 14th edn (Oxford, Oxford University Press, 2008).

D French, S Mayson and C Ryan, *Mayson French and Ryan on Company Law* 27th edn (Oxford, Oxford University Press, 2010).

E Gottschalk et al (eds), *Conflict of Laws in Globalized World* (Cambridge, Cambridge University Press, 2007).

S Grundmann, W Kerber and S Weatherill (eds), *Party Autonomy and the Role of Information in the Internal Market* (Berlin, de Gruyter, 2001).

AG Harryvan and J van der Harst (eds), *Documents on European Union* (London, Macmillan, 1997).

O Hart, *Firms, Contracts and Financial Structure* (Oxford, Oxford University Press, 1995).

TC Hartley, *International Commercial Litigation: Texts, Cases and Materials on Private International Law* (Cambridge, Cambridge University Press, 2009).

BW Harvey and DK Perry, *The Law of Consumer Protection and Fair Trading* 6th edn (London, Butterworths, 2000).

J Israël, *European Cross-Border Insolvency Regulation: A Study of Regulation 1346/2000 on Insolvency Proceedings in the Light of a Paradigm of Co-operation and a* Comitas Europaea (Oxford, Intersentia, 2005).

Justice, *The Protection of the Small Investor* (Cambridge, Justice Educational and Research Trust, 1992).

D Kershaw, *Company Law in Context: Text and Materials* (Oxford, Oxford University Press, 2009).

H Kötz and T Weir (tr), *European Contract Law,* vol I (Oxford, Clarendon Press, 1997).

R Kraakman et al (eds), *The Anatomy of Corporate Law: A Comparative and Functional Approach,* 2nd edn (Oxford, Oxford University Press, 2009).

GF Maasen, *An International Comparison of Corporate Governance Models* (Amsterdam, Spencer Stuart, 1999).

MP Maduro, *We The Court: The European Court of Justice and the European Economic Constitution. A Critical Reading of Article 30 of the EC Treaty* (Oxford, Hart Publishing, 1998).

HJ Musielak and K Schurig (eds), *Festschrift für Gerhard Kegel* (Berlin, Kohlhammer, 1987).

P Nygh, *Autonomy in International Contracts* (Oxford, Oxford University Press, 1999).

M Ooi, *Shares and Other Securities in the Conflict of Laws* (Oxford, Oxford University Press, 2003).

AC Page and RB Ferguson, *Investor Protection* (London, Weidenfeld and Nicolson, 1992).

B Pasa, GA Benacchio and L Orme (tr), *The Harmonization of Civil and Commercial Law in Europe* (Budapest, Central European University Press, 2005).

E Rabel, *The Conflict of Laws: A Comparative Study,* vol II, 2nd edn (University of Michigan, 1960).

S Rammeloo, *Corporations in Private International Law: A European Perspective* (Oxford, Oxford University Press, 2001).

H Rasmussen, *On Law and Policy in the European Court of* Justice (Lancaster, Kluwer, 1986).

A Santa Maria, *European Economic Law* (Netherlands, Kluwer, 2009).

W Sauter and H Schepel, *State and Market in European Union Law: The Public and Private Spheres of the Internal Market before the EU Courts* (Cambridge, Cambridge University Press, 2009).

N Selwyn, *Selwyn's Law of Employment,* 15th edn (Oxford, Oxford University Press, 2008).
A Smith, *The Wealth of Nations: Books I and II* (London, Penguin, 1999).
Stephenson Harwood, *Shipping Finance,* 3rd edn (London, Euromoney Institutional Investor, 2006).
P Vlas, *Rechtspersonen in het internationaal privaatrecht* (Deventer, Kluwer, 1982).
I Ward, *A Critical Introduction to European Law,* 3rd edn (Cambridge, Cambridge University Press, 2009).
T Weir (tr), K Zweigert and H Kötz, *An Introduction to Comparative Law,* 3rd edn (Oxford, Oxford University Press, 1998).
OE Williamson, *The Economic Institutions of Capitalism* (New York, Free Press, 1985).
DA Wittman (ed), *Economic Analysis of the Law: Selected Readings* (Oxford, Blackwell, 2003).

Chapters in Edited Volumes

J Armour, G Hertig and H Kanda, 'Transactions with Creditors' in R Kraakman et al (eds), *The Anatomy of Corporate Law: A Comparative and Functional Approach,* 2nd edn (Oxford, Oxford University Press, 2009).
J Bengoetxea, N MacCormick and L Moral Soriano, 'Integration and Integrity in the Legal Reasoning of the European Court of Justice' in G de Búrca and JHH Weiler (eds), *The European Court of Justice* (Oxford, Oxford University Press, 2001).
M Blair, 'Firm-Specific Human Capital and Theories of the Firm' in M Blair and MJ Roe (eds), *Employees and Corporate Governance* (Washington DC, Brookings Institute, 1999).
G Broggini, 'Regole societarie del nuovo diritto internazionale privato svizzero' in E Brem et al (eds), *Festchrift zum 65. Geburstag von Mario m. Pedrazzini* (Bern, Verlag Stämpfli, 1990).
RM Buxbaum, 'The Origins of the American "Internal Affairs" Doctrine Rule in the Corporate Conflict of Laws' in HJ Musielak and K Schurig (eds), *Festschrift für Gerhard Kegel* (Berlin, Kohlhammer, 1987).
P Cartwright, 'Consumer Protection in Financial Services: Putting the Law in Context' in P Cartwright (ed), *Consumer Protection in Financial Services* (London, Kluwer, 1999).
P Davies, 'Enron and Corporate Governance in the UK and the European Community' in J Armour and JA McCahery (eds), *After Enron: Improving Corporate Law and Modernising Securities Regulation in Europe and the US* (Oxford, Hart, 2006).
L Enriques, 'Company Law Harmonization Reconsidered: What Role for the EC?' in SM Bartman (ed), *European Company Law in Accelerated Progress* (The Hague, Kluwer, 2006).
L Enriques, H Hansmann and R Kraakman, 'The Basic Governance Structure: The Interests of Shareholders as a Class' in R Kraakman and others (eds), *The Anatomy of Corporate Law. A Comparative and Functional Approach,* 2nd edn (Oxford, Oxford University Press, 2009).
L Enriques, H Hansmann and R Kraakman, 'The Basic Governance Structure: Minority Shareholders and Non-Shareholder Constituencies' in R Kraakman et al (eds), *The Anatomy of Corporate Law,* 2nd edn (Oxford, Oxford University Press, 2009).
RE Freeman, 'A Stakeholder Theory of the Modern Corporation' in TL Beauchamp and NE Bowie (eds), *Ethical Theory and Business,* 5th edn (New Jersey, Prentice Hall, 1997).
L French, 'Introduction' in Stephenson Harwood, *Shipping Finance,* 3rd edn (London, Euromoney Institutional Investor, 2006).

H Hansmann and R Kraakman, 'What is Corporate Law' in R Kraakman and others (eds), *The Anatomy of Corporate Law. A Comparative and Functional Approach,* 2nd edn (Oxford, Oxford University Press, 2009).

KJ Hopt, 'Modern Company and Capital Market Problems: Improving European Corporate Governance After Enron' in J Armour and JA McCahery (eds), *After Enron: Improving Corporate Law and Moderninisng Securities Regulation in Europe and the US* (Oxford, Hart, 2006).

PC Müller-Graff, 'Basic Freedoms – Extending Party Autonomy Across Borders' in S Grundmann, W Kerber and S Weatherill (eds), *Party Autonomy and the Role of Information in the Internal Market* (Berlin, de Gruyter, 2001).

J Paterson, 'The Company Law Review in the UK and the Question of Scope: Theoretical Concerns, Practical Constraints and Possible Directions' in R Cobbaut and J Lenoble (eds), *Corporate Governance. An Institutional Approach* (Netherlands, Kluwer Law International, 2003).

P Reymond, 'Les personnes morales et les sociétés dans le nouveau droit international privé suisse' in F Dessemontet (ed), *Le nouveau droit international privé suisse. Travaux des journées d'études organiseés par le Centre de droit de l'entreprise les 9 et 10 octobre 1987, à l'Université de Lausanne* (Lausanne, Cedidic, 1988).

G Rühl, 'Party Autonomy in the Private International Law of Contracts: Transatlantic Convergence and Economic Efficiency' in E Gottschalk et al (eds), *Conflict of Laws in Globalized World* (Cambridge, Cambridge University Press, 2007).

R Schuman, 'The Schuman Declaration of 9 May 1950' in AG Harryvan and J van der Harst (eds), *Documents on European Union* (London, Macmillan, 1997).

SE Woodward, 'Limited Liability in the Theory of the Firm' in DA Wittman (ed), *Economic Analysis of the Law: Selected Readings* (Oxford, Blackwell, 2003).

Journal Articles

TE Abeltshauser, 'Towards a European Constitution of the Firm – Problems and Perspectives' (1990) *Michigan Journal of International Law* 1235.

AA Alchian and H Demsetz, 'Production, Information Costs and Economic Information' (1977) *The American Economic Review* 777.

WA Allwood, 'Article 5(5): meaning of "branch, agency or other establishment"' (1988) *European Law Review* 213.

KJ Alter, 'Who Are the "Masters of the Treaty"?: European Governments and the European Court of Justice' (1998) *International Organization* 121.

M Andenas 'Free Movement of Companies' (2003) 119 *Law Quarterly Review* 221.

B Angelette, 'The Revolution that Never Came and the Revolution Coming – *De Lasteyrie du Salliant, Marks & Spencer, Sevic Systems* and the Changing Corporate Law in Europe' (2006) *Virginia Law Review* 1189.

J Armour, 'Legal Capital: An Outdated Concept?' (2006) *European Business Organization Law Review* 5.

J Armour and WG Ringe, 'European Company Law 1999-2010: Renaissance and Crisis' (2011) *Common Market Law Review* 125.

A Arnull, 'The European Court and judicial objectivity: a reply to Professor Hartley' (1996) *Law Quarterly Review* 411.

C Azzolini, 'Problemi Relativi alle Persone Giuridiche nella Riforma del Diritto Internazionale Privato' (1993) *Rivista di Diritto Internazionale Privato e Processuale* 893.

SM Bainbridge, 'Director Primacy and Shareholder Disempowerment' (2006) *Harvard Law Review* 1735.

T Ballarino, 'From *Centros* to *Überseering*: EC Right of Establishment and the Conflict of Laws' (2002) *Yearbook of Private International Law* 203.

T Ballarino, 'Sulla mobilità delle società nella Comunità Europea. Da *Daily Mail* a *Überseering*: norme imperative, norme di conflitto e libertà comunitarie' (2003) *Rivista delle società* 669.

T Ballarino and A Bonomi, 'The Italian Statute on Private International Law of 1995' (2000) *Yearbook of Private International Law* 99.

C Barnard and S Deakin, 'Reinventing the European Corporation? Corporate governance, social policy and the single market' (2002) *Industrial Relations Journal* 484.

LA Bebchuk, 'The Case for Increasing Shareholder Power' (2005) *Harvard Law Review* 833.

M Becht, C Mayer and F Wagner, 'Where do firms incorporate? Deregulation and the cost of entry' (2008) *Journal of Corporate Finance* 241.

A Belcher, 'The Boundaries of the Firm: The Theories of Coase, Knight and Weitzman' (1997) *Legal Studies* 22.

A Belcher, 'Board Diversity: Can Sex Discrimination Law Help?' (2005) *Northern Ireland Legal Quarterly* 356.

NP Beveridge, 'The Internal Affairs Doctrine: The Proper Law of a Corporation' (1989) *The Business Lawyer* 693.

PI Blumberg, 'The Corporate Entity in an Era of Multinational Corporations' (1990) *Delaware Journal of Corporate Law* 283.

PJ Borchers, 'Contract and tort Law: Categorical Exceptions to Party Autonomy in Private International Law' (2008) *Tulane Law Review* 1645.

J Borg Barthet, 'Online Gambling and the Further Displacement of State Regulation: *A Note on PMU v Zeturf*' (2008) *International and Comparative Law Quarterly* 417.

J Borg-Barthet, 'European Private International Law of Companies after Cartesio' (2009) *International and Comparative Law Quarterly* 1020.

J Borg-Barthet, 'A New Approach to the Governing Law of Companies in the EU: A Legislative Proposal' (2010) *Journal of Private International Law* 589.

CM Bruner, 'The Enduring Ambivalence of Corporate Law' (2008) *Alabama Law Review* 1385.

RM Buxbaum, 'The Threatened Constitutionalization of the Internal Affairs Doctrine in Corporation Law' (1987) *California Law Review* 29.

G Cansacchi, 'Le choix et l'adaptation de la règle étrangère dans le conflit des lois' (1953) II *Recueil des Cours de l'Académie de Droit International* 81.

RH Coase, 'The Nature of the Firm' (1937) *Economica* 386.

D Coester-Waltjen, 'German Conflict Rules and the Multinational Enterprise' (1976) *Georgia Journal of International and Comparative Law* 197.

R Daines, 'Does Delaware Law Improve Firm Value?' (2001) *Journal of Financial Economics* 525.

JC Dammann 'The future of codetermination after Centros: Will German corporate law move closer to the U.S. model?' (2003) *Fordham Journal of Corporate and Financial Law* 607.

JC Dammann, 'Freedom of Choice in European Corporate Law' (2004) *Yale Journal of International Law* 477.

J Dammann, 'A New Approach to Corporate Choice of Law' (2005) *Vanderbilt Journal of Transnational Law* 51.

S Deakin 'Legal Competition and Regulatory Competition: Which Model for Europe?' (2006) *European Law Journal* 440.

DA DeMott, 'Perspectives on Choice of Law for Corporate Internal Affairs' (1985) *Law and Contemporary Problems* 161.

RR Drury, 'The Regulation and Recognition of Foreign Corporations: Responses to the "Delaware Syndrome"' (1998) *Cambridge Law Journal* 165.

R Drury, 'The European Private Company' (2008) *European Business Organization Law Review* 125.

WF Ebke 'Centros – Some Realities and Some Mysteries' (2000) *The American Journal of International Law* 623.

WF Ebke 'The "Real Seat" Doctrine in the Conflict of Laws' (2002) *The International Lawyer* 1015.

WF Ebke, 'The European Conflict-of-Corporate-Laws Revolution: Uberseering, Inspire Art and Beyond' (2004) *International Lawyer* 813.

H Eidenmüller, A Engert and L Hornuf, 'How Does the Market react to the Societas Europaea?' (2010) *European Business Organization Law Review* 35.

MA Eisenberg, 'The Structure of Corporation Law' (1989) *Columbia Law Review* 1461.

L Enriques, 'EC Company Law Directives and Regulations: How Trivial Are They?' (2006) *University of Pennsylvania Journal of International Economic Law* 1.

L Enriques and M Gelter, 'Regulatory Competition in European Company Law and Creditor Protection' (2006) *European Business Organization Law Review* 417.

E Fama, 'Agency Problems and the theory of the firm' (1980) *Journal of Political Economy* 288.

A Fiorini, 'The Codification of Private International Law: The Belgian Experience' (2005) *International and Comparative Law Quarterly* 499.

E Friedler, 'Party Autonomy Revisited: A Statutory Solution to a Choice-of-Law Problem' (1989) *Kansas Law Review* 471.

FJ Garcimartín Alférez, 'La Sentencia «Centros»: una visión a través de los comerntarios' (2001) *Revista Jurídica* 169.

FJ Garcimartín Alférez, 'Cross-Border Listed Companies' (2007) 328 *Recueil des Cours de l'Académie de Droit International* 13.

M Gestri, 'Mutuo Riconoscimento delle Società Comunitarie, Norme di Conflitto Nazionali e Frode alla Legge: il caso *Centros*' (2000) *Rivista di Diritto Internazionale* 71.

AJ Gildea, '*Überseering*: A European Company Passport' (2004) *Brooklyn Journal of International Law* 257.

M Goldman, 'La nationalité des sociétés dans la Communauté économique européenne' (1969) *Travaux du Comité français de droit internationale privé* 215.

F Guillaume, 'The Law Governing Companies in Swiss Private International Law' (2004) *Yearbook of Private International Law* 251.

S Grundmann, 'The Structure of European Company Law: From Crisis to Boom' (2004) *European Business Organisation Law Review* 601.

B Gustin, 'What Law Governs Liability of Shareholders for Corporate Debts' (1914) *Harvard Law Review* 575.

Y Hadari, 'The Choice of National Law Applicable to the Multinational Enterprise and the Nationality of Such Enterprises' (1974) *Yale Law Journal* 1.

T Hartley, 'The European Court, judicial objectivity and the constitution of the European Union' (1996) *Law Quarterly Review* 95.

LL Hansen, 'Merger, Moving and Division Across National Borders – When Case Law Breaks through Barriers and Overtakes Directives' (2007) *European Business Law Review* 181.

H Hansmann and R Kraakman, 'Toward Unlimited Shareholder Liability for Corporate Torts' (1991) *Yale Law Journal* 1879.

H Hansmann and R Kraakman, 'The Essential Role of Organizational Law' (2000) *Yale Law Journal* 387.

H Hansmann and R Kraakman, 'The End of History for Corporate Law' (2001) *Georgetown Law Journal* 439.

H Hansmann, R Kraakman and R Squire, 'Law and the Rise of the Firm' (2006) *Harvard Law Review* 1335.

O Hart, 'An Economist's Perspective on the Theory of the Firm' (1989) *Columbia Law Review* 1757.

K Heine and W Kerber, 'European Corpoate Laws, Regulatory Competition and Path Dependence' (2002) *European Journal of Law and Economics* 47.

A Hinarejos, 'Laval and Viking: the right to collective action versus fundamental freedoms' (2008) *Human Rights Law Review* 714.

K Hofstetter, 'Parent Responsibility for Subsidiary Corporations: Evaluating European Trends' (1990) *International and Comparative Law Quarterly* 576.

EM Iacobucci, 'Toward a Signaling Explanation of the Private Choice of Corporate Law' (2004) *American Law and Economics Review* 319.

MC Jensen and WH Meckling, 'Theory of the Firm: Managerial Behavior, Agency Costs and Ownership Structure' (1976) *Journal of Financial Economics* 305.

A Johnston and P Syrpis, 'Regulatory competition in European company law after *Cartesio*' (2009) *European Law Review* 378.

J Kay and A Silberston, 'Corporate Governance' (1995) *National Institute Economic Review* 84.

C Kersting, 'Corporate Choice of Law – A Comparison of The United States and European Systems and a Proposal for a European Directive' (2002) *Brooklyn Journal of International Law* 1.

EM Kieninger, 'The Law Applicable to Corporations in the EC' (2009) *RabelsZ* 607.

D Komo and C Villiers, 'Are Trends In European Company Law Threatening Industrial Democracy?' (2009) *European Law Review* 175.

V Korom and P Metzinger, 'Freedom of Establishment for Companies: the European Court of Justice confirms and refines its *Daily Mail* Decision in the *Cartesio* Case C-210/06' (2009) *European Company and Financial Law Review* 147.

M Lehmann, 'Liberating the Individual from Battles between States: Justifying Party Autonomy in Conflict of Laws' (2008) *Vanderbilt Journal of Transnational Law* 381.

ER Latty, 'Pseudo-Foreign Corporations' (1955) *Yale Law Journal* 137.

DW Leebron, 'Limited Liability, Tort Victims and Creditors' (1991) *Columbia Law Review* 1565.

A Littler, 'Regulatory Perspectives On The Future Of Interactive Gambling In The Internal Market' (2008) *European Law Review* 211.

D Loftus, 'Capital and Community: Limited Liability and Attempts to Democratize the Market in Mid-Nineteenth-Century England' (2002) 45 *Victorian Studies* 93.

S Lombardo and P Pasotti, 'The *Societas Europaea*: a Network Economics Approach' (2004) *European Company and Financial Law Review* 169.

S Lombardo, 'Conflict of Law Rules in Company Law after *Überseering*: An Economic and Comparative Analysis of the Allocation of Policy Competence in the European Union' (2003) *European Business Organization Law Review* 301.

A Looijestijn-Clearie, 'Centros Ltd – A Complete U-Turn in the Right of Establishment for Companies?' (2000) *International and Comparative Law Quarterly* 621.

P Lortie, 'The Development of Medium and Technology Neutral International Treaties in Support of Post-Convention Information Technology Systems' (2008) *Yearbook of Private International Law* 359.

MP Maduro, 'So Close And Yet So Far: The Paradoxes Of Mutual Recognition' (2007) *Journal of European Public Policy* 814.

DM Majchrzak, 'Corporate Chaos: Who Should Govern Internal Affairs?' (2001) *Thomas Jefferson Law Review* 83.

J Malmberg and T Sigeman, 'Industrial Actions and EU Economic Freedoms: the Autonomous Collective Bargaining Model Curtailed by the European Court of Justice' (2008) *Common Market Law Review* 1115.

J McLean, 'The Transnational Corporation in History: Lessons for Today?' (2004) *Indiana Law Journal* 363.

E Micheler, 'Recognition of Companies Incorporated in other EU Member States' (2003) *International and Comparative Law Quarterly* 521.

SK Miller, 'Piercing the Corporate Veil Among Affiliated Companies in the European Community and in the U.S.: a Comparative Analysis of U.S., German, and U.K. Veil-Piercing Approaches' (1998) *American Business Law Journal* 73.

M Miola, 'Legal Capital and Limited Liability Companies: The European Perspective' (2005) *European Company and Financial Law Review* 413.

CGJ Morse, 'Consumer Contracts, Employment Contracts and the Rome Convention' (2000) *International and Comparative Law Quarterly* 1.

FM Mucciarelli, 'Company "Emigration" and EC Freedom of Establishment: *Daily Mail* Revisited' (2008) *European Business Organization Law Review* 267.

P Muchlinski, 'Corporations in International Litigation: Problems of Jurisdiction and the United Kingdom Asbestos Cases' (2001) *International and Comparative Law Quarterly* 1.

PT Muchlinski, 'Enron and Beyond: Multinational Corporate Groups and the Internationalization of Governance and Disclosure Regimes' (2005) *Connecticut Law Review* 725.

H Muir Watt and LG Radicati di Brozolo, 'Party Autonomy and Mandatory Rules in a Global World' (2004) *International Law Forum* 90.

A Ogus, 'Competition Between National Legal Systems: A Contribution of Economic Analysis to Comparative Law' (1999) *International and Comparative Law Quarterly* 405.

E Örücü, 'Law as Transposition' (2002) *International and Comparative Law Quarterly* 205.

M Pannier, 'The EU Cross Border Merger Directive – A New Dimension for Employee Participation and Company Restructuring' (2005) *European Business Organisation Law Review* 1424.

A Radwan, 'European Private Company and the Regulatory Landscape in the EU – An Introductory Note' (2007) *European Business Law Review* 769.

RG Rajan and L Zingales, 'Power in a Theory of the Firm' (1998) *Quarterly Journal of Economics* 387.

M Reiman, 'Savigny's Triumph? Choice of Law in Contracts Cases at the Close of the Twentieth Century' (2008) *Virginia Journal of International Law* 571.

WG Ringe, 'No Freedom of Emigration for Companies?' (2005) *European Business Law Review* 621.

WG Ringe, 'The European Company Statute in the Context of Freedom of Establishment' (2007) *Journal of Corporate Law Studies* 185.

MJ Roe, 'The Shareholder Wealth Maximization Norm and Industrial Organization' (2001) *University of Pennsylvania Law Review* 2063.
R Romano, 'Law as a Product: Some Pieces of the Incorporation Puzzle' (1985) *Journal of Law, Economics and Organization* 225.
R Romano, 'Answering the Wrong Question: The Tenuous Case for Mandatory Corporate Laws' (1989) *Columbia Law Review* 1599.
WH Roth 'Case note on *Centros*' (2000) 37 *Common Market Law Review* 147.
WH Roth, 'From *Centros* to *Ueberseering*: Free Movement of Companies, Private International Law, and Community Law' (2003) *International and Comparative Law Quarterly* 177.
A Santa Maria, 'Problemi attinenti al diritto internazionale privato e processuale delle società' (1987) *Rivista delle Società* 1473.
SK Schmidt, 'Mutual recognition as a new mode of governance' (2007) *Journal of European Public Policy* 667.
CM Schmitthoff, 'Company Structure and Employee Participation in the EEC – the British Attitude' (1976) *International and Comparative Law Quarterly* 611.
MM Siems, 'The European Directive on Cross-Border Mergers: An International Model?' (2005) *Columbia Journal of European Law* 167.
MM Siems, '*Sevic:* Beyond Cross-Border Mergers' (2007) *European Business Organization Law Review* 307.
E Stein, 'Conflict-of-Laws Rules by Treaty: Recognition of Companies in a Regional Market' (1970) *Michigan Law Review* 1327.
LA Stout, 'Bad and Not-So-Bad Arguments for Shareholder Primacy' (2002) 75 *Southern California Law Review* 1189.
P Syrpis and T Novitz, 'Political and social rights in conflict: Political and judicial approaches to their reconciliation' (2008) *European Law Review* 411.
S Terjesen and V Singh, 'Female Presence on Corporate Boards : A Multi-Country Study of Environmental Context' (2008) *Journal of Business Ethics* 55.
CM Tiebout, 'A Pure Theory of Local Expenditures' (1956) *Journal of Political* Economy 416.
C Timmermans, 'Impact of EU Law on International Company Law' (2010) *European Review of Private Law* 549.
JP Trachtman, 'Embedding mutual recognition at the WTO' (2007) *Journal of European Public Policy* 780.
TH Tröber, 'Choice of Jurisdiction in European Corporate Law – Perspectives of European Corporate Governance' (2005) *European Business Organization Law Review* 3.
G Tuebner, 'Legal Irritants: Good Faith in British Law or How Unifying Law Ends Up in New Divergences' (1998) *Modern Law Review* 11.
C Villiers, 'Achieving Gender Balance in the Board Room: Is it Time for Legislative Action in the UK? (2010) *Legal Studies* 533.
GJ Vossestein, 'Transfer of the registered office: The European Commission's decision not to submit a proposal for a Directive' (2008) *Utrecht Law Review* 53.
JHH Weiler, 'A Quiet Revolution: The European Court of Justice and its Interlocutors' (1994) *Comparative Political Studies* 510.
ML Weitzman, 'Increasing Returns and the Foundations of Unemployment Theory' (1982) *The Economic Journal* 787.
MJ Whincop, 'Conflicts in the Cathedral: Towards a Theory of Property Rights in Private International Law' (2000) *University of Toronto Law Journal* 41.
OE Williamson, 'The Theory of the Firm as Governance Structure: From Choice to Contract' (2002) *Journal of Economic Perspectives* 171.

A Winkler, 'Corporate Law or the Law of Business? Stakeholders and Corporate Governance at the End of History' (2004) 67 *Law and Contemporary Problems* 109.

AW Wiśniewski and A Opalski, 'Companies' Freedom of Establishment after the ECJ *Cartesio* Judgment' (2009) *European Business Organization Law Review* 595.

J Wouters, 'European Company Law: *Quo Vadis*?' (2000) *Common Market Law Review* 257.

Miscellaneous

J Armour, B Black and C Cheffins, 'Is Delaware Losing its Cases?' ECGI Working Paper (2010) http:ssrn.com/abstract=1578404.

T Baums and P Krüger Andersen, 'The European Model Company Law Project: ECGI Law Working Paper No 097/2008' (2008) http:// ssrn.com/abstract=1115737.

WJ Bratton, JA McCahery and EPM Vermeulen, 'How Does Corporate Mobility Affect Law Making? A Comparative Analysis' (2008) ECGI Law Working Paper No 91/2008 http://ssrn.com/abstract=1086667.

The Dutch Ministry of Justice http://english.justitie.nl/currenttopics/pressreleases/archives2006/-Simplified-Formation-of-BVs-for-Smaller-companies-and-Start-up-Businesses.aspx.

J Dammann and H Hansmann, 'Extraterritorial Courts for Corporate Law: ECGI Law Working Paper No 43/2005' (2005) http://papers.ssrn.com/sol3/papers.cfm?abstract_id=724165.

M Friedman, 'The Social Responsibility of Business Is to Increase Its Profits' *New York Times Magazine* (New York 13 September 1970) 32.

KPMG International, 'Euro Tax Flash: Issue 90' (2008) www.kpmg.be/dbfetch/52616e646f6d495613e0c3885001ac474ddc7501a1f057e0258c22de5277b322/euro_tax_flash_2008_06_11.pdf.

XE Kramer, 'Dutch Private International Law – Overview 2002–2006' (2007) Erasmus Universiteit Rotterdam http://hdl.handle.net/1765/9232.

C McCreevy, 'Speech 07/441: Company Law and Corporate Governance Today' (2007) http://europa.eu/rapid/pressReleasesAction.do?reference=SPEECH/07/441&format=DOC&aged=1&language=EN&guiLanguage=en.

CWA Timmermans 'Company Law as Ius Commune?' (2002) Walter van Gerven Lecture, Leuven Centre for a Common Law of Europe www.law.kuleuven.ac.be/ccle/pdf/wvg1.pdf.

INDEX

Alchian, A and Demsetz, H on monitoring and team-production, 32, 33

bifurcation, 56, 89, 107, 130–1, 157–8
Blair, M on firm-specific human capital, 35–6
boards of directors, 160–1
  two-tiered boards, 160
  unitary boards, 160
Brussels I Regulation (2001), 17, 78, 158
Brussels II *bis* Regulation, 17

Cadbury Schweppes judgment (case C-196/04; [2006] I-7995), 123–5
  Cartesio judgment, in, 129
  case details, 125
California Corporations Code, 47, 54–5, 156–7
  directors' accountability, 68
capital requirements in Europe, 63–4
Cartesio Oktató és Szolgáltató bt (C-210/06) judgment, 29, 127–35, 164
  AG Maduro's opinion, 127–31
  European Court of Justice's judgment, 131–5
  fourteenth company law directive (2007), 93–4
Centros Ltd v Erhvervs-og-Selstabsstyrelsen (C-212/97) judgment, 15, 56, 61–2, 64
  Cartesio judgment, in, 129–30, 132–3
  case details, 113–14
  corporate law and, 152–3
  creditor protection, 163
  employee entitlement, 115
  freedom of establishment, 76–7
    judgments, 105–12, 113–17
      introduction, 105–6
  incorporation, 115
  mutual recognition, 116–17
  recognition of companies, 136
  reversal of, 146–7
  right of establishment, 153
  TFEU articles 49 and 54, 114–15
Coase, RH:
  nature of the firm, 30–3, 154–155, 171–2
companies and company law:
  company directors,
    UK, shareholder value, 11
  contracts' roles and, 33–6
  directives see company law directives
  emigration of companies, 124
  European Union treatment of, 172
  governance,
    cross-border mergers, 88
  groups of companies in Germany, 92–3
  intra-company relationships, 23
  legal personality of companies, 118–19
    officers' duties and liabilities, 161–2
  parent company's and subsidiaries' relationship, 162
  public companies' corporate governance, 92
  reincorporation, 87–8
  taxation, 124, 125
  UK, 5
company law directives, 92–4
  eleventh (1989), 116
  EU and, 56–7
  fifth (1972), 92
  fourteenth (2007), 93–4
    Commissioner for the Internal Market's statement, 93
  fourth (1978), 116
  generally, 92
  ninth directive (draft, 1976), 92–3
competition and party autonomy, 40–1
consumers:
  definition, 22
  shareholders as, 22–3
contract law:
  concept of a company, 33–6
  corporate contracts *see* corporate contracts
  corporation law distinguished, 20–1
  party autonomy, 16–17, 19–30
  protection of weaker party, 21–5
Convention on the Mutual Recognition of Companies and Bodies Corporate 1968, 7–8, 106–109
  aim, 7
  ratification, 7–8
corporate choice and contractual principle, 171–2
corporate contracts, 26
  definition, 36
  enforcement mechanisms, 169
  privity of, 169
corporate emigration, 78, 120, 133–5
corporate law:
  California, in, 156–7
  economic analysis, 30–47
    protective mechanisms, 52–69
  contract law distinguished, 20–1

corporate law (*cont.*):
  Delaware of *see* Delawarisation
  divergence, 69–71
  EU *see* European Union
  gender issues, 11, 69–70
  Germany, in *see* Germany
  Hansmann and Kraakman on, 10
  harmonisation *see* harmonisation
  history, 9–10
  legal basis, 150–1
  liberal model of choice, 38–9
  multi-party interests, 79
  party autonomy *see* party autonomy
  regulatory frameworks, 149–69
  supranationalisation, 147–8
  team production, 30–3
    monitoring, 32
  third party rights, 26
  unification, 147–8
corporate liability in Germany, 61–2
corporate shareholders, 58–62
  USA, 59
Council of the European Union:
  1061/11 DRS 84 SOC 432, 99–102
creditor protection, 62–5, 163,
  principles, 62–4
  transnational, 64–5
cross-border mergers:
  Cartesio judgment, in, 134
  company governance, 88
  directive (2005), 56, 87–90
    aims, 87
  Sevic Systems judgment, 125–7
cross-border seat transfers, 164–5
  definition, 164
  fourteenth company law directive (2007), 93–4
  USA, 88

Daily Mail judgment:
  Cartesio judgment, in, 127–9, 132–3
  cross-border seat transfers, 164
  freedom of establishment judgments, 111–12
  Inspire Art judgment, in, 121
Deakin, S on market competition, 41
decision-making, 39–40
Delawarisation, 80, 81–2, 86–7, 156–7
  TFEU article 50, 83
Directive on Shareholders' Rights (2007), 57
directors' accountability, 68–9

EC Treaty:
  article 43 *see* TFEU article 49
  article 48 *see* TFEU article 54
  article 293, 73, 118–20
    Inspire Art judgment, 121
economic analysis and conflict of corporate laws, 30–47

efficiency:
  best law, 39–41
  legal certainty, 41–6
e-Justice initiative, 158–9, 165–6
emigration and immigration, 120, 133–5
employees:
  company stakeholders, as, 65–8
  decision making powers, 91–2
  participation, 88–9, 90–2
    harmonisation, 90–1, 161
    Societas Privata Europaea (2008), 101–2
  party autonomy, 89
  powers, 34
  representation, 67–8
  shareholders in Germany, 67
  shareholders in UK, 66
employment, loss of, 40
enlightenment and private autonomy, 18
entrepreneurship, 30–3
Europe:
  capital requirements, 63–4
  gender issues in corporate law, 11
  party autonomy,
    TFEU regulations, 73–4
European Commission:
  COM (2008) 396/3, 99–102
European Commission Convention on the Mutual Recognition of Companies and Bodies Corporate 1968, 106–9
European Court of Justice:
  corporate law case law, 172–3
European Cross-Border Merger Directive (2005), 65
European Model Company Law Project, 147
European Union (EU):
  company law directives, 56–7
  corporate entity, 60–2
  corporate law,
    current legislation, 143–6
    future development, 142–70
      introduction, 142
  council regulations,
    EC 2157/2001 *see* Societas Europaea (SE) (2001)
  harmonisation effects of directives, 85–6
  member states' relationship with companies, 120, 125
  party autonomy, 73–103
    constitutional aspects, 74–8
    incorporation, 77–8
    introduction, 73–4
'Eurosclerosis', 111

foreign companies, incorporation, 166
France:
  shareholders and CGT, 123
fraude à la loi, 68, 114
freedom of choice and TFEU article 50, 83

freedom of establishment:
  definition, 76
  judgments *see* freedom of establishment judgments
  Societas Europaea (SE)(2001), 97–8
  TFEU article 50, 78–9, 83–4
freedom of establishment judgments, 104–41
  Centros judgment, 105–12, 113–17
  Daily Mail judgment, 11–12
  introduction, 104–5
  legislation, 104–5
  TFEU articles 49 and 50, 109–11
Freeman, R. E. on shareholders, 34–5

Gebhard test, 116
gender issues:
  corporate law, in, 11
  equality issues, 69–70
German Council for Private International Law, 149, 159–60
Germany:
  corporate law, 33
    groups of companies, 92–3
    private international law recommendations, 159–60
  corporate liability, 61–2
  employee participation, 91
  employees as shareholders, 67
  real seat theory, 44, 144–5
Giuliano-Lagarde Report (1980), 20–1
governance:
  company and cross-border mergers, 88
  corporate and public companies, 92
  state, 18

Hague Convention on Choice of Court Agreements (2005), 16–17
Hague Protocol on the Law Applicable to Maintenance Obligations (2007), 17
Hansmann, H on corporate law, 10, 52
harmonisation, 80–1, 82–3
  corporate laws, 135–8, 149–50
  employee participation, 90–1, 161
  generally, 2, 3
  negative *see* negative harmonisation
  party autonomy, 15, 85–94
    USA, 85
  TFEU article 50, 84–5
Hart, O on corporate law, 38–9

immigration *see* emigration and immigration
incorporation:
  Centros doctrine, 115
  electronic solution, 158–9
  European Union and party autonomy, 77–8
  foreign companies, 166
  future development, 143–4
  Societas Privata Europaea (SPE), 101
  TFEU article 50, 82–3
incorporation theory, 4–6, 41–2, 46–7, 51–2, 107–8, 150, 155
  definition, 51
  E. R. Latty's modification (1955), 155–8
    consequences, 156–7
    details, 155–6
  history, 5–6
  Italy, in, 50–1
  party autonomy, 13–14
  USA, in, 155–7
Inspire Art judgment (2003, C -167/01), 56, 61–2, 65, 120–2
  Cartesio judgment in, 129–30
  case details, 121
  corporate law and, 152–3
  incorporation and, 77
  internal affairs doctrines, 122, 133–5, 144
international unification, 6–8
intra-company relationships, 23
involuntary creditors, 70–1
iSupport, 158
Italy:
  incorporation theory, 50–1
  real seat theory, 44, 50–1
  shareholder protection, 163–4

Jensen, MC on contractual relationships, 34

Kamer VanKoophandel en Fabrieken voor Amsterdam v Inspire Art see Inspire Art judgment
Kraakman, R on corporate law, 10, 52
de Lasteyrie du Saillant judgment, 123–5
  case details, 23

Latty, ER on pseudo-foreign corporations (1955), 155–8
legal certainty, 41–6, 165–6
  Cartesio judgment in, 130, 146–7, 149–50, 151–2
legal personality, 60–2
lex contractus, 20–1
liberalisation, 145–6
  liberal incorporation, 155
  outreach statutes and, 121–2
Liechtenstein AG BGH (1986), 45
limitation of private ordering, 154–5
limited liability, 53, 58–9
Lubbe et al v Cape Industries (1977), 60–1

Maduro, AG:
  Cartesio judgment opinion, 127–31
Maduro, MP on legal competition, 40–1
Marks and Spencer judgment, 123–5
  case details, 124
Meckling, WH on contractual relationships, 34

Muchlinski, P on legal personality, 60–1
mutual recognition, 75–6, 172
  Centros judgment, 116–17

negative harmonisation, 127, 138–9, 143
  fourteenth company law directive (2007), 93–4
Netherlands:
  creditor protection, 65
New York Corporations Code, 55
non-compliance, 45–6
novation, 27–9

outreach statutes, 46–7
  liberalisation and, 121–2

Paramount Communications v Time (1989 US case), 11
party autonomy, 13–48, 171–2
  constitutional aspects, 74–8
  contract law and, 16–17, 19–30
  corporate law, 139–40, 154
  efficiency, 39–41, 41–6
  employees, 89
  enlightenment, 18
  EU and, 74–6
    incorporation, 77–8
  Europe, in, 73–103
    introduction, 73–4
    TFEU regulations, 73–4
  harmonisation, 15, 85–94
    USA, 85
  introduction, 13–16
  legislative and judicial references, 15
  limitations, 49, 86
  outreach statutes, 46–7
  private international law, 16–19
  real seat theory, 14
Powell Duffryn PLC v Petereit (1989), 19, 21, 23
price mechanism, 31
private international law:
  exceptions, 69–71
  Inspire Art judgment, 121
  party autonomy, 16–19
  Societas Europaea (SE), 98–9
property rights and shareholding, 36–9
prorogation clauses, 17
  Powell Duffryn judgment, 19
pseudo-foreign companies, 120–2, 136

The Queen v HM Treasury and Commissioners of Inland Revenue ex p Daily Mail and General Trust PLC (1987) see *Daily Mail* judgment

Rajan, RG on employees' power, 34
real seat theory, 4–6, 14, 42–6, 50–1, 150, 155
  application of, 167–9
    formulae for, 167–8
  Austria, in, 144–5
  Convention on the Mutual Recognition of Companies and Bodies Corporate 1968, 7
  creditor protection, 62–3
  definition, 50
  Germany, 44, 144–5
  history, 5–6
  Italy, 44, 50–1
  Societas Europaea (SE)(2001), 96–7
  Überlagerung principle, 157
regional unification, 6–8
reincorporation, 27–9
  Cartesio judgment, 135
  cross-border mergers, through, 87–8
  TFEU article 50, 82–3
residual control rights, 38–9
right of establishment and *Centros* judgment, 153
risk, 31, 53, 62
  transfer of, 62
Rome I Regulation (2008), 20, 22,
  reincorporation, 27
Rome III Regulation (2010), 17

SE *see* Societas Europaea (2001)
Sevic Systems AG (C-411/03, 2005), 125–7
  Cartesio judgment, in, 129, 134
  case details, 125
shareholder primacy model, 9
shareholder protection, 163–4
shareholders, 23–5
  autonomy, national rules for, 39–41
  generally, 22–3
  liability,
    limits, 57–62
      principles, 57–8
  minority, 24–5, 28–9
    standard form contracts, 25–7
  non-shareholder constituencies (USA), 10
  property rights, 36–9
  rights, 52–7
    principles, 52–4
    Societas Privata Europaea (SPE) (2008), under, 100–1, 102
  value, 11
    UK, in, 11
Shares, 37–8
  definition of, 37
  treatment in private international law, 38
Societas Europaea (SE) (2001), 95–9, 154
  legal basis, 95
  private international law aspects, 96
  purpose of, 96
  real seat theory, 96–7
  restrictions on use, 98
  take-up rate, 97–8

Societas Privata Europaea (SPE) 2008 (COM (2008)396/3), 99–102, 154
aims and purposes, 99–100
development, 99
employee participation, 101–2
incorporation, 101
private international law aspects, 100
shareholders' rights under, 100–1, 102
stakeholders, 34–5
model, criticism of, 35
standard form of contract, 25–7
Statute for a European Company (SE) (2001, EC 2157/2001) *see* Societas Europaea
supranational business vehicles, 95–103
introduction, 95
supranationalisation and corporate law, 147–8
Swiss Private International Law Code (1987), 46–7, 58
company officers' liability under, 162
directors' accountability, 68–9

taxation of companies, 124, 125
team production, 30–3
TFEU *see* Treaty on the Functioning of the European Union
théorie du siège réel, *see* real seat theory
third party rights:
corporate law, 26
party autonomy, 18
Treaty on the Functioning of the European Union (TFEU) (2009):
article 49, 73–4, 135–8
freedom of establishment judgments, 109–11
article 50, 78–85, 172
Centros judgment, after, 81–5
historical development, 79–80
article 54, 73–4, 111–12, 122, 135–8,
Cartesio judgment,
European Court of Justice on, 132–3
freedom of establishment judgments, 109–11
article 81, 172
Treaty of Lisbon:
Repeal of article 293 EC, 137–8

Überseering BV v Nordic Construction Company Baumanagement GmbH (NCC) [2002], 117–20
Cartesio judgment, 132–3
case details, 118–19
corporate law and, 152–3
incorporation, 77
unification of corporate law, 147–8
United Kingdom (UK):
capital requirements, 63–4
company law, 5
corporate liability, 60–1
employees as shareholders, 66
gender issues in corporate law, 11
shareholder protection, 163–4
shareholder values, 11
co-directors' discretion, 11
USA:
corporate shareholders, 57
cross-border seat transfers, 83
incorporation theory, 155–7
non-shareholder constitutencies, 10
party autonomy,
harmonisation 85

Williamson, OE on corporate governance, 35
Works Council Directive, 90–2

Zingales, I on employees' power, 34

www.ingramcontent.com/pod-product-compliance
Ingram Content Group UK Ltd.
Pitfield, Milton Keynes, MK11 3LW, UK
UKHW021907150926
475560UK00003B/229